NEVER WITHOUT
HONOR

NEVER WITHOUT HONOR:

STUDIES OF COURAGE IN TRIBUTE
TO BEN H. PROCTER

*With an introduction
by Archie P. McDonald*

DAVID MURPH

WATSON ARNOLD

ROGER TULLER

MICHAEL COLLINS

MARK BEASLEY

MARY KELLEY SCHEER

EDDIE WELLER

STEPHEN F. AUSTIN STATE UNIVERSITY PRESS
NACOGDOCHES ★ TEXAS

For information contact:
Stephen F. Austin State University Press
1936 North Street, LAN 203,
P.O. Box 13007
Nacogdoches, Texas, 75962.
sfapress@sfasu.edu

Distribution by Texas A&M University Press Consortium
www.tamupress.com
1.800.826.8911

First Edition: May 2013

CONTENTS

CHAPTER 6

CHAPTER 7

IN MEMORY OF BEN H. PROCTER

Our beloved mentor and faithful friend who taught us most of what we know about the practice of history and even more about life.

INTRODUCTION

By Archie P. McDonald

*(Editor's note: The Introduction was written before the passing of Drs.
Procter and McDonald, thus the usage of first person.)*

But I'm a Procter student, too!

That was my unspoken reaction when asked to contribute to a
volume honoring my close friend and collaborator Ben Procter,
adding that I would be the only writer involved who had not been one
of Ben's students. The caller that day meant graduate students enrolled
at Texas Christian University, and on that technicality he was correct.
In a broader sense, however, I am also Ben's student and in this essay I
am representing a legion of historians and political activists scattered
across the United States.

Ben's influence and reach extended across the country because
he was the ultimate "organization man." He rarely missed annual
meetings of the Texas State Historical Association, Southern Historical
Association, Southwestern Social Science Association, Western
Historical Association, Phi Alpha Theta, and other professional
historical organizations. Ben virtually required graduate students, and
urged his "non-traditional" students, to attend the business sessions
of such organizations because "That's where decisions are made," and
anyone who wanted to be a player in those associations should be
present, involved, and vocal.

Ben did not just attend such gatherings. He and Phoebe, Ben's
college sweetheart and still cheerleader wife, usually drove to the host
city in a big Buick (later Cadillac), which gave him "wheels" despite
the sometimes great distances from Fort Worth. With mobility, Ben
usually arranged a dinner on the least busy night of the convention,
always away from the headquarters hotel and any official function of
the organization.

Ben invited a great number of historians to these Dutch-treat dinner gatherings and provided or arranged transportation for those needing it. The food—Italian, Tex-Mex, Chinese, or more likely barbeque—mattered little; comradeship counted most. Another premium, many felt, was "the most food for the least money," but Ben never consumed that many calories anyway. He was too busy visiting, "working the room" in politician-speak, asking on behalf of graduate students whose departments were hiring this year, who could get one of his people on programs or perhaps arrange for them to write a review for their journal. This one-man public relations—Godfather—mentor forever promoted his students, whether TCU or "non-traditional." Ben made sure everyone met everyone else by presiding over a go-around with each one introducing themselves and identifying their institutional affiliation.

Ben also prowled the book exhibit hall and corridors outside meeting rooms on a similar mission but always found time to attend sessions if old friends or graduate students numbered among the presenters. He attended presidential dinners faithfully, and often threatened the speaker that he intended to "accidently" drop silverware during some crucial moment in their presentation—but he never did so. Most were friends who likely owed their election to high office to Ben's perpetual influence on the nominating committee of every professional organization in which he participated. Ben found satisfaction in the success, service, and achievements of all his students.

The Advanced Placement program of the Educational Testing Service, headquartered at Princeton University, enabled Ben to broaden his friendships in the history profession to a national scale. Among the pioneers of the annual essay "reading" of high school hopefuls who wanted "advanced" college credit in U.S. history, Ben drove each June to New Jersey and spent a week "ranking" (ETS forbids using the term "grading") essays on a prescribed scale. At first, readers gathered at Rider College, then moved to Trenton State College, and still later to Clemson University in South Carolina and Trinity University in San Antonio.

Ben quickly became one of the "table leaders," or straw bosses, who made certain their table of readers remained "locked in" on standards for "ranking" and worked steadily enough to meet unofficial quotas. Table leaders could also move around to visit, an ideal assignment for one so gregarious as Ben. But Ben, as always, was competitive, so soon he was driving his rankers to read more essays than those at any other table—and placing bets with other table leaders on the outcome!

Evenings, after an institutional dinner in the college cafeteria, were reserved for poker. Here, too, Ben was often the "table leader" if not the big winner. He always arranged at least one dinner off campus, just like those promoted at professional meetings, and John Belohavek remembers a Chinese restaurant in New Jersey named The A Kitchen that Ben favored because the food flowed abundantly but the price remained low year after year. This would be the one evening that Ben might change from the brown jumpsuit he habitually wore to the readings. Some bet that Ben wore the same suit every day, while others assumed he had multiple but identical jumpsuits. This mystery was never resolved.

I became a reader/ranker in the 1980s through Ben's sponsorship, and he mentored me in the mysteries of "reading" AP essays. He also smoothed the way when I was summoned to New York in the middle of a reading to appear, with wife Judy, on "CBS This Morning." This was owed to my publishing a cookbook about our lifestyle: Judy was mayor of Nacogdoches and rarely had time to cook, but I always arrived home first in the evening and so took up the chore—which expanded to other mealtimes as well. It is strictly forbidden to arrive late, depart early, or take leave in the middle from the reading. My absence would hardly take twenty-four hours, but rules are rules—at least until Ben told Chief Reader Bob Warren that I was going, period. He even took off time to take me to the train station in Trenton, and Phoebe picked me up the next day and returned me to my table.

Ben Procter, a native Texan, was born in Temple on February 21, 1927. An excellent student, he was graduated from Austin High School in 1945 and enlisted and served in the U.S. Navy for fifteen months. Upon discharge in September 1946 he entered The University of Texas that same fall. Ben played end on the Longhorn football team and earned a place on an All-America football team—and a Phi Beta Kappa key in the same semester. His athletic record included gaining 1,382 yards for an average of 16.8 yards per catch and scoring thirteen touchdowns. In 1949, Ben's Longhorns defeated the TCU Horned Frogs in no small part because he caught more passes and scored more touchdowns than any player had done in any game in Southwest

Conference history to that time.

Ben graduated from The University of Texas in 1951 and the following year also received his master's degree from the same institution. He played professional football with the Los Angeles Rams until injured, then enrolled in the graduate program in history at Harvard University in Cambridge, Massachusetts. Frederick Merk directed Ben's dissertation, a biography of John H. Reagan, but Ben also studied with such outstanding scholars as Samuel Eliot Morison and Arthur Schlesinger, Sr., and Arthur Schlesinger, Jr., and received the Doctor of Philosophy degree in 1961. Ben joined the faculty at Texas Christian University in 1957.

Historians, particularly those who practice their craft through appointments in higher education, fall into distinct categories: those known for publications; those who concentrate on teaching; and those who excel in teaching and sharing the yield of their research with others through spoken and written words. Ben Procter's record places him firmly in the latter camp. His book, *Not Without Honor: The Life of John H. Reagan*, published by The University of Texas Press in 1962, remains the definitive biography of this Texas surveyor, political leader, and postmaster general of the Confederacy. *Not Without Honor* won the Summerfield G. Roberts Award as best book on Texas history in 1963. Next came *Texas Under a Cloud*, co-written with journalist Sam Kinch Jr, published by Pemberton Press in 1972, which won the Texas Writer's Roundup Award in 1973. The Texas State Historical Association published Ben's *Battle of the Alamo*, a monograph on the battle that remains the crucible of Texas history, in 1986, and Eakin Press published his *Just One Riot: Episodes of 20th Century Texas Rangers*, in 1991. This was followed by his edition with foreword of *A Texas Ranger*, written by N.A. Jennings, published by R.R Donnelley & Sons, in 1993.

Partners and co-writers Jim Pearson and William Conroy joined Ben in writing *Texas: The Land and Its People*, a seventh-grade textbook published by Hendrick-Long in 1969, with revised editions issued in 1978 and 1986, which dominated the public school market for nearly two decades. In 1980, Ben and I complied *The Texas Heritage*, a reader to accompany university- and college-level texts, published by Harlan-Davison, which remains in use in its fourth edition in 2010.

Ben's magnum opus is *William Randolph Hearst: The Early Years*,

1863-1910, and *William Randolph Hearst, The Later Years, 1911-1951*, published by Oxford University Press in 1998 and 2007; the latter publication won the Phi Alpha Theta Best Book Award. When I called Ben while he was doing the research for these volumes he would be pouring over microfilm copies of newspapers published by Hearst and others from San Francisco to New York. In addition, Ben published articles and book reviews in journals such as the *Encyclopedia Britannica, American West, Journal of Southern History, Southwestern Historical Quarterly, Arizona and the West, The Historian, Journal of American History, Southwest Social Science Quarterly*, and the *East Texas Historical Journal*, and arranged Phi Alpha Theta sessions for the annual meeting of the Southwest Social Science Association for decades.

Honors and accolades for more than forty years of professional achievements cluttered the walls and shelves of Ben's home office as well as his quarters on the TCU campus. For example, he chaired the T.R. Fehrenbach Award Committee of the Texas Historical Commission, served on the editorial boards of *Arizona and the West* and *Journal of the West*, was an associate editor of the *New Handbook of Texas*, and was elected president of the Southwestern Social Science Association, 1971-1972; Texas State Historical Association, 1979-1980; and national Phi Alpha Theta, 1980-1982. In 1973 Ben received the Minnie Stephens Piper Award for outstanding achievement in teaching, and TCU's Favorite Teachers Award in 1995. Outside of academe, but related to his standing as a historian, Ben was named an Admiral in the Texas Navy in 1965, an honorary member of the Sons of the Republic of Texas in 1987, and a Knight of San Jacinto, a part of SRT, in 1993. He served on the board of The Texas Humanities Committee (later Humanities Texas), and the State Board of Review for the National Register of Historical Places, a division of the Texas Historical Commission. I was privileged to sit beside him during meetings of both, plus the executive council of TSHA and other historical organizations for nearly three decades.

Many years have passed since I met Ben during an annual meeting of TSHA in Waco. The introduction came via the good offices of F. Lee Lawrence, an attorney from Tyler, Texas, and the unofficial but powerful leader of the non-academic members of the Association. I knew Lee through the East Texas Historical Association, which he had helped to organize in 1962, long before he nominated me to be ETHA's director and editor in 1972. Now Lee was leaving the Council of TSHA prior to returning the next year as second vice president and the ladder to the presidency. Lee feared for the fate of the Association without another East Texan aboard, so he nominated me for a place on the Council and asked Ben, who dominated the proceedings of the Nominating Committee for years, to insure my selection. So our meeting in Waco was my "audition" to learn if I was worthy.

First: this arrangement is testimony to the strong bond between Ben and Lee, a bond which literally held the Association together during troubled times ahead. Second: Ben wasn't buying anyone—even with Lee's endorsement—sight unseen, hence our meeting in Waco. Ben was in his "Kojak" mode that day. Kojak was a television police detective played by bald actor Telly Savalis, whose shtick was a Tootsie Roll sucker in the corner of his mouth. So balding Ben greeted me with a sucker stick poking out next to his cheek. We boarded his Buick (this was before oil wells and Cadillac's), and got to know each other while touring flat and not terribly scenic Waco. With Lee's endorsement, I must have passed muster: Ben persuaded the committee to nominate me and we were off on a partnership of more than three decades during which he became my closest professional friend, hero, and eventually a man whom I could comfortably say I loved. No one in the profession, not even Lee Lawrence, whose memory I cherish and whose support and friendship I valued greatly, has meant more to me than Ben. He opened many doors for speaking and publication opportunities for me, bucked up my spirits when I needed it, and "had my back," sometimes when I knew about it and even more when I did not.

Such affection is shared by a legion of genuine academic "Procter students" at Texas Christian University, mostly graduate students, now friends. For example, Jeff King, Class of 1981, remembered, in an article published in *TCU Magazine*, "Ben Procter—my favorite out of several world-class professors.... With reading glasses atop his head, and his shirttail hanging out, he towered over his students while he graphically described various torture techniques employed by the Comanches." And Bob Carlson, Class of 1983, said, "Ben Procter, American History. What a terrific storyteller!. . .He was tall and balding and balanced his eyeglasses on the tip of his nose. I can still hear him saying, "Fire when ready, Gridley!""

Mary Kelley Scheer, Ben's graduate assistant in 1998 and later a professor at Lamar University, sat in on his freshman classes but also worked in his office. Scheer recalls many things about her time at TCU, including the "countless hours" Ben spent with students who needed help, and her valiant but futile efforts to clean up his office because "he didn't throw anything away." A veteran of three seminars Ben directed, Scheer was sometimes the subject of what graduate students called being "Procterized." Procterization involved having one's written work examined, word by word and sentence by sentence, and the use of clichés, the passive voice, or finding a paragraph without a topic sentence produced a scowl and perhaps greater criticism. Mike Collins, another of Ben's students, says he still cringes at the memory of Ben exclaiming, "Class, Mr. Collins has a split infinitive!"

While working in the office Scheer also recalls Ben constantly calling colleagues at other universities seeking jobs for his students, and once promising to "...come and teach those classes until they could find someone else" if his student did not perform satisfactorily. Once Ben "accepted you," says Scheer, you became part of his family. "He cared about you. I enjoyed visiting his home on many occasions, getting to know Phoebe and going out to one of his favorite restaurants, Angelos, to eat barbeque."

Collins, who serves as professor and administrator at Midwestern State University in Wichita Falls, Texas, says that Ben "was more than simply a mentor, and more than a role model for his students. He was our inspiration.... I can honestly say that, while he taught me virtually everything I know about the practice of history, he taught me even more about life, about being a man. In that respect, he has always been a second father to me."

Colleague Light Cummins, professor of history at Austin College, located in Sherman, Texas, recalls his first meeting with Ben, "a giant of a man with a stern and no-nonsense visage...accentuated by 'half-glasses' perched halfway down his nose in a seemingly very defiant manner. The effect created by his suit, white shirt, and dark solid tie—... which I would learn constituted his 'official uniform,' except for fishing trips, only adds to his overpowering any room in which he appears among other historians." Cummins later participated in many of Ben's two-day fishing expeditions on Lake Texoma.

Ben orchestrated fishing trips the way he organized dinners

at the AP readings or professional meetings. Regulars, in addition to Cummins and Collins, included John Crain of the Summerlee Foundation, publisher Andrew Davidson, former students Dave Murph and Mark Beasley, Ken Hendrickson of Midwestern State University, and others who happened to call or drop by when Ben was in his organizing mode. All had tales to tell when these weekend adventures ended—about how Ben made them all fish from one side of the boat while he dominated the other side; complaints that he always "limited out" first and made them throw back smaller catches so he could go on fishing; rigged bets on biggest catch or some such wager, which Ben always won; worst guide, or overnight accommodations, or chow—but they reenlisted every time Ben issued an invitation.

John Belohavek, a colleague from AP readings and professor at the University of South Florida, in Tampa, recalls riding with Ben from Fort Worth to Galveston, one of Ben's favorite retreats, with "Ben powering his big Buick across the two lanes of the Lone Star State. With blue belles [bluebonnets] blowing in the breeze and pickups hurling by...Ben would insist on telling his favorite story about where you were...and what happened there a century ago.... What made any such trip exciting was that he wasn't really looking at the road. Instead, he would plop his right arm over the top of the seat, steer with his left hand, and gaze into the back seat.... Phoebe, who had witnessed such behavior for decades, seemed to handle this all with ease but the novice traveler might see his premature demise somewhere on a Texas back road."

Belohavek also believes that "the term 'yellow dog Democrat' was crafted with Ben Procter in mind." Belohavek thinks that Ben's "commitment to a progressive democracy, inclusive and compassionate, has been a hallmark of his thinking." Democrats, "although sometimes haltering in their programs—have remained in his mind dedicated to that domestic goal. In contrast, Republicans, especially Texas Republicans, drive him to distraction." Belohavek claims that visits with Ben on the telephone inevitably turn to politics, and that although Ben has witnessed Texas "shifting from the days of Sam Rayburn and LBJ to Republican dominance, he has remained faithful to the party, its candidates, and his ideals."

Two close friends, Speaker Jim Wright and writer Jeff Guinn, also value their association with Ben. Wright credits Ben with suggesting that he make notes about the momentous events in which he participated as a congressman, majority leader, and speaker of the House of Representatives. "Ben became aware of my somewhat leisurely and haphazard habit of writing thoughts and observations by longhand in a journal," so he prodded Wright into a more systematic approach. At first, Ben "debriefed" Wright when he returned to Fort Worth and Phoebe would type a transcript of their exchange. Then Ben took to riding to the airport with Wright to tape his thoughts, and finally he convinced Wright to carry a small tape recorder with him daily to register first hand reactions to national and international crises and ordinary experiences. Wright says that such a record enabled him to write two volumes of memoires and that neither Ben nor Phoebe ever breached the confidential nature of the project so essential to its success.

Guinn, formerly a columnist for the Fort Worth Star-Telegram, remembers a disagreement with Ben over accusations of plagiarism alleged against a prominent historian. Guinn thought the historian only "sloppy" in his failure to credit two sources, while Ben believed the offence more serious. When Guinn wrote a column expressing his view, he claims that the ink was not dry on the newsprint before Ben called to chide him. Their conversations on the matter continued though several more calls, but Guinn says that their exchanges of views, while intense, never became personal. Soon afterwards, Guinn took two TCU student assistants to dinner. Seeing Ben at another table, Guinn went over to say hello. When he returned, one student said, "You KNOW Dr. Procter?" "Yes," said Jeff, "we are friends." "Dr. Procter has friends," the student asked in wonder? Jeff said, "You shouldn't be afraid of him. He and I have been having a running argument for six weeks, and as you can see, we're still fine with each other." After a pause the student asked, "You argued with Dr. Procter and you lived?"

And so it has ended. All the torches and talismans of leadership have passed to younger laborers. Students in Ben's classes over four decades—especially graduate students—carry his lamp of learning forward through classrooms of their own in published biographies, monographs, and textbooks, and by presenting papers for professional and lay audiences. Wherever they go, whatever they do, Ben goes with them. He is in their mind in what they teach and in their heart in how they do so. And they will pass it on, lending his great spirit of immortality as long as they labor.

We others, we non-traditional students, are joyed to have been a Friend of Ben. The poet Yeats said it best for me (with just a slight rewriting):

Think where my glory begins and ends
And say that my glory was that I was a friend of Ben's.
Ben Procter Crossed The Bar on April 17, 2012.

NEVER WITHOUT HONOR

CHAPTER 1

John Peter Smith

Founder of Fort Worth, From the Old Frontier to the New

By David Murph

On a North Texas December afternoon, a young man, having hitched a wagon ride for the final few miles into Fort Worth, stepped down and looked around for the first time at what would become home for the rest of his life. He had come a long way, starting in Kentucky, traveling south by boat and foot, looking for a place to settle. Eventually reaching New Orleans and finding himself in the midst of a cholera epidemic, he had hurried to Shreveport where he joined a wagon train to Dallas.[1]

Something about Dallas disappointed him. He called it "a muddy village that had grown up to be a trading post." So he continued to head west—this time on foot—toward Fort Worth. On the second day of walking, he stopped at the Jack Durrett place. Durrett was preparing to deliver some deer meat to Fort Worth and offered him a ride the rest of the way. It was 1853. New arrival John Peter Smith was twenty-two years old. No one, including him, could have imagined the impact he would have.[2]

So who in the world was John Peter Smith? Such is the passage of time that today, if Fort Worth residents were asked that question, chances are, most responses would be—"Oh, that's our charity hospital." And they would be right. John Peter Smith Hospital is the most prominent and one of the few places his name is to be found these days. How ironic. No one could have had more influence on the development of Fort Worth than he. His was a fascinating, energy-filled life that paralleled and literally shaped the city's first fifty years. Fort Worth would not be the Fort Worth of today had he not arrived.[3]

His story is also the story of late frontier America. His early years are easily described. In 1831, he was born in Owen County,

Kentucky. Both parents died when he was young, and an older cousin, W. H. Garrett, became his guardian. Garrett sent him off to Franklin College in Indiana where Smith spent one year before transferring to Bethany College in Virginia—now in West Virginia. Here he studied under Alexander Campbell, primary founder of the Christian Church (Disciples of Christ). Smith graduated with honors in ancient languages and mathematics in 1853. He returned to Kentucky to study law but, fascinated with the West, grew restless and decided to see it for himself. In November of that year he set out on his journey.[4]

He stepped off of that wagon in Fort Worth, college degree in hand, at an important time. The army post, having been founded in the summer of 1849, had just been abandoned that fall after only four years of existence. The army was moving its line of forts westward, and only weeks before had ridden out of Fort Worth, leaving its empty buildings on the high bluff above the Trinity River.[5]

Years later John Peter Smith (now called Peter by his friends) described his first impressions of this place. He recalled that "Indians of the Caddo (and) Waco…tribes were scattered through the section, their camp fires dotting the prairies at night in every direction around Fort Worth." When he arrived "not more than 30 people, young and old, were in the settlement. They occupied homes which had been deserted by the soldiers, and the embryo city was launched just west of the present courthouse square." Smith immediately believed he had come to a great place. "It seemed I had never seen a more beautiful spot. The magnificent hills, now crowned with elegant homes, and the lovely valleys, which have always been a favorite theme of mine, attracted me and I resolved to make my home here." [6]

What no one could have known that December, including Smith, was that Fort Worth would indeed become his lifetime home, and he would have such a huge hand in developing it, that one would be hard to imagine without the other. He would live to be seventy years old and to witness the beginning of the twentieth century. He would invest himself in and make lasting contributions to almost every facet of the town's life. He was Fort Worth's Amon Carter years before Amon Carter. But for this young, new settler, these days were still far in the future.[7]

Apparently one of Smith's first Fort Worth decisions involved guns. They were common in this setting he was about to call home, but something about carrying one bothered him. He was not comfortable with a gun and told fellow settler Middleton Tate Johnson, "I don't want to kill anybody and I certainly do not want to be killed. What's the answer?" "Well, Peter," advised Johnson, "if that's your idea, don't wear a gun. Nobody's going to shoot you if you ain't armed." That was good enough for Smith. He never wore one.[8]

Shortly after arriving, Smith decided to become a school teacher and, in so doing, became Fort Worth's first. With a college education, he was a natural for the job. What had been the fort's hospital building was in the best shape of all the abandoned structures, with a good clapboard roof and a fireplace at each end. Receiving permission to use the building, Smith opened it as a school and welcomed twelve students of various ages, most of whom could not even read.[9]

This venture was short lived. "The role of pedagogue did not please me," he recalled. After teaching for only three months he became ill, closed the school, and the old hospital building soon housed the Male and Female Academy, often called the first permanent educational enterprise in Fort Worth. Smith soon took up pursuits common to a number of young men on the frontier—store clerking, surveying and studying law. For several months he worked in the general store of Brinson and Daggett which had opened while the army was there and then moved into one of the empty fort buildings. He was also learning to survey and received an appointment as deputy surveyor of the Denton Land Department. Most of this work was in Jack and Palo Pinto counties. Since surveyors often received land as payment, this job enabled him for the first time to own some land. In the meantime, he had also decided to become a lawyer, and with Fort Worth attorney A. Y. Fowler, began studying law.[10]

By now Smith's energy and ambition were evident in one venture after another. While surveying and studying law, he also became a Mason and helped found Fort Worth's Masonic Lodge, even serving as High Priest. Also, in 1855 he became a charter member of First Christian Church, the town's earliest congregation. And somehow he found time for politics, getting heavily involved in the raucous campaign that would move the Tarrant County seat from Birdville to Fort Worth.[11]

It was quite an election. Some Fort Worth citizens, eager to wrest the seat of county government from Birdville in 1856, persuaded the Texas Legislature to set a special election in November. Election day would become memorable, not only because the outcome was important, but also because it turned into a contest to see which community could "out whiskey" the other. Determined to win that battle, the Fort Worth citizens set barrels of whiskey, dippers included, in front of two mercantile stores on the square. Beside them were buckets of sugar for those who liked their whiskey sweetened. Birdville leaders had planned to do the same but were outsmarted. They placed a barrel in a live oak grove, but on election eve some Fort Worth men, wise to the plan, slipped over to Birdville under the cover of night, poured the whiskey into their own barrel and added it to their supply. Fort Worth won the election by seven votes and became the new county seat.[12]

Birdville refused to accept this verdict as final, especially newspaper publisher A. G. Walker who, as state senator, tried to invalidate the election. He claimed that there were fewer male voters in the county than the number of ballots cast. John Peter Smith, along with J. C. Terrell of Fort Worth, happened to be in Austin when Walker made this charge before a legislative joint committee. They intervened and persuaded the legislators to support a compromise measure: hold another election in 1860 and choose among three options for the county seat—Fort Worth, Birdville, or a spot in the center of the county. By that time Birdville's cause was hopeless. On April 18, 1860, Birdville was defeated by even a non-existent entity. Fort Worth received 548 votes, "the center" 301 and Birdville only four.[13]

Something about Smith seemed to keep him in perpetual motion. Though calm and judicious by nature, he never stopped. There was always something else to be done, another challenge or opportunity, another way to achieve something. Through all his involvements he had continued to study law under A. Y. Fowler and by 1858 was admitted to the bar. But even this new venture would soon be interrupted by another. In 1860, with Indian problems mounting along the Red River, attorney Smith headed north and signed up with a group of rangers determined to end the violence. After several weeks, satisfied with the results, he returned home to practice law.[14]

Events far beyond Smith's control, however, were about to postpone his legal career. In 1860, as the Civil War loomed, a meeting of Fort Worth residents was called by Smith, Middleton Tate Johnson and E.

M. Daggett. A majority of those present adopted a resolution requesting Governor Sam Houston call a special session of the legislature to vote on secession. Their hope was that Texas would secede but remain independent, not affiliating with other southern states. Houston also opposed linking Texas with the Confederacy, but to no avail.[15]

Regardless of the course chosen, Smith was determined to do his duty as he understood it. He would follow the will of his fellow Texans. So when Texas voted to leave the Union and join the Confederacy, he recruited 120 men and helped form Company K under the command of Colonel William Steele. On November 15, 1861, he reported for duty in San Antonio as second lieutenant, Company K, 7th Texas Calvary, Sibley's Brigade.[16]

Smith would see plenty of action in the war. One of his earliest experiences was also one of the hardest. Henry Hopkins Sibley had convinced Jefferson Davis that invading the New Mexico Territory was a good idea and would lead to a "greater Confederacy." Davis made him a Brigadier General and authorized what would become a disastrous mission. It started well enough in January, 1862, as Sibley led Lieutenant Smith and more than 2,000 men out of El Paso northward along the Rio Grande. By the end of February Sibley's forces had defeated Union troops at Valverde, Albuquerque and Santa Fe. But then everything changed. Although the Rebels held their ground in a six-hour battle at Glorietta Pass on March 28, a group of Union troops discovered and destroyed Sibley's supply train, leaving him in an isolated, almost hopeless position.[17]

The situation had shifted quickly from success to survival. With all other choices gone, Sibley and his men began the long march back to Texas from Glorietta in what became one of the tragedies of the war's first year. Smith and his comrades were a weary, bedraggled lot. Day after day they trudged on. Baked by the sun, hungry and thirsty, many collapsed and died along the way, their bodies eaten by wolves. Not until late in May, their pitiful caravan now strung out for fifty miles, did the surviving remnant stagger into El Paso.[18]

But that was not the end. Smith had been given the assignment to escort several wagonloads of wounded survivors all the way back to San Antonio. And what an assignment it was as the wagons creaked and bounced along through sand, brush, gullies and rugged terrain. Upon reaching El Paso, Smith encountered a Mexican with a herd of goats and quickly saw some possibilities. He convinced the man to bring his goats and join the wagon train. It must have been some sight as this unlikely string of horses, men, wagons and goats grindingly made its way over a vast expanse of Texas. Though apparently never learning to like goats' milk, the men drank it anyway, and by the time they reached San Antonio the health of some had actually improved. Miraculously, none had died. Years later his granddaughter said that he "was prouder of getting the wounded men back from Glorietta than anything he ever did." After this debacle, Henry Hopkins Sibley would never again receive another significant command.[19]

Smith could not rest long. In that fall of 1862, Union forces captured Galveston, and Confederate General John McGruder was determined to liberate it. His plan was to launch an attack with a five-hundred-man land force supported by two armed steamboats---the Bayou City and the Neptune. Smith and several fellow Texans from the New Mexico nightmare were to be aboard the Neptune. At the Houston docks both the Bayou City and the Neptune were covered with cotton bales for protection. The operation began in the early hours of New Year's Day, 1863, as the land troops crossed over to the island and the two padded vessels steamed down Buffalo Bayou to encounter four Union gunboats. While the Confederates engaged the Federals in heavy fire, Smith's Neptune and the Bayou City were dramatically effective in neutralizing the enemy's naval force. (However, one of the four gunboats exploded without any enemy help.) The Neptune was heavily engaged, striking one of the Union boats hard enough to break its own nose. But by that time, both the naval and land battles were ending in victory and the three Massachusetts companies on shore surrendered en masse. Smith and his cohorts had liberated Galveston.[20]

He would serve throughout the war, spending the last half of it in Louisiana. Although escaping injury in New Mexico and Galveston, he would not be so lucky in Louisiana. In June, 1863, in the fighting near Donaldsonville, Smith was severely wounded and, as he put it, "was unable for duty for six months." Then, in April, 1864, he was wounded again, this time not so seriously, at the Battle of Mansfield, an important encounter that thwarted Union General Nathaniel Banks's efforts to march into Texas. Smith was promoted to Colonel and on May 18 of the following year, at the war's end, disbanded the 600 men under his command at a Trinity River landing in Navarro County called Wild Cat Bluff.[21]

Then occurred one of the strangest, most uncharacteristic episodes in John Peter Smith's life. Fearing what might happen to former Confederate officers, he fled for the Mexican border. He and fourteen other former officers agreed to meet in Austin early in June and from there travel to Mexico City. The exact plan is not clear, but apparently they hoped to meet with Emperor Maximilian and request large tracts of land where they could begin new lives. They met as planned and on June 18 set out for Mexico, carrying a letter of introduction to Maximilian from Texas Governor Pendleton Murrah extolling their exemplary qualities.[22]

Despite all the optimism, Smith must have known that he had embarked on a treacherous trip. General Philip Sheridan had been sent to the Rio Grande with more that 50,000 troops to display American discontent with the French occupation of Mexico. Making matters even tougher was the bounty on these Texans' heads for any Mexicans who captured and turned them over to the Americans. As they reached the Rio Grande, their problems became evident. Several Mexicans, pretending to befriend them, suggested some places to cross the river. No one could be trusted. Finally, choosing their own spot, they crossed to the Mexican side at Mier. No sooner had they entered town than they were rounded up and jailed. Their Mexican land dreams appeared to be at an end. However, they must have been good negotiators, because the next morning the Mexican officer in charge considered the gifts of a horse and pistol enough payment to release them.[23]

But the night must have been long and discussion filled, for looking at what the future might hold, they were no longer in agreement about what to do. Smith obviously had second thoughts about their grandiose scheme because, while twelve of the men left for Mexico City, he and two others split off and skirted the Mexican side of the Rio Grande, riding more than 100 dangerous miles to Matamoros. Then, crossing the river at Brownsville, they finally encountered Federal forces. They were recognized and held as former Confederates, but for how long is not known. What is clear is that on July 17, 1865, Smith signed a document claiming that as a "Prisoner of War" he "surrendered to Maj. General E. R. S. Canby, USA" and gave his "solemn PAROLE OF HONOR" that he would not hereafter "serve in the Armies of the Confederate States…against the United States of America…" That was enough to free him. He and his two companions sold their horses at Brownsville and caught a cargo boat to Galveston. From there Smith began the long journey toward home and by September he was back in Fort Worth.[24]

From every indication Smith never said much about this adventure. Maybe it was embarrassing. Maybe it defied explanation. Who but he alone could have known his thoughts? To be sure, it was a sharp break from the kind of life he had been building, but then, so was the war. For four tumultuous years his life had been rearranged and rerouted. He had decided to run, but it was more than running from something. He was also running toward something---a future that at one point seemed to hold magnificent, even dreamlike possibilities but that in the bright light of a Mexican morning quickly faded. So he returned to the place and people he knew best.[25]

Colonel Smith soon plunged back into the bustling life of frontier Fort Worth. Just before the war, he and J. J. Jarvis, another civic-minded local attorney, had formed a law partnership that was now beginning to thrive. Realizing the value of land, Smith continued to acquire as much as possible and was quickly becoming a major landowner. As if this were not enough to keep him occupied, he also agreed to teach school again. In 1866, a small, new school opened its doors, and he could not resist volunteering. This teaching experience proved more to his liking than the first.[26]

Now in his mid thirties, Smith was still a bachelor. But that was about to change. In October, 1867, he married Mary Fox, the widow of pioneer Fort Worth physician F. A. Fox. She and her husband had come from Mississippi. In addition to her young son, she and John Peter Smith would eventually bear five children---four sons and a daughter.[27]

This post-war, adopted home town to which Smith had returned and in which he would fully invest himself was far from tame. In fact, it was wilder than ever. B. B. Paddock's Fort Worth Democrat newspaper drew a disturbingly clear picture of Fort Worth in these years. He included items such as: "Night before last at a late hour, a party of roughs, eighteen or twenty in number, came into town and made strong demonstrations toward liberating the prisoners in the jail." He began another story with "Female Bruisers and General Hair Pulling and Scratching" and told of two women he described as the "demi monde" of the city. One had "something like a map of Mexico on her face and the absence of a few ringlets from her poll."[28]

Dance halls were a special problem. Paddock announced that "Blood has been shed at the dance houses…close them out" and "The Red Light dance house is in full blast. Hundreds of cowboys, frontiersmen and gangsters frequent it nightly." Actually, the dance halls, though troublesome, had become so prevalent that the city council, tired of passing ordinances prohibiting them, voted to license them for $100.00 a quarter, payable in advance. This measure lasted about a month until the mayor decided to oppose it and the council agreed, returning the dance halls to their wide-open status. "It is utterly impossible," said Paddock, "for our citizens to bear much longer with the rowdy element in our midst. We have a distinct class of men existing here who have no more respect for their own or another man's life than a real civilized man would have for the life of a fly."[29]

The lawlessness was not restricted to dance halls. Twice in the span of two weeks, in a ravine fourteen miles west of town, the Yuma stagecoach was robbed. And one summer, both the east and west stagecoaches were held up on the same day in broad daylight. That was not all. Paddock admonished his readers "Stop shooting at night. We have glass windows at our house, and even when the balls don't go through the wall, it creates unpleasant reflections to hear them pattering against the weatherboarding."[30]

In addition to dance halls, robberies and gunfire, Indian raids were still near enough to be frightening. In 1873, just northwest of town, two Indian chiefs, Santana and Big Tree, hit a wagon train carrying supplies to Fort Griffin. In the melee wagons were burned, mules and horses stolen, and several men were killed. Both chiefs were captured and tried for murder at Jacksboro, and all this not quite far enough away from anxious Fort Worth residents.[31]

Despite Fort Worth's raw, boisterous life, it seems to have embodied the dichotomy that characterized a number of frontier communities---a violent, unsettled element somehow living alongside, even with, softer, more cultured currents. At the same time Santana and Big Tree were raiding nearby wagon trains and killing settlers, newspaper editor Paddock was announcing that Fort Worth "now has a dancing school…holding forth in the courthouse." He was also not above declaring that the town needed a tailor and a milliner. "We don't care so much about the tailor; but a young and pretty milliner is preferred." Paddock, a fellow veteran and close friend of Smith's who had seen his share of violence, could not help but extol the beauty of their town. "It is impossible to present by description a true picture of the beautiful landscape views and natural scenery that are open to view upon the romantic bluffs and grassy plains in and around the city of Fort Worth." Violence and beauty, side by side, even intermingled.[32]

In these same years Smith also witnessed some of the great cattle drives that came through Fort Worth on the McCoy Trail. These large, combined herds entered town from the south, slowly made their way to what are now Broadway and South Main, then up Jones Street and from there northeast through the edge of the business district to Cold Springs Road and across the river. These drives were major events as they lumbered through town. Nearly all business ceased; children were kept inside; doors and windows of houses were shut tight as huge clouds of dust filled the air. Making matters worse, the possibility of stampedes was always real. In one two-year period, more than 200,000 head of cattle were driven through town.[33]

During all these happenings, John Peter Smith had become prominent. Reported to be the largest landowner in town, by 1870 he owned 2,000 acres in Tarrant County. He also began generously giving much of it away to benefit Fort Worth. No gift was more publicized and important than one he made in January 1877 when he donated five acres of land to build a hospital for the poor. It was dedicated to "the common use and benefit of the destitute sick of the city and county." A contemporary account of this gift called it "a magnificent site for a hospital...on a beautiful eminence about a mile south of the depot... Such gifts, in such times, speak volumes of praise for the generous donor. Go thou and do likewise." Two years later, aware that a growing Fort Worth needed a cemetery, Smith gave twenty wooded, rolling acres near downtown to create Oakwood Cemetery. Special sections were established for Negroes, Catholics and Confederate veterans. In addition, he donated land for a Jewish cemetery and a sizeable tract for a park stretching from the city bridge to the forks of the Trinity.[34]

Throughout the 1870s, as Fort Worth grew from fewer than 2,000 citizens to more than 6,000, Smith seemed to have a hand in almost every major development. Along with Thomas Tidball who had come from Missouri, Kliever Van Zandt and J. J. Jarvis, he helped organize a bank that would become the Fort Worth National Bank. It began in a small storeroom on the courthouse square with Smith's office upstairs, above the enterprise. In 1874 he even helped light the town by leading the way in organizing the Fort Worth Gas and Light Company and, at almost the same time, formed the Fort Worth Street Railway Company. This operation used a single track, stretching from the courthouse to the train depot, on which mules pulled passenger cars. Along the way, drivers often stopped at saloons and went in with riders to get a drink before continuing the journey.[35]

Fort Worth celebrated the nation's centennial in 1876 with dramatic new links to the rest of the world. For several years city leaders had worked to obtain railroad service. Smith, along with B. B. Paddock, helped lead fundraising rallies and contributed generously from his own pocket. Success eventually came, but in a wilder, more unpredictable way than most could have predicted. The westward progress of the Texas and Pacific Railroad had been stalled at Eagle Ford, just east of Fort Worth. The Texas Legislature had promised the T&P sixteen sections of land for every completed mile of track, but had also imposed an almost impossible deadline. Railroad executives, becoming increasingly frantic, disregarded normal procedures and threw every worker possible into the track-laying effort. While one Fort Worth legislator, by his single vote, kept the House of Representatives in session and stalled the deadline, several city businesses released employees to join the railroad crew and work around the clock to complete the track. On the morning of July 19, 1876, on wobbly rails, the first train arrived in Fort Worth, setting off huge rounds of cheering and fireworks. And just three months later, from a small office downtown, a telegraph operator, with the mayor at his side, sent a message to Dallas and actually got a reply. Fort Worth was now connected to a wider world. Its economy would not be far behind.[36]

Though prominent, John Peter Smith was not above the law, as evidenced by an embarrassing 1878 newspaper article entitled "Practice Your Precepts." Swimming in certain sections the Trinity River was one of several Sunday activities prohibited by the city. "Our worthy citizen, J. P. Smith," the story began, "among other bountiful blessings, has been endowed with a family of children and among the number are two very promising lads who have been in the habit of refreshing themselves---by bathing in the running waters of the Clear Fork. Their favorite hole happened to be within the corporate limits of the city and acting upon the caution of their father who pictured to them the legal penalty of...swimming there, they obediently sought and found another hole beyond the limit prescribed by law for such sports. Mr. Smith himself," it continued, "feeling in the humor of bathing, sought out the self same forbidden hole Sunday morning, stripped and took comfort in the waters deep. One of the police happening along about that time, espied the gentleman and in the mayor's court yesterday morning he paid the penalty set apart for such carelessness. We're never too old to learn by experience."[37]

Smith rose from appearing in the mayor's court to becoming mayor in 1882. He would be elected to a second term, and serve four years characterized by strong, visionary leadership. He had long been an advocate of public education, and during his tenure Fort Worth public schools were begun with him serving as ex-officio president of the board. Also, the city charter was amended to allow taxes up to 2 ½ percent, making possible many improvements. For instance, the city's first sidewalks were built, the fire department was reorganized, the first sanitary sewers were dug, and a municipal water system was created. In addition, Main and Houston Streets were paved all the way from the courthouse to the train depot. Fort Worth was becoming a real city.[38]

As Smith prepared to leave office, he faced his most difficult mayoral experience. The railroad strike of 1886, instigated by the Knights of Labor, had spread to Fort Worth with the result that all trains coming in or out of town, except one daily run, were stopped. A month into the strike, railroad officials decided to break the blockade with an armed train that made it out of town, only to encounter a group of strikers and be derailed. In a gunfight that ensued, a guard was killed. Smith acted immediately. At his request, Governor John Ireland sent 300 state militiamen to Fort Worth to prevent further violence. The strike soon ended, but the tension it created would linger.[39]

A contemporary account related a telling personal description of Mayor Smith. "He is a fine specimen of western manhood, generous, liberal and benevolent to a fault; yet his generosity to the poor seems to add to his prosperity. He is remarkably patient, never losing his temper. He is industrious and though constantly employed is never in a hurry." It called him "firm," claiming that "when his judgment is convinced, it is not easy to move him from his purpose." He was labeled "a public spirited man," a "useful" man. "The death of no one in his community would create a larger vacancy or one more difficult to be filled."[40]

That industriousness, coupled with determination and love for his home town, brought him notice beyond Fort Worth. After Smith had visited the Roseville quarries in central Texas in 1887, B. B. Paddock quoted the *Austin Statesman* as saying: "It is not known whether Col. Peter Smith made an offer to move the granite quarries to Fort Worth or not." He claimed that a Dallas leader once said Smith "tried to buy the Chicago Water Works for that purpose" and added: "That sort of pluck has made Fort Worth what she is."[41]

Smith was again elected mayor in the summer of 1890, this time to fill the unexpired term of the incumbent who had resigned. He had just finished leading an effort to create the Spring Palace, a large, fanciful building that served as the centerpiece of an enterprise promoting agricultural and dairy products. The Spring Palace would not last long. Attracting visitors not only from neighboring states but also other countries, it survived just one year before being destroyed by fire. Mayor Smith, named by a Kansas newspaper as Fort Worth's first and only millionaire, was not discouraged. He once again focused his influence and energy on the betterment of his town whose population now exceeded 25,000. Under his leadership, funds were appropriated for a new city hall, the city's boundaries were extended to a six-mile square, a new sewerage system and fire station were created, and major improvements were made to the public water works.[42]

Although his last stint as mayor ended in 1892, his active role in improving and promoting Fort Worth did not. By this time he had become a significant donor to Fort Worth University, was on the city's Board of Trade, had given land rent-free to the Farmers' Alliance Cotton Yards, was serving as president of the Fort Worth Shoe and Leather Company, president of People's Mutual Gas Company, and also leading a movement to establish the city's first stockyards. He seemed to be everywhere.[43]

And he was not slowing down. In 1901, although a number of railroads had now come to Fort Worth, seventy-year-old Smith traveled to St. Louis to see if he could lure one more. One evening, while walking back to his hotel following a meeting, he was attacked, beaten and robbed of thirty dollars. Falling to the pavement, he broke a tooth. Blood poisoning set in, and after a few days in a St. Louis hospital, John Peter Smith died on April 11.[44]

Fort Worth citizens were stunned. The response was overwhelming. Such was his prominence that a Fort Worth newspaper's large, bold headline said simply "He is Gone." A local delegation left immediately by train for St. Louis to accompany his body back home. Upon its return, hundreds gathered at the train station and stood silently to receive him and pay their respects. His funeral was the largest Fort Worth had ever seen. It was held at his home near where First United Methodist Church now stands. Swarms of people filled the house, yard and even streets in every direction for two blocks to pay tribute to this man who had arrived as a twenty-two-year old in a village of thirty people perched on the river bluff around an abandoned army fort, who had gone off to war and returned to become the very life blood of their town. His body was carried to Oakwood Cemetery, to land he had donated years earlier, and was buried in a ceremony that included a special tribute from his fellow Confederate veterans.[45]

A visitor to his gravesite today would find no clue to his prominence, for he desired no special monument or marker. His small, flat gravestone is identical to other simple markers of family members---one among several in the Smith plot. However, his fellow citizens demanded more. John Peter Smith was not only respected but also loved. His modesty, his kindness and generosity endeared him to others, and soon after his death a number of civic leaders launched a fundraising drive to build a monument in his honor. As a result of this effort in 1906, a statue was dedicated in the park north of St. Patrick's Cathedral, adjacent to prime land Smith had sold to the church for $100.00.[46]

That same year, young Amon Carter would arrive in Fort Worth and begin his rise to wealth and fame. But rather than finding an abandoned fort, he would inherit a well-grounded, vibrant city, ready to move into the twentieth century. Whether he knew it or not, he would owe much to John Peter Smith. From schools, hospitals and churches, to railroads, water and cattle, Smith had led the way. He was one of those remarkable people who see themselves connected to and responsible for others, who see their resources as intended to be used for the betterment of those around them. His generosity—both of spirit and dollars—laid the foundation on which others would build a great city. Fort Worth is his town. He, perhaps more than anyone else, built it. As his last surviving granddaughter said, "He was absolutely crazy about this town." She must have been right, because everywhere you look, it shows.[47]

Endnotes

1   Julia Kathryn Garrett, *Fort Worth: A Frontier Triumph* (Austin: Encino Press, 1972), p. 124. Hereafter cited as Garrett, *Frontier Triumph*; interview with Josephine Terrell Smith Hudson (John Peter Smith's last surviving grandchild) by author, Fort Worth, Texas, July 15, 1999. Hereafter cited as Hudson interview; *The Encyclopedia of the New West* (Marshall, Texas: United States Biographical Publishing Company, 1887), p. 471; *Research Data, Fort Worth and Tarrant County*, Fort Worth Public Library, 110, 111, 883, 808. Hereafter cited as *Research Data*.

2   Garrett, *Frontier Triumph*, p. 124; Oliver Knight, *Fort Worth: Outpost on the Trinity* (Norman, University of Oklahoma Press, 1953), p. 38. Hereafter cited as Knight, Fort Worth; Bill Fairley, *Star-Telegram*, July 23, 1997.

3   Duane Gage, *Star-Telegram*, October 19, 1985; Bill Fairley, *Star-Telegram*, July 23, 1997; Mary Daggett Lake, "The Story of John Peter Smith, Pioneer Teacher and City Builder," unidentified article, November 21, 1926. Hereafter cited as Lake, "The Story of John Peter Smith."

4   *Catalogue of the Officers and Students of Franklin College*, 1849-50, Archives, Franklin College Library, Franklin, Indiana (Printed by John D. Defrees, 1850), p. 8; *Catalogue of the Officers and Students of Bethany College, for 1852 and 1853*, Together with the *Course of Study and Annual Announcement for 1853-'54* (Wheeling: Printed at the Daily Intelligencer Job Office, 1853); letter to author from B. Jeanne Cobb, Archivist and Coordinator of Special Collections, Bethany College, Bethany, West Virginia, October 22, 1999; Garrett, *Frontier Triumph*, p. 124; John Henry Brown, *Indian Wars and Pioneers of Texas* (Austin: L. E. Daniell Publishing Company, 1880), p.754. Hereafter cited as Brown, *Indian Wars and Pioneers*.

5   *Encyclopedia of the New West*, p. 471; Knight, *Fort Worth*, p. 25.

6   *The News Tribune*, Fort Worth, May 16, 1975.

7   Duane Gage, *Star-Telegram*, October 19, 1985; *New Handbook of Texas*, vol. 5 (Austin; Texas State Historical Association, 1996), p. 104.

8   *The News Tribune*, Fort Worth, November 28, 1980; James Young Smith (son of John Peter Smith), typed manuscript in author's possession, unknown origin and date.

9 Garrett, *Frontier Triumph*, p. 124; Knight, *Fort Worth*, p. 39;
Encyclopedia of the New West, p. 471; Research Data, 1128, 2031, 2291.

10 Duane Gage, "John Peter Smith," unpublished biographical sketch,
1980, p. 2; Hereafter cited as Duane Gage, "John Peter Smith." Star-
Telegram, November 21, 1926; Garrett, *Frontier Triumph*, p. 124;
Brown, *Indian Wars and Pioneers*, p. 754; *Research Data*, 112.

11 Knight, *Fort Worth*, pp. 40-42; *Star-Telegram*, November 21, 1926;
Research Data, 2032, 18192.

12 *Research Data*, "Fort Worth City Guide," n.d., p. 338; *Research Data*,
147, 250, 3274, 3430; Garrett, *Frontier Triumph*, pp. 141-144; Knight,
Fort Worth, pp. 40-41.

13 *Dallas Herald*, April 18, 1860; Knight, *Fort Worth*, pp. 43-44, 281;
Research Data, "Fort Worth City Guide," n.d., p. 338.

14 *Encyclopedia of the New West*, p. 470; *Research Data*, 112, 194. Smith
was said to be joining "rangers."

15 T. R. Fehrenbach, *Lone Star: A History of Texas and the Texans* (New
York: Macmillan, 1968), pp. 344-347; *Encyclopedia of the New West*, p.
471; Hudson interview; Bill Fairley, *Star-Telegram*, July 23, 1997.

16 *Encyclopedia of the New West*, p. 471; Hudson interview; Brown,
Indian Wars and Pioneers, p. 754; Bill Fairley, *Star-Telegram*, July 23,
1997.

17 Robert Paul Jordan, *The Civil War* (Washington, D.C.: National
Geographical Society, 1969), pp. 80-81. Hereafter cited as Jordan, *The
Civil War*. David Rubel and Russell Shorto, editors, *The Civil War
Chronicle: The Only Day-by-Day Portrait of America's Tragic Conflict
As Told by Soldiers, Journalists, Politicians, Farmers, Nurses, Slaves,
and Other Eyewitnesses* (New York: Crown Publishers, 2000), pp. 141-
142. Hereafter cited as Rubel and Shorto, *Civil War Chronicle*; *Dallas
Morning News*, May 12, 2002; Garrett, *Frontier Triumph*, pp. 205, 221.

18 Jordan, *The Civil War*, pp. 80-81; Rubel and Shorto, *The Civil War
Chronicle*, pp. 141-142; Hudson Interview.

19 Letter from Josephine Terrell Smith Hudson to Duane Gage, n.d.
Hereafter cited as Hudson to Gage. *Research Data*, 4009; Duane Gage,
"John Peter Smith," p. 3; Rubel and Shorto, *Civil War Chronicle*, pp.
141-142, 163; Garrett, *Frontier Triumph*, pp. 205, 225; Jordan, *The Civil
War*, pp. 80-81.

20 Shelby Foote, *The Civil War, A Narrative: Fredericksburg to Meridian* (New York: Random House, 1963), pp. 57-58. Hereafter cited as Foote, *The Civil War, A Narrative*; Garrett, *Frontier Triumph*, p. 221.

21 *Research Data*, 318, 3948, 3949, 4009; Brown, *Indian Wars and Pioneers*, p. 754; Rubel and Shorto, *Civil War Chronicle*, pp. 398-399; Foote, *The Civil War, A Narrative*, pp. 138, 599; Garrett, *Frontier Triumph*, pp. 225, 229-230.

22 Bill Fairley, "A Reluctant Confederate," *Star-Telegram*, March 1, 2000; Garrett, *Frontier Triumph*, pp. 230-231.

23 Ibid.

24 PAROLE OF HONOR, July 16, 1865, copy in author's possession; *Star-Telegram*, March 1, 2000; Garrett, *Frontier Triumph*, pp. 231-232; *Encyclopedia of the New West*, p. 471.

25 Hudson interview.

26 Addison Clark, one of the founders of Texas Christian University, eventually replaced Smith as teacher. Research Data, 343, 4045, 4071, 18343; Fort Worth *Democrat*, September 20, 1873, February 7, 1874; *Star-Telegram*, October 19, 1985.

27 Hudson interview; *Encyclopedia of the New West*, p. 471.

28 Fort Worth *Democrat*, July 19, 1876, September 5, 1876; *Research Data*, 3458.

29 Fort Worth *Democrat*, January 16, 1877, July 10, 1878, August 14, 1878, September 3, 1878, September 11, 1878; *Research Data*, 3466, 3467, 3468.

30 Fort Worth *Record*, September 20, 1914; Fort Worth *Democrat*, April 19, 1873.

31 Fort Worth *Democrat*, August 16, 1873, September 6, 1873; *Research Data*, 1083, 1084.

32 Fort Worth *Democrat*, January 25, 1873.

33 *Research Data*, 4072, 4082; Knight, *Fort Worth*, pp. 59-61; Garrett, *Frontier Triumph*, pp. 315-317.

34 *Research Data*, "Fort Worth City Guide," n.d., 474; *Star-Telegram*, April 7, 1981; Hudson interview; Hudson to Gage; Fort Worth Daily Democrat, October 19, 1977.

35 *Research Data*, 17, 226, 470, 2537, 2538, 4087; "Fort Worth City
    Guide," n.d., pp. 169, 176; Fort Worth *Daily Democrat*, November 28,
    1878; Fort Worth *Daily Gazette*, March 8, 1884, April 18, 1884; *Star-
    Telegram*, April 26, 1931.

36 *Research Data*, 1089, 1090, 1097, 1099, 2495, 2496, 2510; Fort Worth
    Democrat, May 24, 1873, April 20, 1876, May 27, 1876; *Star-Telegram*,
    April 23, 1931, January 18, 1950, April 2, 1955.

37 Fort Worth *Democrat*, April 23, 1878.

38 *Research Data*, 914, 915, 3406, 3407, 4049; Austin *Daily Statesman*,
    June 3, 1883; *New Handbook of Texas*, vol. 5, p. 104; Lake, "The
    Story of John Peter Smith," Sioux Campbell, "Fort Worth City Guide,
    Monuments-Memorials," in *Research Data*, 17822.

39 *Research Data,* 4072; Knight, *Fort Worth*, pp. 127-129.

40 *Encyclopedia of the New West*, p. 470.

41 Fort Worth *Daily Gazette*, March 31, 1887.

42 Denton C. Limbaugh, "Fort Worth City Guide, City Government," n.d.,
    in *Research Data*, 17982; *Research Data,* 17985, 2822; *Star-Telegram*,
    October 31, 1979. Smith is cited as millionaire in clipping from
    Wichita *Eagle,* Wichita, Kansas, n.d.

43 "Fort Worth City Guide," n.d., p. 294; *Research Data*, 294, 2810, 2913;
    Fort Worth *Daily Democrat*, September 2, 1876; Fort Worth *Daily
    Gazette*, November 23, 1890; Knight, *Fort Worth*, p. 137.

44 Fort Worth *Register*, April 12, 1901; *Research Data*, p. 316; Hudson
    interview.

45 Fort Worth *Register*, April 12, 1901, April 14, 1901.

46 Sioux Campbell, "Fort Worth City Guide," "Monuments-Memorials,"
    Research Data, 17822.

47 *Research Data*, 1497; Hudson interview; Bill Fairley, *Star-Telegram*, July
    23, 1997; *Star-Telegram*, December 2, 2003.

CHAPTER 2

ASHBEL SMITH

SETTING THE HIGHEST OF TEXAS STANDARDS

By Watson Arnold

Galveston was not a pretty place in 1848. The city had grown from the scattered buildings that sheltered Henry Smith and the Republic of Texas government from the armies of Santa Anna in 1836 to a city of about three thousand inhabitants spread several miles up and down the island. The business section, the Strand, consisted of an unpaved, sandy street filled with the dung from the innumerable animals that daily trod its path. It stretched a half mile lined with brick and wooden buildings that backed up to the mud flats of the bay. Wooden wharfs stretched hundreds of yards over the shallow water to the deeper channel and ships docked several deep on each side. Below the wharves, the shallow waters filled with the garbage and sewerage of the city, the refuge from the docked ships, and the carcasses of dead animals and fish. The bay waters, rocked by the waves from passing shipping and the gentle bay tides, rarely removed the offal from the mud flats. Only the occasional storm washed out the litter and, more often than not, flooded it onto the city streets. Passengers from the boats hurried down the wooden planks to escape the terrible stench that arose from the pollution below.

On the streets that ran beside the Stand clustered the cabins, shacks, and hovels of the new immigrants, the dockworkers, and the poor. Unique to Galveston, the houses of the slaves faced the alleyways and a subculture of saloons and tradesmen catering to blacks had grown along the rank muddy back lanes. The city streets were also unpaved, sandy and swampy. Vegetation was scarce. There existed neither sewage nor water systems. Cisterns filled with rainwater draining from the roofs furnished drinking water. Because the water table lay only a few feet below the surface, pollution from the shallow privies contaminated the wells. Flies and mosquitoes bred in the tepid, fecund waters of the bay, in the privies, and in the puddles in the streets. The ocean breezes kept them from the larger homes but they collected in the homes adjacent to the Strand.[1]

On the Gulf side of the island lay the scattered houses of the wealthier residents. They lived in large one and two-story wooden houses with unscreened windows stretching from the floor to the ceiling and always open to the cooling ocean breezes. Wide verandas and porches shaded by oleanders and carefully cultivated trees wrapped around the houses. Down the island for several miles stretched the farms and dairies that fed the city. Galveston Island was prosperous and healthy, but a tempest that was to paralyze and nearly close the new city was approaching.

Such was the condition of Galveston early in September 1839 when Ashbel Smith traveled to the island to recover from a prolonged and debilitating bout of "moderate fever." Brother George Smith, who was studying medicine with Ashbel traveled with him. They stayed at the house of his friend, General Moseley Baker. Shortly after his arrival, Smith noted in a letter to his friend Barnard E. Bee, "Yellow fever is raging tremendously in New Orleans." Three weeks later, the epidemic reached Galveston. Ashbel Smith would play a crucial role when Yellow Fever struck the island.[2]

At this time, Ashbel Smith was perhaps the most educated man in Texas and had traveled a long way from his birthplace of Hartford Connecticut in 1805. After attending Yale University, obtaining a BA and MA degree when nineteen years old, graduating Phi Beta Kappa, he obtained a MD degree, also from Yale. He pursued his medical career by studying surgery in Paris. While there in 1842, an epidemic of cholera swept the city, and Smith wrote a paper on the disease--in French.[3]

Ashbel Smith remained close to family throughout his life. Smith had a half brother, Curtis, from his father's previous marriage, brothers Henry and George and a sister, Caroline. Brother George followed him to Texas, training as an apprentice physician with his brother. Caroline resided in Connecticut, taking care of their parents and keeping close contact with her brothers. Smith, however, remained estranged from his brother Henry, who lived in Memphis, for many years. They eventually reconciled. Smith eventually entered the medical profession. After graduating from Yale in 1824, Smith moved to Salisbury, North Carolina, serving as a tutor for the children of Colonel Charles Fisher and as headmaster in a private school. He returned to Hartford to attend medical school in 1828. In 1831, Smith traveled to Paris to study surgery, then returned to Salisbury in 1832, establishing a thriving medical practice. Smith became restless in Salisbury and in 1837, he moved to Texas. Shortly after his arrival in the city of Houston, he became roommates with Sam Houston, President of the Republic of Texas. Smith nursed Houston through a serious though unspecified illness in 1837. They began a friendship that lasted the rest of their lives. Houston appointed Smith as Surgeon General of the Army of the Republic of Texas. Shortly afterwards Smith became ill with a chronic relapsing fever and traveled to Galveston to recover.[4]

When Yellow Fever struck Galveston Island on September 20, 1839, over half the island's ten resident physicians and an equal proportion of the civilian population fled the city. Certainly, with his poor health, Smith had every reason to leave, but he put aside his personal problems and plunged into treating the victims of the epidemic. He did send his brother George out of harm's way.[5]

A Galveston resident described the epidemic in a letter to her mother in Maine. "We are fortunate in having an excellent physician, Doctor Smith. He has been sometime in the country and was Surgeon General of the Army during the war. About the middle of the town, there is a strip of low marshy land. . . . It is a perfect mud hole, never dry, the filthiest part of the city and the smell is dreadful. It (the epidemic) lasted about six weeks and over that time there were 205 deaths. The bad air occasioned the sickness. The city authorities and the most influential men were advised by the physician who had the first cases (Dr. Smith) to have this low place spot of land filled. But it would cost over a thousand dollars and people would not believe it was yellow fever. . . . Dr. Smith has opened up nine bodies, has several phials of the black vomit and has tasted of it. Dr. Smith is perfectly well and has never had any symptoms of the disease and if it was contagious, I think he would."[6]

Without delay Smith began to treat the victims of the epidemic. He wrote, on September 28, 1839, "Immediately on my arrival the yellow fever broke out and I plunged into practice." And later, "A good deal of excitement has prevailed here on the subject of Yellow Fever. Seventy to eighty cases have occurred. . . . From three to six are dying daily. . . . It is limited to the Strand. . . .The large property holders have endeavored to conceal the fact of its existence for fear of damaging the trade." Smith had noted the poor sanitation in the swampy area around the Strand, the central business center of Galveston, and he advocated filling in the low-lying areas and treating the swamps with lime. The Galveston city council did not want to spend the money needed to clean up the city and businessmen tried to suppress news of the epidemic. Smith "set them at defiance," publishing truthful accounts of the progress of the epidemic.[7]

Yellow Fever proved a dreaded disease of unknown origins that had a sudden onset, ineffective therapy, and high mortality. The initial symptoms consist of high fevers, often with delirium. After four or so days, the fever temporarily abates and the patient feels quite well. At this point most began their recovery. The prognosis becomes guarded, however, in those who suffered a recurrence of the fever. These patients continued to deteriorate and just before death turned yellow (jaundiced) and began to vomit black, blood stained material. Death follows shortly thereafter. Even for those who survived, treatment for Yellow Fever was ineffective and often harmful. Generally, physicians prescribed purgatives, especially calomel, a mercury compound with considerable toxicity. Other treatments consisted of rhubarb and sienna. Mortality rates varied from twenty to sixty percent.

The epidemic was devastating to Galveston and the surrounding area. All commerce ceased and most of the population fled. Eventually a majority of the city's population of 2000 souls were afflicted with Yellow Fever and 250 died. While the epidemic raged in Galveston, the nearby town of Houston also experienced an epidemic. President Sam Houston and his family fled the town for their home at Cedar Point and escaped infection. Houston's epidemic was shorter, milder and with less mortality.[8]

By December 5, Smith had written the preliminary copy of a paper on Yellow Fever, noting in a letter he had "taken several samples of black vomit" from patients. Smith reported thirty-three cases, on eight of which he had performed autopsies. He carefully noted the symptoms, treatment, and outcome of each case and detailed the results of each autopsy. He proved that Yellow Fever was not contagious from contact with the sick by collecting specimens from the patients and even tasting the notorious "black vomit" without adverse effects. Smith published his report privately, distributing copies to several hundred of his friends and collogues, writing the first medical treatise in "our new Republic." Later he published an abbreviated report in the *North American Journal of Medical Science,* early in 1840. Greensville Dowell, who later wrote on Yellow Fever epidemics in Galveston, noted, "Dr. Smith's account is the most complete history I have found of any epidemic that has yet occurred." He noted most of the victims lived on the Strand or in the ally ways adjacent to the area. Smith recognized the relationship of the epidemic to water, weather, temperature and described the ideal conditions for mosquitoes—though he missed the vector—the mosquito. Instead, he related the cause to "putrid airs" arising from the fetid marsh along the Strand.[9]

Smith later wrote that by the end of the epidemic he felt better than he had for "quite some time" and had "made a bit of money" besides. He noted he had decided to practice medicine in Galveston, a new town in a new republic. On December 1, after the epidemic had passed, Smith was on his way to Austin with General J. B. Henderson and Colonel Bee.[10]

During the Eighteenth and Nineteenth centuries, Yellow Fever was the scourge of American ports, particularly those along the Gulf of Mexico, such as Galveston. Imported along trade routes from Africa and the West Indies, the disease was not native to the Americas but little was known about the cause of the disease. One of the first well documented epidemics occurred in Philadelphia in 1793. Benjamin Rush, at the time the preeminent physician in America, wrote a monograph on the epidemic and, unfortunately, recommended copious bleeding as therapy. The epidemics ceased in the Northern ports when the slave trade stopped.[11]

One of the deadliest and most well documented Yellow Fever epidemics occurred in Memphis, Tennessee in 1878. Researchers have traced the source of the outbreak to Africa where the disease is endemic. It traveled aboard slave ships to Havana, probably with mosquito larva in water casks filled in the African ports and then to New Orleans, arriving in that city in September 1878. New Orleans suppressed news of the epidemic to prevent panic and to keep business as usual in the port city. Nevertheless, news leaked up the Mississippi to Memphis and other inland ports and they knew the epidemic would probably spread up river. From New Orleans, the epidemic reached Memphis in October, carried by a passenger on a steamboat.[12]

When Yellow Fever reached the city, the population stood unprepared and the city panicked. During the prelude to the local outbreak, the Memphis town council spurned the advice of the medical community on sanitation and refused to clean up the city. After the first case occurred along the waterfront, the infection spread slowly from building to building and from the riverside shanties and then inland to the more affluent neighborhoods. As long as the disease was only in the lower class neighborhoods, the business community tried to suppress information about the extent of the epidemic. Nevertheless, once the news broke that Yellow Fever was present in Memphis, panic ensued. Those that could, fled and thousands evacuated the city. Some communities quarantined the city and denied its residents permission to stay in their cities or even to disembark from railroad cars, least the epidemic spread.

The epidemic paralyzed Memphis business, right at the peak of the cotton harvest with disastrous consequences. Memphis, perched on the bluffs overlooking the Mississippi River, the major north-south trade artery to New Orleans and European ports and located at the crossroads of the east-west and north-south rail and road systems, dominated the Southern cotton trade. During the epidemic, no goods moved into or out of the city and cotton began to flow to Atlanta and other non-affected markets. This epidemic probably caused the demise of Memphis as a major cotton export center, and the city never recovered its dominance in the cotton trade. That business moved to Atlanta, a city not afflicted with periodic Yellow Fever epidemics. Atlanta subsequently became the major city of the South and came to control the inland cotton market.[13]

Modern investigators have determined that the common house mosquito, *Aedes aegypti*, carries Yellow Fever and has peculiar habits. It prefers an urban habitat and breeds best in relatively clean, still water in warm, humid conditions. Cisterns and water barrels are favored nesting grounds. The female is a voracious feeder, biting only during the day. It can fly only short distances—literally from house to neighboring house. It also is not a highflying insect, generally not rising over six feet above ground. During the Memphis epidemic, the population noted that the prison located in the midst of a low-lying neighborhood, did not report any cases, probably because the wall around the prison was over ten feet in height. The female can transmit infection to its eggs and larvae and epidemics may wane as adult mosquitoes die from sudden cool weather, only to reemerge several weeks later after warmth has recurred and the larvae have hatched. Finally, cold weather kills the mosquito and its larvae, explaining why epidemics abate after the first frosts in October and November. Ashbel Smith described these features in his monograph but did not recognize the mosquito as the vector spreading the illness.[14]

Following the Spanish American War, Walter Reed and his team of researchers in Cuba completed our understanding of Yellow Fever and outlined effective preventive measures. They proved the mosquito to be the vector for Yellow Fever and that the mosquito became infectious four to ten days after biting a Yellow Fever patient. Using this information, the chief medical officer in Cuba, William Gorgas eliminated the mosquitoes from Havana by fumigating buildings and eliminating standing water and Yellow Fever cases fell precipitously. Gorgas later used the same measures during the construction of the Panama Canal. Presently, with a vaccine, Yellow Fever rarely causes epidemics or deaths.[15]

Later in the nineteenth century, Yellow Fever nearly cost Galveston the Texas cotton export trade. Houston, taking advantage of the epidemics and threats of epidemics, repeatedly quarantined Galveston and closed the rail lines into the port. The closures usually occurred at the peak of the cotton harvest, leaving Houston as the sole Texas port, via Buffalo Bayou, for export of the cotton to European markets. Finally, Galveston merchants, tired of the game, built their own railroad, bypassing Houston, into the Cotton Belt as far north as the Oklahoma line. The Galveston, Colorado, and Sante Fe Railroad operated for several decades before joining the Atchison, Topeka and Sante Fe system. By building its own railroad, Galveston missed the lot of Memphis and remained the major cotton exporting port in Texas.[16]

After providing care to the patients of Galveston and publishing his seminal article, Smith became active in politics in the new Republic of Texas, serving in a number of offices over the years and remaining close friends with Sam Houston, Mirabeau Lamar, and Anson Jones, an unusual occurrence in those days of bitter political divisions. Houston appointed and Lamar reappointed Smith as Surgeon General of the Texian army. Lamar and Houston sent Smith to Europe as ambassador to France and Great Britain. President Anson Jones appointed him as Secretary of State of the Republic of Texas during the negotiations with the United States, Britain, France, and Mexico prior to annexation to the United States. Smith resigned as Secretary of State shortly before annexation when reappointed ambassador to France and Great Britain and sent to explain the impending union to the republic's European allies. In addition, Smith served several terms in the House of Representatives and Senate of the Republic.

Smith became widely known for a violent temper when provoked. In 1839, while serving as Houston's senator in the congress of the Republic of Texas, Senator S. H. Everitt repeatedly called Smith a "liar" on the Senate floor. Smith responded by horsewhipping Everitt in the senate chamber. After the attack Everitt demanded an investigation. Instead, the senate censored Everitt for bad behavior and only admonished Smith for delivering a well-deserved response. Smith, however, resigned his offices. Still Everitt continued in office and later launched a series of vindictive investigations of Smith's expenses as Surgeon General. The investigations came to naught.

Although he returned to the practice of medicine, Smith continued to dabble in politics for most of his life. He became an important power player in Democratic Party politics, attending most of the state conventions. Harris County reelected him to the state senate in 1853. He served on local school boards and in a number of appointed governmental positions, primarily those establishing institutions of higher learning.[17]

While United States Senator, Houston ensured that his old friend, Ashbel Smith, was appointed to the Board of Visitors at West Point. While traveling through Memphis in route to inspect the academy, Smith found that city in the grip of a cholera epidemic. Called upon for assistance, he stayed to treat the victims (He had been considered and expert on cholera since his paper in Paris). At the conclusion of this memorable trip he delivered a stirring oration to the graduating seniors at West Point.

Ashbel Smith's Civil War career proved somewhat unfortunate as he was repeatedly placed in loosing situations. Like many Unionists in Texas, he opposed secession, but when Texas seceded, he felt honor bound to support his adopted state and his neighbors. Even though fifty six years old, Smith organized a local militia, the Bayland Guards, and became its colonel, training his troops on his plantation near Brazoria. His soldiers adored this diminutive, peculiar, intellectual physician. They knew Smith would always protect them and fight alongside them. He demonstrated his courage at Shiloh, and during the fierce fighting at the Texas Redoubt during the siege of Vicksburg, Smith fought shoulder to shoulder alongside his troops as they repeatedly repealed assaults from federal troops. Despite their regard, the recruits enjoyed provoking Smith into one of his famous rages, firing at his feet, then laughing as he yelled, cursed, and hopped from foot to foot. They knew the spectacle would be short lived and Smith would be contrite immediately afterwards.

Smith's unit was popular and contained the sons of former presidents Anson Jones and Sam Houston. One day while Smith was drilling his unit at his Evergreen Plantation, San Houston—who lived nearby—visited the drill field. At Smith's request, Houston happily officiated as drill master. According to one source, Houston shouted "Eyes Right." The recruits responded and Houston commanded, "Do you see Louis T. Wigfall?" They responded "No, Sir." Houston then commanded, "Eyes left." The soldiers obeyed and Houston inquired, "Do you see William S. Oldham?" They answered "No, Sir." Houston gave a third command. "Eyes Front" and asked, "Do you see either of them in front?" They replied, "No, Sir." Houston responded "No, nor you never will," and walked off.[18]

The Confederate Army mustered his brigade as part of the Second Texas Infantry into the command of Albert Sidney Johnson in Tennessee and Mississippi as part of the Second Texas Infantry. Smith arrived just in time to participate in the battle of Shiloh where Johnston was killed and the Confederates defeated, forced to retreat into Mississippi. Smith suffered a wound in the arm during the engagement. After recovering from his wound, he then led a combat regiment, commander rather than as a physician. In fierce fighting during the Vicksburg campaign, he led his troops in defending the Texas Redoubt against repeated Union attacks. After the Confederate surrender of Vicksburg, Smith remained a captive in a prisoner-of-war camp until exchanged.[19]

On Smith's return to Texas, Governor Pendleton Murrah designated him as the commander of the Confederate garrison at

Galveston and, in 1864, shortly after Smith assumed that command, Murrah ordered him to New Orleans to negotiate Texas' surrender to Union forces. The victorious Union command, however, refused to negotiate with Smith. Confederate General E. Kirby Smith had already surrendered the Confederate armies of the Trans-Mississippi, and the federal forces demanded unconditional surrender from Texas. Smith returned to Galveston just in time to surrender the city to the Union forces of General Gordon Granger on June 19, 1865.[20]

After the war, Smith returned to his medical practice and his beloved Evergreen Plantation. Whatever interested Smith he embraced with fervor. He loved agriculture and throughout his life devoted himself to making his plantation entirely self-sufficient, and he continually introduced new crops and equipment, most of which failed. For example, his attempt to raise grapes for the French ended using the local mustang grapes for a wine that he fiercely defended. Most of his new varieties of cotton did not thrive in the costal environment. He ate only what he raised but was only partially successful by practicing Spartan living and eating a monotonous diet. Visiting friends despaired of his food.

In 1852, Smith served as superintendent for the first State Fair of Texas held in Corpus Christi. He brought samples of the meat biscuit he had developed with Gail Borden and, though the long distance of Corpus from the center of Texas population decreased attendance, Smith considered the event a "highly respectable" success. Later, Smith attended the Paris International Exposition in 1878 as one of the Texas commissioners and unabashedly promoted Texas agricultural products. French officials even appointed him one of the judges for agricultural products.[21]

Like some of his earlier experiments, the meat biscuit did not prove a success. While surgeon general, Smith had reluctantly gone into partnership with his friend, Gail Borden, producing a meat biscuit for army and navy consumption. Borden and Smith received a gold medal at the Crystal Palace Great Exhibition in London, which Smith accepted for him. Despite the award, Borden's project failed and Smith closed their plant in Galveston. Borden later developed the evaporated milk product that made his fortune.[22]

Smith never married, though he had several romances in Salisbury, where he perhaps even fathered a child. Shortly after several Salisbury women rejected his marriage proposals, Smith moved to Texas. When asked why he never married, he always stated he was "too short and too ugly" to attract a wife. Later in life, Smith supported a local orphanage and offered free medical care to the children. He even brought one little girl to his home so he could give her twice a day treatments for an eye infection. She enchanted the old man and he adopted her. She became his housekeeper and eventually inherited his estate.[23]

Ashbel Smith always took a keen interest in medical affairs. In 1837, President Mirabeau B. Lamar appointed him to head the Texas Board of Medical Examiners, and in that role he strongly supported licensing of physicians to eliminate fraudulent and untrained practitioners. Smith participated in the establishment of the Texas Medical Society in 1856, its reorganization in 1869 and eventually served as president of the society in 1882. He also led the medical community in support of a medical school in Galveston in 1874, and later served as trustee of the Texas Medical College and Hospital there, fostered the Galveston City Hospital, recruited faculty and students, and spoke to each of the graduating classes. On March 15, 1876, he presided over the conferring of medical degrees by the Texas Medical College and gave the graduation oration.

Ashbel Smith likewise promoted higher education for Texas throughout his career. This brilliant, remarkable man, one of only two Phi Beta Kappa members in Texas during its formative years, believed deeply that, in order to grow, Texas must have institutions of higher education of the highest quality. His dedication to education never wavered throughout his life. In 1837, Smith, with Mirabeau Lamar, founded the Philosophic Society of Texas to further the education of the leading men in Texas. He also helped found the Texas Literary Society in 1846 to advocate for education in Texas.

His first attempt to establish a proprietary medical school in 1881 failed but laid the foundation for a state medical institution. Despite this initial failure, Smith continued to champion the formation of a medical school in Galveston. He led the campaign in the referendum of September 6, 1881 that placed the state's medical school at Galveston and the undergraduate university in Austin. Smith eventually persuaded the legislature to appropriate the funds necessary to support the college. Fittingly, when the University of Texas Medical School at Galveston opened in 1881, Ashbel Smith was there to lay the cornerstone for 'Old Red,' which was named in his honor.[24]

Smith also supported universal public education and played an important role in persuading Lamar and later the 1870 constitutional convention to set aside portions of Texas public land for support of educational institutions. In 1856, while serving in the Texas House of Representatives, Smith sponsored a public education bill that eventually went down to defeat. Another of Smith's bills passed in 1858 as an act authorizing the establishment of a "first class" university in Texas. In 1858, he became a member of the board of directors and eventually superintendent of the Houston Academy, a school dedicated to improving education in the Bay area. In 1874, now seventy years old, Smith joined the board of commissioners for the Harris County School District and, as superintendent, he established one of the first publicly funded school systems in the state. A few years later, Smith was appointed as one of three commissioners to establish the "Agricultural and Mechanical College for Colored Youths," which eventually became Prairie View A&M.[25]

Near the end of his life, Ashbel Smith was able to start that university "of the first class" that he had advocated for so many years. In 1881, Governor Oran Roberts appointed Ashbel Smith to the board of regents responsible for establishing the University of Texas, and in that capacity he took a leading role in building the new campus and supervising faculty recruitment. Smith became the first president of the Board of Regents and directed the establishment of the campus at Austin with his usual vigor, though he was now seventy-six years old. Smith and the regents began to chose faculty and construct buildings at Austin. Smith depended on Alexander Penn Wooldridge, a local Austin attorney, to handle the day-to-day activities of the building campaign and, though in his eighties, Smith traveled from his home near Houston to Austin to assist in supervising building construction, recruiting professors, and delivering diplomas to graduates at Austin. The University of Texas opened on September 15, 1883, with 166 students and Smith was on hand to pass out the first diplomas.[26]

Ashbel Smith was a physician who put the care of his patients above his own personal safety and well-being. Aside from being an educator who was determined that Texas develop first-class institutions of higher and public education, he earned his reputation as a powerful orator in demand across the state. He wrote numerous articles on a wide variety of subjects. Smith was to establish and serve on the first board of regents, monitor construction and establish the Prairie View School for blacks, the University of Texas Medical Branch at Galveston and the University of Texas at Austin. As one history summarized his life and contributions, "In medicine, education and honorable dignity Ashbel Smith did much to establish Texas Standards." He died in 1886 at eighty-one years of age and is buried in the State Cemetery at Austin.[27]

Endnotes

1   Gary Cartwright, *Galveston A History of the Island*, New York: Atheneum, 1991, pp. 72-75ff.

2   Ashbel Smith (AS) to Daniel Seymour, September 3, 1839. Ashbel Smith Papers, University of Texas, Barker Library, Austin, Texas (hereafter noted as ASP), Box 2G 230; AS to Colonel Bee, September 26, 1839, ASP Box 2G 230.

3   Ashbel Smith, "The Cholera Spasmodica in Paris in 1832," ASP, Box 2G237; Box 2G230.

4   Elizabeth Silverthorne, *Ashbel Smith of Texas*, College Station: Texas A&M Press, 1982, pp. 9-36ff.

5   Ferris, Sylvia Van Voast and Eleanor Sellers Hope, *Scalpels and Sabers*, Austin: Eakin Press, 1965, pp. 70-73ff.

6   Lucy Shaw to Jane N. Weston, December 3, 1839, Rosenberg Library, Galveston, Texas; Ferris, *Scalpels and Sabers*, pp. 70-73.

7   AS to William Lacke, December 5, 1839, ASP Box 2B37; AS to T. P. Anderson, October 18, 1839, ASP, Box 2G230.

8   For a discussion of the effects of yellow fever epidemics on Galveston commerce see: Greensville Dowell, *Yellow Fever and Malarial Diseases Embracing A History of the Epidemics of Yellow Fever in Texas*, Philadelphia: Medical Publications Office, 1876.

9   Ashbel Smith to Isaac Hayes, December 6, 1839, ASP, Box 2B37; Ashbel Smith, "An Account of Yellow Fever Which Appeared in the City of Galveston, Republic of Texas in the Autumn of 1839; With Cases and Dissections," *North American Journal of Medical Science*, vol. iii, p. 213, 1839. Though the date of the journal is 1839, this edition was printed and distributed in 1840; Greensville Dowell, *Yellow Fever*, p. 135.

10   Ashbel Smith to Isaac Hayes, December 6, 1839, ASP, Box 2B37; AS to G. Wister Pennack, November 21, 1839, ASB 2G230 (Pennack was editor of the *Medical Journal of Philadelphia*).

11   Molly Caldwell Crosby, *The American Plague The Untold Story of Yellow Fever, The Epidemic That Shaped Our History*, New York: The Berkley Publishing Group, 2006, pp. 12-14.

12   Crosby, *The American Plague*, p. 45.

13 Crosby, *The American Plague*, pp. 14-15.

14 Crosby, *The American Plague*, p. 14; For a summary of the facts know about yellow fever in 1870s see Greensville Dowell, *Yellow Fever*.

15 Crosby, *The American Plague*, pp. 201-228ff.

16 James Marshall, *The Railroad That Built an Empire*, New York: Random House, 1945, pp. 213-214

17 Ezra Prad to Ashbel Smith, January 28,1839, ASP, Box 2B37

18 Wigfall and Oldham were two of the firebrands that led Texas into secession and war, a move Houston bitterly opposed. Joseph E. Chance, *The Second Texas Infantry*, Austin: Eakins Press, 1984, pp. 4-5.

19 Silverthorne, *Ashbel Smith of Texas*, pp. 148-159ff.

20 Silverthorne, *Ashbel Smith of Texas*, pp. 163-169ff.

21 Silverthorne, *Ashbel Smith of Texas*, pp.127-128, 198-199.

22 Silverthorne, *Ashbel Smith of Texas*, p. 54.

23 Silverthorne, *Ashbel Smith of Texas*, pp. 184-185.

24 Commencement program, ASP, Box 2G 237; Chester Burns, *Saving Lives. Training Caregivers, Making Discoveries A Centennial History of the University of Texas Medical Branch at Galveston*, Austin: Texas State Historical Association, 2003, pp. 9-20ff; Pat Ireland Nixon, *A History of the Texas Medical Association 1853-1953*, Austin: University of Texas Press, 1953, pp. 10, 31-40, 100.

25 Silverthorne, *Ashbel Smith of Texas*, pp. 194-195.

26 Silverthorne, *Ashbel Smith of Texas*, pp. 221; Burns, *Saving Lives*, pp.1-22ff; Ruth Ann Overbeck, "Alexander Penn Wooldridge," *Southwestern Historical Quarterly*, vol. 57, no. 3, p. 342. After hurricane Ike, a question has risen if the Board of Regents could unilaterally either move or abolish the Galveston Medical School, which was placed in the city by a plebiscite.

27 Chauncy Leake, Introduction to *Yellow Fever in Galveston*, p. xiii.

CHAPTER 3

FRANK HAMER

FACING DOWN THE MOB DURING THE SHERMAN RIOT

By Roger Tuller

As an angry lynch mob determined to "get" their intended victim crowded the corridors of the Grayson County, Texas, courthouse on May 9, 1930, Texas Ranger Captain Frank Hamer demonstrated equal resolve to thwart them. Earlier that morning George Hughes, 41, an itinerant African American farm hand, had gone on trial for the sexual assault of a white woman. Before the first witness had completed his testimony the mob charged toward the courtroom and broke down its doors. Captain Hamer ordered his men—three other Rangers and a handful of local officers—to detonate teargas grenades, driving back the would-be lynchers. The lawmen successfully beat back two more assaults while hook-and-ladder units evacuated jurors, witnesses, and county officials overcome by the acrid fumes. After securing Hughes in a concrete vault that served as the County Clerk's Office, Hamer redeployed his men at the top of the stairs leading to the second-floor courtroom. Bracing for another attack, he ordered them "to hold their fire until [he] gave orders to shoot." Now buoyed by false rumors that Governor Dan Moody had ordered the Rangers to "'protect the negro [*sic*] if possible, but don't shoot anybody,'" the throng swarmed up the stairwell yet again. "'You can't shoot us,'" some cried as they surged forward. But Frank Hamer, unaware of such rumors, unyielding in his resolve, and unafraid of the consequences, leveled his shotgun and fired.[1]

By 1930, Frank Hamer was a legend in Texas law enforcement whose record of service spanned a quarter-century. "Utterly fearless," he was a "crack shot," with "the patience, the physical equipment (6'3 and 198 pounds), and definitely the know-how to track down any fugitive." His friend and admirer, the renowned historian Walter Prescott

Webb, described Hamer as a lawman who could not be "scared, bought, or fooled." From his early days battling bandits and rustlers on horseback to his later years chasing car thieves and confronting boomtown mobs, Hamer established a fearsome reputation for "protecting the innocent and punishing the guilty, if need be, personally and without mercy." Texas Department of Public Safety Director Homer Garrison recalled that Hamer "participated in probably more gunfights than any other Ranger of his times, was wounded seventeen times, was left for dead four times, and never once backed away from a fight." "There is not a criminal in Texas who does not fear and respect him," Webb wrote in 1935. "If all criminals in Texas were asked to name the man that they would most dread to have on their trail, they would probably name Captain Frank Hamer, without hesitation." In defending George Hughes from the Grayson County lynch mob, Hamer exemplified the principles that had shaped his career and built his legend.[2]

Francis Augustus Hamer was born into a frontier family on March 17, 1884, near Fairview in Wilson County, Texas. His father, also named Frank, journeyed to Texas from West Virginia as a trooper and blacksmith in Colonel Ranald McKenzie's Fourth U.S. Cavalry after the Civil War. In 1874, following his military service, he married Lou Emma Francis, whose forbears had migrated from Virginia and Tennessee. Their union produced five boys and three girls: Estill, Francis Augustus, Clinton (called "Sant" in the family), Harrison, Patricia, Alma, Flavius, and Grace. They relocated to San Saba County in 1890, where the father supported them as a blacksmith on the Welch Ranch. Four years later the elder Frank uprooted his growing brood once more, this time to open a blacksmith shop at Oxford, in Llano County.[3]

Growing up on the West Texas frontier late in the nineteenth century helped to   mold Frank Hamer both mentally and physically. Although he would "brag" later in life "that he had an Oxford education"—based on geography rather than the university's name, obviously—Hamer attended only through the sixth grade in the rudimentary public schools available to him. Yet despite its short duration, his formal education nevertheless revealed and contributed to aspects of his adult character. He was "a precocious student, especially in mathematics," displaying the logic and reason that would serve him so well as a peace officer in the future. School first exposed him to J. W. Wilbarger's

1889 account of early frontier conflict, *Indian Depredations in Texas*. After reading the nearly 700-page tome, young Frank was inspired, not so much by the hardy pioneers who battled to claim the region, but by their relentless Native American foes; he therefore "decided to be as much like an Indian as [he] could." This pronouncement led to extended, solitary hunting trips in the woods and on the plains of Llano County, often for a week or more at a time if he could escape his chores on the family farm and in his father's blacksmith shop. Alone in the wilderness and dependent only on himself for food and safety, he watchfully studied his prey and meticulously honed his sensory powers. Later in life, admirers and family members would agree that Frank Hamer's vision and hearing were uncannily acute; they credited him with being able to "see the bullet" in flight, and to hear an approaching airplane half a minute before anyone else present. By the time he left home at age seventeen, young Frank possessed the traits that later contributed to his legend: native "intellect, expanded in school and extended by . . . life in the woods"; "muscles formed and hardened by back-breaking work in the blacksmith shop"; powerful senses enhancing exceptional abilities as a hunter, tracker, and marksman; and a familiarity with—perhaps even a preference for—solitude.[4]

But the young man who rode away from Oxford in 1901 had no plans for a career in law enforcement. Rather, Frank left home to become a cowboy, perhaps after killing a man. According to Hamer family oral histories, a neighbor named Dan McSwain approached him with an offer to pay the youth $100 to kill "a prominent rancher." Hamer not only refused, but informed the intended victim of McSwain's deadly intentions. Soon after, McSwain fired a load of buckshot into Frank Hamer's back, seriously wounding but not killing him. Dragged to safety by his younger brother, Harrison, he fled toward the junction of the Pecos and the Rio Grande Rivers and "hid out" for several weeks until his wounds had healed sufficiently to retaliate. Then, according to his great-nephew, "Bud" Hamer and other family members, "Uncle Frank come [sic] back after he got well from being shot. And did kill him, killed McSwain." Whatever the reasons, in 1901 both Frank and Harrison Hamer signed on as wranglers at the ranch of Berry Ketchum, near Sheffield in Pecos County, Texas. 1903 found the brothers working cattle on the McKenzie Ranch, near Marathon. And by 1905 Frank was working on the Carr Ranch, between Sheffield and Fort Stockton, when a chance telephone conversation steered him toward his future as a lawman.[5]

Among the distantly scattered residents of West Texas at that time, the telephone provided more than a means of communication; it served likewise as a form of amusement when they eavesdropped on each others' conversations. Idling away the hours on an October evening by listening to the party line at Carr Ranch Headquarters, Hamer overheard the conversation that ultimately changed his vocation: Pecos County Sheriff D. S. "Dud" Barker requesting aid from a former deputy, Charley Witcher. A thief had stolen a horse in Fort Stockton and had fled in Witcher's direction. With Sheriff Barker too busy tending the county jail to pursue and the former deputy unable to assist, Frank Hamer interrupted their call and volunteered to intercept the thief, who would almost certainly cross the Carr property on his present escape route. "Staking out" the only waterhole on the ranch, Hamer waited through the night for his quarry. As expected, early the next morning a rider matching the thief's description appeared. When he dismounted to water "his" horse, Hamer sprang from his hiding place, Winchester in hand, and announced "you're under arrest." It would prove the first of many such moments.[6]

"I sure felt good that morning," Hamer recalled nearly thirty years later, "riding up and down the long slopes with that thief ahead of me." After he turned his prisoner over, the sheriff asked the fateful question: "Frank, how'd you like to be a Texas Ranger?" The idea appealed to the young cowboy, and Barker could help to arrange an appointment. Having battled Indians, Mexicans, and outlaws for seventy years, the Rangers established a legendary image among Texans; the prospect of joining their ranks thrilled Hamer. And as a former Ranger who had distinguished himself fighting the "San Saba Mob" of vigilantes ten years earlier, Barker retained both the stature and connections to recruit a promising newcomer into the force. Acting on Barker's evaluation, Ranger Captain John H. Rogers—one of the famous "Four Great Captains" who strengthened the force in the late nineteenth century—ordered Hamer to report to Sergeant Jim Moore at Sheffield. On April 21, 1906, Francis Augustus Hamer enlisted as a private in Company C of the Texas Rangers. He stood six feet, three inches tall, weighed 193 pounds, and was 22 years old.[7]

The state legislature had reorganized Texas Ranger Force in 1901, with an authorized strength of eighty-nine men divided into four mounted companies. This was not the celebrated Frontier Battalion of Indian-fighting lawmen, but the "Four Great Captains" of that renowned unit led the reconstituted Ranger Force and passed down its tactics and traditions. Thus Frank Hamer's early service and training followed the best practices and highest principles of the Ranger legacy. Certainly physical courage exemplified the Rangers; in the same year that Hamer joined the force a U. S. Army major stationed in Brownsville remarked that Ranger Captain Bill McDonald was so fearless that he would "charge hell with a bucket of water." Few could hope to match the integrity of Hamer's own Captain, John H. Rogers, a soft-spoken, tee-totaling Presbyterian church elder who commanded his men through moral authority and ultimately resigned his commission after twenty-eight years of service because he could not serve under a "wet" governor. Meanwhile, Captain John R. Hughes exemplified the tenacity of the best Rangers in his obsessive pursuit of Geronimo Parra, who killed Ranger Sergeant Charles Fusselman in 1890. For nearly ten years Hughes followed every possible lead and used every available resource to bring Parra to justice. Finally, with the cooperation of the famous New Mexico lawman Pat Garrett, Hughes delivered Parra for trial and finally witnessed his hanging on January 5, 1900. And Captain John A. Brooks conspicuously demonstrated "a high sense of duty." Whether shooting it out with the outlaw Conner family in East Texas or chasing the forces of revolutionist Catarino Garza through the unforgiving landscape of South Texas, Brooks served bravely for twenty-three years until his retirement in November of 1906. Even then, he continued to serve his neighbors, first as a state legislator and then as a judge in the county that bears his name. Such were the men who set the standards that Frank Hamer strove to copy throughout his career.[8]

The young Ranger's early assignments focused on interdicting banditry along the Rio Grande border, aiding local law enforcement in the wild border town of Del Rio, and quelling labor unrest. Governor S. W. T. Lanham dispatched Company C to augment "Federal troops who had been unable to maintain order" in the region. They arrived at Del Rio—their new headquarters, "a no-man's-land to which crooks and riffraff from both Mexico and the United States flocked whenever things got too hot elsewhere"—on September 29, 1906. Early in December of that year, Hamer joined Captain Rogers and three other

Rangers and local officers in ending a standoff with accused murderer Ed Putnam, who had barricaded himself in Sharp family's home on the outskirts of Del Rio. Despite lawmen pouring over 300 shots into the house, Putnam refused to surrender. Concealed behind a hackberry tree, Private Hamer waited patiently until he saw an opportunity, then squeezed off a single shot from his .30-30 Winchester to end the standoff. Although he "tasted the sweet reward of a city's appreciation" for killing Ed Putnam, his duties during 1907 and 1908 proved less rewarding as he and other Rangers split three-month shifts guarding mining operations in Terlingua against labor organizers.[9]

In the Fall of 1908, Hamer left the Rangers for a position, "at a much larger salary," as City Marshal in Navasota, Texas. He would certainly earn the extra money, because the town of three thousand desperately needed someone tough enough to keep the peace. Local newspapers had recorded "literally dozens" of shootouts over the previous three years in which "at least a hundred citizens met violent deaths." Furthermore, one source reported that the community was "ripped by racial strife," with the population including "a large percentage of sharecroppers and negroes [sic] who were constantly at odds with illiterate bullies from the old families." So many African Americans filled the streets of Navasota "on Saturdays and holidays . . . that a white woman hardly dared walk on the sidewalk," according to another. In such a charged environment, the previous City Marshal had served for "exactly one week."[10]

Frank Hamer, on the other hand, proved equal to the task and retained his position for almost three years. Although the racial dynamics of Navasota were new to him, he approached law enforcement there with the same principles he had imbibed from the "Four Great Captains." "Everybody looks alike to him," the local paper opined. White toughs who abused African Americans "felt the heel of the Hamer boots—and some the toe," according to Walter Prescott Webb. Black suspects likewise faced toughness; at least one died of gunshot wounds incurred while resisting the new marshal. Hamer recalled years later how he maintained order among large gatherings of African Americans:

I'd go over to this man . . . [who] was the unofficial boss of all the rest down there . . . and say 'Now, Sam, I'm gonna [sic] make you the parade marshal. I want you to keep all the rest of the boys in line, so pick out three or four helpers and make sure everyone behaves. . . . All of the time that I was there, we never had a problem at a negro [sic] celebration, thanks to Sam.

Soon racially conscious white "women found plenty of room to go where they pleased," while "many of the town's wide-open dice and poker games quietly closed down," and "word spread that Navasota had a City Marshal who was not afraid to perform his duty." In fact, he had performed so efficiently that "by 1911 . . . he had worked himself out of a job."[11]

Walter Prescott Webb wrote in 1935 that Hamer's exploits in Navasota "would read like a chapter from the life of Wyatt Earp." Recent scholarship suggests a more poignant parallel: like the legendary frontier "town tamer," Frank Hamer appears to have married and—tragically—buried a spouse at an early age. "His first wife was named Molly," great-nephew Harrison III told historian Robert Nieman. The family retains a postcard from Molly to Frank's mother, dated March 20, 1911 (less than a month before Hamer resigned as Town Marshal), which states "'Dear Mother, we were married Sunday . . . will return to Navasota in a few days.'" Molly Hamer appears to have died about six months" after her wedding, apparently drowning at a Sunday school picnic. Her untimely passing could help explain a restless, unsettled period that followed in Hamer's life, much in the same way biographers account for Earp's peripatetic wanderings following the death of his first wife, Urilla.[12]

From 1911 to 1918 Hamer was an itinerant lawman, serving intermittently as a police officer in Houston, a range inspector in the Texas hill country, a Texas Ranger on the border, and a private bodyguard—or "hired gunman," as one historian characterized him—among feuding ranchers in West Texas. In Houston he held the title "Special Officer" from April 1, 1911 until April 20, 1913, serving under the authority of Mayor Baldwin Rice. In this capacity he helped track down a gang responsible for killing several Houston policemen, captured at least two prison escapees, and slapped a *Houston Press* reporter who falsely reported criticism of the mayor's special officers. "Politics came into the picture," his biographers reported, and he "resigned in disgust." Next he returned to the range work he knew so well, pursuing horse thieves, cattle rustlers, and fence cutters in the vicinity of Junction. He rejoined the Texas Rangers on March 29, 1915, soon after Mexican Revolutionaries and discontented Tejanos had joined forces behind the Plan de San Diego, a frightening, if fanciful, program seeking to establish an independent republic in the lands formerly held by Mexico and to kill every Anglo male over the age of sixteen in the process. Hamer was once again posted to Del Rio, where he avoided both the sporadic raiding by revolutionaries from both sides of the border in the Lower Rio Grande Valley and subsequent brutal retaliation against Tejanos by Rangers and other Anglos in the so-called "Bandit War." By November of 1915, however, Hamer had once again left regular Ranger duties—this pattern of on-again-off-again service was common among Rangers of his generation—but retained an appointment as a Special State Ranger when he resumed his activities as a brand inspector, this time for the Texas Cattle Raisers Association. This assignment would introduce him squarely into the middle of a bitter feud among West Texas ranchers.[13]

The trouble originated with the divorce of Gladys Johnson Sims, the daughter of a "wealthy and powerful ranching family in Scurry County," from Edward Sims, "a prominent cattleman" from adjoining Garza County. It soon devolved into violence, requiring the intervention of state authorities and producing surprising results. The custody battle over the Sims' two daughters turned so bitter that, on December 16, 1916, Gladys and her brother, Sydney Johnson, shot and killed Edward Sims after he tried to take the girls away from her. Both shooters surrendered and posted bond; they were later acquitted. But while they remained free awaiting trial, they feared retaliation and therefore hired three bodyguards: TCRA brand inspector Frank Hamer, his younger brother Harrison (now a deputy game warden), and a man named Hallman. All three men unnerved local officials by "carrying six shooters but claiming to be State rangers . . . with big cartridge belts and guns, making rather a display of their arms." Scurry County Attorney W. W. Weems complained to Governor James Ferguson that such "extra guards and gun displays [were] only agitating trouble." Acting on the county attorney's request, Governor Ferguson dispatched two Rangers, John D. White and A.G. Beard to the county seat of Snyder, where they remained through the March, 1917 term of the district court and prevented further violence. In the meantime, the controversy forced Frank Hamer to resign his position as brand inspector, and with it his Special Ranger commission. Although he (temporarily) gave up his state authority, he remained on the Johnson payroll as a bodyguard. And that position provided him even greater benefits when, on May 12, 1917, he married Gladys Johnson Sims.[14]

On October 1, 1918, Frank Hamer resumed regular—and ac-tive—service as Sergeant of Company F of the Texas Rangers, based in Brownsville. Within ten days he engaged in a fatal shootout; just over two months later, he embroiled himself in a political contro-versy that threatened the entire Ranger Force. The shooting occurred on the night of October 10, the result of a joint operation between the Rangers and Cameron County Sheriff W. T. Vann to break up the operations of suspected smuggler Encarnacion Delgado, who tried to shoot his way out of the trap set for him. Sergeant Hamer and Sheriff Vann killed Delgado, but not before he fired a single shot that fatally wounded Ranger Sergeant Delbert Timberlake.[15]

Although the Delgado killing was clearly justifiable, many Ranger actions in the lower Rio Grande Valley over the previous three years were not, which had produced growing political opposition to such ex-cesses. One of the leading Ranger critics was State Representative Jose T. Canales, who clashed publicly with Hamer on December 12, 1918. During a heated discussion of a recent incident in which a Canales kinsman had been detained—and allegedly abused—by Rangers, the lawman threatened the legislator: "You have been hot-footing it here, between here and Austin and complaining to the governor and the ad-jutant general about the Rangers, and I am going to tell you that if you don't stop that you are going to get hurt." Hamer then compounded his blunder, not only by repeating the threat (at Canales' request!), but also by admitting to a witness that he had used those precise words.

Clearly the intimidating language resulted from the rising anger of an escalating argument and was characteristic, in that Hamer directly and unequivocally confronted and admonished his foe. Nonetheless, the incident added to increasing public pressure on the Rangers. When Canales returned to Austin for the January, 1919 legislative session, he introduced a law reforming and reducing the Ranger Force. This action in turn led to extensive hearings, which featured accusations against Hamer for menacing the representative. Although the reforms that finally passed in 1919 were watered down to the point that Jose Canales declared of the final bill "I do not recognize my child," and

Ranger supporters viewed the results as a victory for the force, the episode remained an embarrassment for Frank Hamer.[16]

But the Canales incident ultimately did little to deter Hamer's continuing service to the Rangers or his growing reputation among the public. In 1922, three years after the reform bill passed, Governor Pat Neff promoted Francis Augustus Hamer to Ranger Captain commanding the Headquarters Company in Austin, a position Hamer held for most of the following decade. Within weeks of his promotion, Hamer was leading law enforcement operations against bootleggers, gamblers, and prostitutes who had all but taken over the oil boom town of Mexia. To support these efforts, the Governor declared martial law in the county and sent in National Guard troops; by the end of February, 1922, Mexia had been "cleaned up" and, "more important . . . stayed clean." He performed similar duties at Borger, a Panhandle boom town, in 1929. In the meantime, Captain Hamer continued to pursue and capture violent felons, con men, and car thieves throughout the decade. By 1927, with bank robbery a growing problem, he confronted unwanted "assistance" that produced even worse lawbreaking. Sick of holdups, the Texas Bankers' Association offered the following reward: "FIVE THOUSAND DOLLARS FOR DEAD BANK ROBBERS [;] NOT ONE CENT FOR LIVE ONES." In response, enterprising felons in West Texas induced several inexperienced thieves to burglarize small, local banks at night, then tipped off local law enforcers, who shot and killed the burglars and quietly split the reward money with the "tipsters." After investigating these killings, Hamer informed the Bankers' Association that the reward contributed to "a perfect murder machine," but they refused to withdraw or modify the bounty; anyone who could be induced to attempt bank robbery, they argued, deserved their fate.

Receiving no cooperation on that front, the lawmen enlisted aid from an unlikely ally: the press. Usually reticent with reporters, Hamer called his first press conference on March 12, 1928, to expose both the murder scam and the bankers' refusal to cooperate. Within a matter of weeks the perpetrators were in custody and the Bankers' Association had modified its conditions for payment. Frank Hamer seemed able to combat any level of criminal activity. Thus, when racial violence threatened in North Texas in 1930, he seemed the obvious choice to prevent it.[17]

On Thursday morning, May 8, 1930, Captain Frank Hamer arrived at Sherman, the seat of Grayson County, bordering Oklahoma north of Dallas. Accompanied by Sergeant J. B. Wheatley and Rangers J. E. McCoy and J. W. Aldrich, his assignment was to provide additional security and to prevent mob violence the next day, during the trial of George Hughes, a black field hand accused of sexually assaulting his (white) employer's wife. But despite the lawmen's truly heroic efforts to preserve order, on May 9 the situation devolved into a full-scale riot, one of the worst incidents of racial violence in the United States that year, and in the words of historian Robert Utley, "one of the most brutish and shameful episodes in the history of Texas."[18]

Surely the crime that triggered these events was a brutal one, the kind guaranteed to arouse the ugliest passions among whites in "Jim Crow" Texas. At about 10:00 A.M. on Saturday, May 3, Hughes, described in newspaper accounts as "coal black, about five and one-half feet tall and weigh[ing] about 160 pounds," appeared at his employer's farm "about five miles southeast of Sherman on the Luella Road" to collect six dollars in wages. The farmer's wife informed him that her husband had gone to Sherman for the day and Hughes left the property.

He returned about forty-five minutes later, armed with a double-barreled shotgun. According to the wife's statement to Grayson County District Attorney Joe P. Cox, the assailant forced her into a bedroom and, despite her fierce resistance, raped her repeatedly. When her hysterical five-year-old son tried to climb onto the bed to stop the attack, Hughes roughly shoved the boy out of the room, locked the door, and resumed the assault. But the rapist soon became distracted, fearful that the boy might seek help. The child had already fled the house, however, when the perpetrator interrupted his assault to stalk him in the barn. In the meantime, the boy's mother escaped to a neighbor's home to "sound the alarm." When passersby retrieved the boy and returned with him to the farm, Hughes fired at them (no one was hit) and fled "toward the bottoms of Choctaw Creek," a few hundred yards away; they pursued at a safe distance and "kept him under surveillance" until Grayson County Deputy Sheriff Bart Shipp arrived on the scene to arrest him.[19]

Because of the inflammatory nature of the case, the possibility of mob violence loomed over the legal process from the beginning, although Grayson County officials pressed forward with all the speed possible under Texas law. As one historian has succinctly summed up the situation in that era:

> Jim Crow reigned in Texas as unshakably supreme as in the other states of the Old South . . . . Beatings and lynchings occurred regularly. Sometimes local lawmen or Rangers headed them off. More often, mobs did their work despite or with the complicity of local police before Rangers could be summoned.

Under such circumstances, swift and decisive judicial action was necessary to prevent worse and widespread retaliation. Thus District Attorney Cox filed complaints against Hughes with Justice of the Peace W. M. Blaylock immediately on Saturday afternoon. "No threats of mob violence were heard" in the neighborhood where the assault had occurred, the *Sherman Daily Democrat* announced hopefully in its Sunday edition. Nevertheless, Fifteenth District Judge R.M Carter swiftly convened a special session of the grand jury at 11:00 A.M. on Monday, May 5. By 12:15 P.M., the jurors had indicted George Hughes on three counts of "criminal assault"—the rape—and two counts of "assault to murder"—shooting at his pursuers. Judge Carter set Friday, May 9, for the trial, the earliest date permissible under Texas rules of judicial procedure for a felony case. The *Democrat's* Monday headline trumpeted reassuringly, "Quick Trial Promised for Negro."[20]

But despite this pledge, demands by some whites for less formal and more immediate "justice" multiplied over the next few days and forced the intervention of state authorities. Exaggerated descriptions of the victim's injuries and false reports that Hughes was "diseased" spread among rural families. Jeff "Slim" Jones (later indicted for his leading role in the riot and suspected of longstanding Ku Klux Klan affiliations) spread such tales around outlying portions of Grayson and adjoining counties, arousing wider outrage. Even the weather contributed to rising tensions as heavy rains drove many farmers from their fields and into Sherman. On Monday evening, May 5, a small group of young men—most of them around twenty, but some still in high school--appeared outside the county jail insisting that Hughes be turned over to them. A larger group congregated on Tuesday with the same demand. In both cases, County Sheriff Alfred Vaughan and Deputy Shipp dispersed the crowds easily, but the gatherings portended greater troubles. As the crowds grew and their mood became "increasingly ugly," Judge Carter telephoned Governor Dan Moody and requested Rangers to augment local forces and prevent a progressively more likely lynching. Consequently Captain Hamer, Sergeant Wheatley, and Rangers McCoy and Aldrich boarded a northbound train in Austin on Wednesday, May 7; they reached Sherman the next morning.[21]

On Friday, May 9, the trial began smoothly with strong security measures in place. Captain Hamer and several deputies escorted Hughes from the county jail to the courthouse "early Friday," before most onlookers had awakened, let alone assembled. As Judge Carter opened court at 9:00 A.M., the Rangers, Sheriff Vaughan, and "several deputies" barred anyone not directly connected with the case from the courtroom. Therefore the space was "only half full" when both the prosecution and defense declared themselves "Ready" to proceed at 9:30. The opposing attorneys had agreed upon twelve jurors by 11:45; the judge swore them in at 12:00 noon.[22]

From this point on the situation degraded as the growing crowds outside the courtroom devolved into an angry mob. By the time jury selection was underway, onlookers had "packed and jammed" the Grayson County Courthouse "from the entrance to the courtroom corridor down the stairways to the doors of the building." Just before noon, Hughes's victim arrived by ambulance to testify. Enraged by the sight of the woman being born upstairs on a stretcher, the crowd attempted to force their way into the courtroom. They retreated quickly, however, when the Rangers and deputies brandished rifles and shotguns. At 12:10, District Attorney Cox read the indictment, to which Hughes immediately pleaded guilty. All that remained now was the sentencing phase, which surely would have resulted in the death penalty. But as Cox's first witness testified, the angry throng forced its way into the courtroom corridor. Judge Carter ordered the jury removed from the courtroom while the officers struggled to drive out the intruders, prodding them with the butts and barrels of their weapons, but "without firing." After about ten minutes of inconclusive scuffling, Hamer ordered his men to discharge teargas grenades at 12:30, once again forcing the mob out.[23]

Although the teargas had effectively disbursed the second assault, its lingering effects necessitated suspending the trial; clearly the situation was becoming more and more tenuous. Firefighters arrived to evacuate those overcome by gas fumes, guiding them down ladders from the courtroom windows. District Attorney Cox led Hughes to the most secure spot in the building--a two-story, steel and concrete, fireproof vault that served both as the County Clerk's office and storage for county records—and locked him in. At about 1:00, the mob charged the courtroom once more, and again the officers repelled them with teargas. Meanwhile, Judge Carter, "a young man, newly elevated to the bench" who was outside the depth of his experience here, called a conference for a change of venue in his chambers. There, Hamer informed him flatly that "the trial could not be held" in Sherman "without bloodshed."[24]

Thanks to the circulation of a false rumor, Hamer would prove his point within "a few minutes." Word had spread among the crowd that Governor Moody had instructed the Rangers to "Protect the negro [sic] if you can, but don't shoot anybody." Thus emboldened, the crush in the courthouse stairwell surged forward for a fourth time, their taunts of "you can't shoot us" echoing in the stairwell. But Hamer belied the report and repulsed them yet again when he fired a shotgun loaded with birdshot directly into the mass, "wounding two men," at least one of whom later sought medical assistance. "This stopped the mob" Hamer laconically reported to the Governor.[25]

The respite was only temporary, however; within minutes the would-be lynchers had reassembled at the foot of the stairs, still demanding that George Hughes be turned over to them. When Captain Hamer informed them forcefully that he would not comply, one of the leading "agitators" announced, "'well we are coming up and get him.'" "'Any time you feel lucky, come on'" the Ranger replied defiantly, "'but when you do there is going to be many funerals in Sherman.'" This warning (no doubt combined with the shots fired during the previous assault) caused the group to reconsider; they withdrew from the building and, "for twenty or thirty minutes, things were quiet."[26]

Actions both among the crowd and the lawmen during that short lull proved fateful in escalating an attempted lynching into a race riot. Apparently convinced that the mob had been permanently driven from the courthouse, Sheriff Vaughn led his men to the street to reconnoiter the throngs there and plan his next move, leaving only Captain Hamer and his three Rangers to protect Hughes. Meanwhile members of the mob, frustrated in their attempts at a frontal assault and egged on by female onlookers who derided them for their "yellowness," as well as youths who questioned whether they had "red enough blood to do something about a nigger who raped a white woman," vented their frustrations on the courthouse building itself. At first they hurled rocks, breaking windows throughout the building. Then, around 2:30 P.M., two boys "about 17 or 18 years old" threw an open can of gasoline into the County Tax Collector's office in the southeast corner of the first floor. Another youth threw in a lighted match, but it failed to ignite the fuel. Yet another boy climbed through a broken window and lit the gasoline. He escaped the building just as the fire flared up, exulting "Now the damned old courthouse is on fire." By 2:45, witnesses reported that "flames broke through the top of the courthouse."[27]

Those still inside the building had no choice but to flee or burn with the building. Judge Carter and County Clerk Gafford escaped "when the flames burst forth." Captain Hamer reported that "all at once the flames from the lower story . . . swept up the stairways and on up to the ceiling over our heads. The flames cut us off from the vault" where George Hughes was locked. Unable to rescue their prisoner, the Rangers finally climbed out a second-story window, the last to leave the building. "Myself and men barely escaped," Hamer reported a few days later. Hughes, unfortunately, stayed trapped in the vault as the courthouse burned around him. By 4:00 PM, the "building stood in ruins," completely gutted; only the brick walls and the vault remained.[28]

After he fled the burning courthouse, Hamer sized up the crowds on the streets as a serious threat for more mayhem. He needed to report this assessment to the Governor, but doing so would prove far more difficult than expected. Thousands of people now lined the square surrounding the flaming structure, many merely onlookers speculating on the fate of George Hughes, others participating in or urging on the destruction. When firefighters attempted to douse the blaze, some mob members hacked their hoses in two as others cheered "Don't worry, the taxpayers will build a new one." Already the situation had spun far beyond the control of four Rangers and a handful of local deputies. Fortunately, Captain Hamer found a sympathetic onlooker who drove him out of Sherman to contact Governor Moody. Upon reaching the small town of Howe, the Ranger placed a call to Austin. But while waiting for a response, he overheard the operator say "'I am glad they burned the courthouse.'" Not wanting a politically sensitive conversation overheard (or potentially repeated) by a supporter of the rioters, Hamer hung up and pressed his driver back into service, now on the road toward Dallas. When they reached McKinney, thirty-five miles south of Sherman, he finally spoke by telephone with Governor Moody at 5:08 PM. He learned that state militia troops from Denison and Dallas were already en route to Sherman to restore order.[29]

But the small contingents that arrived during the evening of May 9th were insufficient to contain the Sherman Riot, which instead intensified over the following hours. Shortly after 6:00 P.M. "about a dozen guardsmen arrived from Denison"; they were immediately routed by the mob and forced to protect themselves in the county jail. Fifty-two more militia from Dallas reached Sherman at 7:00 and soon faced similar circumstances. The mob hurled rocks, bricks, and virtually anything else available at the troops until they too sought the safety of the jail. One woman "in the forefront of the group" attacking the militiamen "held her baby high over her head with the challenge 'Shoot it, you yellow nigger lovin' soldiers, shoot it!'"[30]

While one group of rioters held legally constituted authority at bay inside the county jail, the remainder returned their attention to George Hughes, bringing the riot to its brutal, if not inevitable, conclusion. Using an acetylene torch and dynamite to breach the vault, the mob removed Hughes's lifeless body at 11:40 PM; whether he had perished as a result of the fire or the explosion remained unclear. Regardless of the cause of his death, members of the mob now wrapped a chain around his neck and dragged his corpse behind a car to the African American business district. There they sexually mutilated the body: "They cut his organ off and stuck it in his mouth," a witness recalled sixty years later. Then "they tied him to a tree and burnt him up." "I could feel the heat and hear flesh sizzle," another onlooker remembered. Fuel for the pyre came from the fixtures of a nearby, black-owned drug store. Such looting quickly spread to other businesses, then turned into arson. By the time an additional 200 troops arrived from Fort Worth, 4:00 A.M. on Saturday, May 10, the entire African American business district was ablaze. Their hoses having been slashed during the courthouse fire, local firefighters were unable to quench the flames if they had been willing to do so—or if the mob would have permitted it.[31]

Early on Saturday morning, May 10, 1930, rain fell on the still smoldering remains of the Grayson County Courthouse and Sherman's black businesses, as well as the "charred and shriveled body" of George Hughes, "which mutely but forcefully evidenced the penalty the inexorable law of racial separation exacts of violators," according to the *Sherman Daily Democrat*. Indeed, such desolation aptly represented the aftermath of the Sherman Riot; little justice resulted for anyone following this brutal episode. Governor Dan Moody imposed martial law in Sherman on the night of May 10. Under that jurisdiction a military court of inquiry opened on May 12, and a week later presented its findings to the Fifteenth District Grand Jury, which in turn indicted fourteen men on May 20 for participating in seventy specific crimes during the rampage, ranging from burglary to "rioting to commit murder." But when those cases came to trial (in November) in Dallas, sixty of sixty-eight potential jurors "declared they would not convict the first defendant . . . even if the evidence against him were conclusive." A second change of venue to Austin finally produced two convictions in 1931, but only a single individual ultimately served prison time for the Sherman Riot—a two year sentence.[32]

Perhaps the only individuals in Texas law enforcement who could claim any pride for their conduct at Sherman were Frank Hamer and the team of Rangers and local deputies who supported him in driving the mob from the courthouse. In leading the defense of George Hughes, Hamer adhered to the principles he had followed since first joining the Rangers. His obvious courage remained unquestioned after successfully defying the mob, fearlessly standing his ground with less than a dozen men against hundreds of half-crazed lynchers. No matter what his personal feelings about African Americans, Hamer attempted to protect Hughes—as well as law and order—even after the rapist had pled guilty and his fate was all but inevitable. And he tenaciously continued those efforts even after arsonists had set the courthouse ablaze; only when the flames "cut [them] off from the vault" and rose "up to the ceiling over [their] heads" did Hamer and the other Rangers finally flee the burning building. But even after doing all that duty could require to save his prisoner, the lawman still persisted in forcing his way through the crowd, commandeering a car and driver, and traveling thirty-five miles to inform the governor of the deteriorating situation.

Clearly, Captain Hamer and his men rose to the highest standards of Ranger conduct in their actions at Sherman.

Such honorable service was widely praised, yet it failed to save George Hughes or prevent the riot, a bitter irony that Hamer never forgot. Soon after the riot, a committee of 132 Sherman citizens passed a series of resolutions to "profess our deep appreciation and gratitude to the . . . members of the Texas Ranger Force upon their fearless and efficient behavior during . . . the recent catastrophe." The citizens further resolved that "special commendation be made of the Rangers [as well as the Texas National Guardsmen still occupying Sherman] . . . for their magnificent display of courage, judgment, tact, and discretion." National Guard commander Colonel Lawrence McGee likewise praised the Rangers "for their cooperation" in restoring order and investigating the riot. But such tributes could not mollify Hamer; his frustration was evident in the statement on Sherman that he submitted to Governor Moody. "We had them [w]hipped off and they could not have taken the prisoner from us . . . only by burning the courthouse as they did," he reported. "And we never dreamed of the gang doing that until the building was enveloped in flames." Consequently, according to biographers H. Gordon Frost and John Jenkins, his "disgust at the cowardly actions of the townspeople of Sherman never abated as long as he lived."[33]

Frank Hamer's long career did not end at Sherman; to the contrary, his most famous exploit—the tracking and killing of Texas outlaws Clyde Barrow and Bonnie Parker—still lay ahead of him in 1930. "Hamer remains in both scholarly and popular perception the man who ran down Bonnie and Clyde," notes Ranger historian Robert Utley. But recent scholarship has revealed that the reality, as usual, was far more complex. Retired from the Ranger Force for a year, Hamer joined the hunt in February, 1934, at the request of Texas prison system general manager Lee Simmons, soon after the fugitive couple had orchestrated a bloody January prison break in which a guard was killed. Hamer teamed up with Dallas Deputy Sheriff Bob Alcorn and followed a trail of clues to Bienville Parish, Louisiana, where Sheriff Henderson Jordan offered them an opportunity to put Clyde and Bonnie "on the spot." Henry Methvin, one of the Texas escapees freed in the January breakout, would betray the couple in exchange for a full pardon from Texas Governor Miriam A. "Ma" Ferguson. "Thereafter, Hamer's major role was to obtain Governor Ferguson's pledge to pardon Henry Methvin." The retired Ranger delivered her promise, in writing, by the end of February. "Throughout March, April, and until the final scene on May 23, 1934, Sheriff Jordan guided the effort to get the outlaw pair." To be sure, Hamer continued to trail them, and he (along with Jordan and four other lawmen) participated in the ambush that ended the lawless couple's career. But he "did not run down Bonnie and Clyde." Still, he publicly accepted that distorted credit—and with two good reasons. Because he was almost always identified as a Texas Ranger in media accounts, such attention helped the public image of the Ranger Force, which had fallen over the past year due to the political appointment of inept Special Rangers by the Ferguson Administration. More importantly, being portrayed as "*the* man" who brought down Barrow and Parker diverted attention from and provided protection for Henry Methvin and his family, all of whom were plainly terrified of retaliation from friends or relatives of the slain duo.[34]

Having turned fifty during the Barrow manhunt, Hamer was not yet ready for full retirement. Instead, in 1936 he formed a security company with former Houston Chief of Police Roy T. Rogers. That business, established to "protect oilfields, refineries, chemical plants, docks, and shipping firms from sabotage and illegal striking," would occupy his professional interests for thirteen of his remaining twenty-one years; family and friends comprised his private life. When World War II began in 1939, Hamer quickly offered his services, along with "fifty ex-Rangers," to defend costal England against saboteurs and other German infiltrators, but U.S. neutrality prevented him from following through. The war confronted Frank Hamer with the greatest personal loss of his life when his younger son, Billy, died fighting on Iwo Jima in 1945. Three years later, the retired lawman played a minor role in the famously disputed U.S. Senate race between Lyndon Johnson and Coke Stevenson when he forcefully escorted Stevenson into a Jim Wells County bank vault to inspect the ballots in the infamous Box 13. A year later, in 1949, he sold his share in the security business and retired to Austin. There, with his surviving son and his family living in nearby San Marcos, Hamer enjoyed the familiar comforts of family and friends—including such Texas literary luminaries as Walter Prescott Webb and J. Frank Dobie—until his death on July 10, 1955. He was buried in the State Cemetery at Austin.[35]

Frank Hamer's career in law enforcement began on horseback, carrying six-shooters and Winchesters; it ended in automobiles, armed with semiautomatic pistols and Browning Automatic Rifles.

Historians and biographers have assessed him variously, depending on the time and context in which they wrote. "Captain Frank Hamer's natural gifts are such as would have made him distinguished as a Texas Ranger at any time in the history of the force, whether fighting Indians, Mexicans, or bandits," wrote Walter Prescott Webb. He included a laudatory chapter on Hamer in his classic (but now dated in interpretation) *The Texas Rangers: A Century of Frontier Defense*, first published in 1935 as the Ranger Force was folded into the newly created Texas Department of Public Safety. Webb's personal relationship with Hamer—they played poker together weekly for years—certainly influenced his evaluation. H. Gordon Frost and John Jenkins cribbed large pieces of Webb's chapter, supplemented with Hamer family interviews and press clippings, for their highly favorable *I'm Frank Hamer: The Life of a Texas Peace Officer*, published in 1968. The book appeared almost as an antidote to the motion picture *Bonnie and Clyde*, which swept to popularity partly by casting Frank Hamer as its "villain," driven by wounded pride to hunt down and kill its more attractive young "heroes."

Writing in the early 1990s, Ben Procter provided more balance, praising the lawman's courage and determination while acknowledging that in early twentieth-century Texas "the law was as unsophisticated as the people . . . and so was Hamer." Robert Utley, in his *Lone Star Lawmen*—the second of two volumes on the Rangers that seem destined to supplant Webb as the standard account—provides a similarly balanced treatment, praising Hamer's achievements and criticizing his shortcomings. Charles H. Harris III and Louis R. Sadler are more critical in their exhaustive study, *The Texas Rangers and the Mexican Revolution*, concluding, regarding Hamer, that "as often happens, his reputation was inflated."[36]

Indeed, reputations are frequently inflated; but that fact is not sufficient evaluation for three decades of service. Certainly Frank Hamer was not the perfect paragon of law enforcement that Webb or Frost and Jenkins portrayed. Their accounts completely ignored his adventures as a "hired gun" in Scurry County, as well as his threatening of Representative Canales, while they distorted the pursuit of Bonnie and

Clyde. But the fact that Hamer did not live up to an artificial reputation, largely created by others after the fact, cannot negate his true accomplishments. For most of his adult life, Frank Hamer enforced the law by adhering to a set of professional virtues that represented the best traditions of Texas Rangers: courage, integrity, tenacity, and duty. And on May 9, 1930, standing at the head of the stairs in the Grayson County Courthouse, firing into the lynch mob, defying them to "come on up," protecting a confessed rapist until the building was in flames around him, he not only exemplified those virtues, but he also rose to and transcended his public reputation.

Endnotes

1   Frank A. Hamer, "Statement, May 13, 1930" Governor's Records—
    Moody, Adjutant General Department—Sherman Affair, May 9-13,
    1930, Texas State Archives and Records Division (hereafter cited as
    Hamer Statement), 1.

2   Ben Procter, *Just One Riot: Episodes of Texas Rangers in the 20th Century*
    (Austin, TX: Eakin Press, 1991), 8-9; Walter Prescott Webb, *The
    Texas Rangers: A Century of Frontier Defense*, (1935; 2nd ed., Austin:
    University of Texas Press, 1965), 519; H. Gordon Frost and John H.
    Jenkins, *I'm Frank Hamer: The Life of a Texas Peace Officer* (Austin:
    Pemberton Press, 1968), 1-2.

3   Frost and Jenkins, *I'm Frank Hamer*, 4-5, 283; Webb, *The Texas Rangers*,
    521; Robert Nieman, "Interview with Bud Hamer, Bobbie Hamer,
    & Harrison Hamer, Texas Ranger Descendents" conducted at Texas
    Ranger Hall of Fame and Museum, Waco, Texas, September 23, 2000,
    www.texasranger.org/E-Books/Oral%20History%20-%20Hamer%20
    Family.pdf, (hereafter cited as Hamer Family Interview) 7, 8, 11,13;
    Robert Nieman, "20th Century Shining Star: Frank Hamer" *Texas
    Ranger Dispatch Magazine* II (Summer, 2003), www.texasranger.org/
    dispatch/11/Pages/Hamer.htm. Although Frost and Jenkins list Francis
    Augustus as the third-born son (based on a 1967 interview with his
    widow, Gladys), three surviving descendants interviewed by Ranger
    historian Robert Nieman agree that he was the second-eldest.

4   Frost and Jenkins, *I'm Frank Hamer*; 5-7; Webb, *The Texas Rangers*, 521-
    522, 523-524; J. W. Wilbarger, *Indian Depredations in Texas: Reliable
    Accounts of Battles, Wars, Adventures, Forays, Murders, Massacres,
    Etc., Etc., Together With Biographical Sketches of the Most Noted Indian
    Fighters and Frontiersmen of Texas* (Austin: Hutchings Clearing House,
    1889); Hamer Family Interview, 15, 23-25, 35, 37-40.

5   Frost and Jenkins, *I'm Frank Hamer*, 8-20; Hamer Family Interview,
    15-17. Jenkins and Frost also recount the McSwain episode based on a
    1967 interview with Harrison Hamer, but biographers and historians
    have yet to produce any documentation corroborating these family ac-
    counts.

6   Frost and Jenkins, *I'm Frank Hamer*, 20-21; Webb, *The Texas Rangers*, 525-526.

7   Frost and Jenkins, *I'm Frank Hamer*, 21-24; Webb, *The Texas Rangers*, 526; Robert M. Utley, *Lone Star Justice: The First Century of the Texas Rangers*, 260-263.

8   Charles H. Harris III and Louis R. Sadler, *The Texas Rangers and the Mexican Revolution: The Bloodiest Decade, 1910-1920* (Albuquerque: University of New Mexico Press, 2004), 17-26; Utley, *Lone Star Justice*, 253-273; Webb, *The Texas Rangers*, 457-461.

9   Frost and Jenkins, *I'm Frank Hamer*, 28-31.

10   Webb, *The Texas Rangers*, 526; Frost and Jenkins, *I'm Frank Hamer*, 31; Nieman, "20th Century Shining Star," 3.

11   Frost and Jenkins, *I'm Frank Hamer*, 37-43; Webb, *The Texas Rangers*, 527; Nieman, "Shining Star," 3.

12   Hamer Family Interview, 12; Casey Tefertiller, *Wyatt Earp: The Life Behind the Legend* (New York: John Wiley and Sons, 1997), 4. The historiography on Wyatt Earp is both voluminous and contentious; Tefertiller's book is well-balanced and has emerged as the standard biography.

13   Frost and Jenkins, *I'm Frank Hamer*, 44-47, 50, 56; Webb, *The Texas Rangers*, 527-528; Harris and Sadler, *The Texas Rangers and the Mexican Revolution*, 210-213, 215, 220-221, 276, 295, 532, 22; Procter, *Just One Riot*, 4. Recent scholarship has superseded the "Bandit War" interpretation of the 1915-1916 border raids and the retaliation that followed. For an excellent overview, see Benjamin H. Johnson, *Revolution in Texas: How a Forgotten Rebellion and Its Bloody Suppression Tuned Mexicans into Americans* (New Haven: Yale University Press, 2003) and Harris and Sadler, *op cit.*

14   Harris and Sadler, *Texas Rangers and the Mexican Revolution*, 317-318; 532, 617; Utley, *Lone Star Lawmen*, 93.

15   Harris and Sadler, *Texas Rangers and the Mexican Revolution*, 532, 419-420; Webb, *The Texas Rangers*, 528-529.

16   Harris and Sadler, *Texas Rangers and the Mexican Revolution*, 429-430,
      432-461 ff.; Utley, *Lone Star Lawmen*, 73, 76-83; Procter, *Just One Riot*,
      4-7.

17   Frost and Jenkins, *I'm Frank Hamer*, 102-104, 111-112, 121-123, 131-
      32, 135; 141-144, 147-154, 157-160; *Webb, The Texas Rangers*, 533-538.

18   Arthur F. Raper, *The Tragedy of Lynching* (Chapel Hill: University of
      North Carolina Press,1933; reprint, New York: Dover Publications, Inc.,
      1970), 319-355; Utley, *Lone Star Lawmen*, 134-140.

19   *Sherman* [TX] *Daily Democrat*, May 4, 1930, 1; May 5, 1930, 1, 3; Raper,
      Tragedy of Lynching, 319-321; Utley, *Lone Star Lawmen*, 134-135.

20   *Sherman Daily Democrat*, May 4, 1930, 1; May 5, 1930, 1, 3; May 6,
      1930, 5; Utley, *Lone Star Lawmen*, 133; Raper, *Tragedy of Lynching*, 320-
      321.

21   *Sherman Daily Democrat*, May 6, 1930, 5; May 7, 1930, 1, 7; Hamer
      Statement, 1; Raper, *Tragedy of Lynching*, 320-22, 331; Utley, *Lone Star
      Lawmen*, 135; Frost and Jenkins, *I'm Frank Hamer*, 164.

22   *Sherman Daily Democrat*, May 9, 1930, 1, 14; Hamer Statement, 1;
      Raper, *Tragedy of Lynching*, 322; Utley, *Lone Star Lawmen*, 135.

23   *Sherman Daily Democrat*, May 9, 1930, 1, 14; Hamer Statement, 1;
      Raper, *Tragedy of Lynching*, 322; Utley, *Lone Star Lawmen*, 135-136.

24   *Sherman Daily Democrat*, May 9, 1930, 1, 14; Hamer Statement, 1;
      Raper, *Tragedy of Lynching*, 322-323; Utley, *Lone Star Lawmen*, 135-136.

25   Hamer Statement, 1; Utley, *Lone Star Lawmen*, 136; Raper, *Tragedy of
      Lynching*, 323; *Sherman Daily Democrat*, May 11, 1930, 1. Although
      Hamer later stated that he fired buckshot into the crowd, birdshot
      seems more likely. The *Sherman Daily Democrat* reported one "Dan
      Shero . . . shot with birdshot while at the courthouse," and Raper's book,
      based on extensive interviews conducted in Sherman immediately fol-
      lowing the riot, mentions only birdshot wounds.

26   Hamer Statement, 1; Utley, *Lone Star Lawmen*, 136-137.

27   *Sherman Daily Democrat*, May 9, 1930, 1, 14; Hamer Statement, 2;
      Raper, *Tragedy of Lynching*, 323-324.

28   *Sherman Daily Democrat*, May 9, 1930, 1, 14; Hamer Statement, 2.

29   Hamer Staement, 2; "Record of L. D. Telephone Calls from Gov. Dan Moody on May 9th, 1930," Governor's Papers—Moody, Adj.Gen. Dept.—Sherman Affair, May 17-20, 1930, Texas State Archives and Records Division; Utley, *Lone Star Lawmen*, 137.

30   *Sherman Daily Democrat,* May 11, 1930, 1; Raper, *Tragedy of Lynching,* 325-326; Utley, *Lone Star Lawmen,* 137-138.

31   *Sherman Daily Democrat,* May 11, 1930, 1, 12; "Courthouse Burning Remembered," *Sherman Democrat,* Grayson County Sesquicentennial Edition, March 17, 1996, Sec. 2, 11; Claudia Kolker, "A Painful Present as Historians Confront a Nation's Bloody Past," *Los Angeles Times,* February 22, 2000, Sec, ?, ?. Raper, *Tragedy of Lynching,* 326-329; Utley, *Lone Star Justice,* 138-139;

32   *Sherman Daily Democrat,* May 11, 1930, 1, 12; Raper, *Tragedy of Lynching,* 330-334; Utley, *Lone Star Lawmen,* 138-139.

33   "Resolutions passed by the citizens of Sherman in connection with the recent disturbances," Governor's Papers—Moody, Adj. Gen. Dept.—Sherman Affair, June 10-July 11, 1930, Texas State Archives and Records Division; Utley, *Lone Star Lawmen,* 139; Frost and Jenkins, *I'm Frank Hamer,* 168.

34   Utley, *Lone Star Lawmen,* 160-165, contains an excellent summary account of Hamer's actual role in the manhunt. Harris and Sadler, *The Texas Rangers and the Mexican Revolution,* 532. For more detail, see Bryan Burrough, *Public Enemies: America's Greatest Crime Wave and the Birth of the FBI, 1933-1934* (New York: Penguin, 2004), 350-361, and John Neal Phillips, *Running with Bonnie and Clyde: The Ten Fast Years of Ralph Fults* (Norman: University of Oklahoma Press, 1996). Walter Prescott Webb's account in *The Texas Rangers,* 538-544, varies considerably from the more recent and heavily-documented accounts mentioned above. Frost and Jenkins, *I'm Frank Hamer,* 178-248, essentially follows Webb.

35   Frost and Jenkins, *I'm Frank Hamer,* 264-279; Nieman, "20th Century Shining Star: Frank Hamer," 5.

36   Webb, *The Texas Rangers,* 545; Nieman, "Twentieth Century Shining Star: Frank Hamer," 5; Procter, *Just One Riot,* 9; Harris and Sadler, *Texas Rangers and the Mexican Revolution,* 222.

Boris B. Gordon-1946

CHAPTER 4

HATTON W. SUMNERS

LEADING THE FIGHT AGAINST FDR'S COURT-PACKING PLAN

By Michael Collins

A chilling, northerly wind swept into Washington on the morning of Friday, February 5, 1937. By the time cabinet members and congressional leaders began arriving for a 10:00 meeting at the White House, a light dusting of snow was beginning to blanket the ground. As Vice President John Nance Garner's black limousine pulled off of Pennsylvania Avenue and rolled to a stop under the portico, Congressman Hatton W. Sumners of Dallas, chairman of the powerful House Judiciary Committee, stared straight ahead, offering no words, only a puzzled glance at his colleague from North Texas, House Majority Leader Sam Rayburn. Sumner's eyes must have betrayed the question that no one dared to ask: why were they being summoned by the president to a meeting called on such short notice? Bundled in a heavy woolen overcoat, Sumners peered up as he stepped first from the car. He could not help but notice that a canopy of clouds hung low over Washington. Perhaps as he studied the darkening skies he wondered if this might be a portent of a gathering storm. The entire scene presented an ominous portent for the "Indian summer" that Garner had forecast for himself and the "Boss," President Franklin Delano Roosevelt.[1]

When Congressman Sumners entered the cabinet room shortly before ten o'clock, only his counterpart, Senate Judiciary Committee Chairman Henry F. Ashurst, had taken a seat. "Why are you here?," Sumners inquired. Ashurst shrugged his shoulders, asking the bald, square-jawed Texan the same question. Within minutes, the entire cabinet, with the exceptions of Secretary of State Cordell Hull and Secretary of the Treasury Henry Morganthau, gathered at the table, alongside Senate Majority leader Joe T. Robinson of Arkansas and

Speaker of the House John Bankhead of Alabama. No one–not even Vice President Garner–seemed to know anything specific about the nature of the meeting. No one, that is, except the president and Attorney General Homer Cummings.[2]

One thing appeared certain, however. Only the previous evening Sumners had received an unexpected telephone call from the White House, requesting his presence at a "very important" cabinet meeting the next morning. While unexpected, the call also came as no great surprise. For the politically astute, fifty-one year-old Texan had long anticipated that the constitutional clash between FDR and the United States Supreme Court would escalate. Not even two years had passed since the "Nine Old Men," as the press had dubbed them, had stricken down the two pillars of FDR's economic recovery programs. Roosevelt supporters had named them the black-robed "Four Horsemen" of the Supreme Court: Justices Willis Van Devanter, Pierce Butler, James McReynolds and George Sutherland. Together, they had formed a core of conservative opposition to New Deal programs. All four had joined to strike down the National Recovery Administration in the case of *Schecter Poultry v. the United States* (1935) and to dismantle the Agricultural Adjustment Administration in *United States v. Butler* the following year. In both cases they had applied a strict interpretation of congressional authority to regulate interstate commerce, and in the latter case to tax one segment of the American population to benefit another.

To head off a full-speed, frontal collision between the two branches of the federal government, therefore, Sumners had already offered a measure that he hoped would create two immediate openings for judicial nominations and, hopefully, enough to satisfy a president determined to change the composition of the nation's highest court. And the compromise proposal would not alienate Republicans, whose ideological conservatism still stood in opposition to the full range of the New Deal. After all, four years into his presidency FDR had yet to enjoy the opportunity to nominate a single justice. In fact, not since Woodrow Wilson placed the name of Louis D. Brandeis before the United States Senate in 1916 had a Democratic president been in the position to change the composition of the Supreme Court. Simply put, Sumners's two-year-old plan would have offered all Supreme Court justices seventy years of age and older the opportunity to retire with full compensation and continued benefits for life. The Texan had good reason to believe that, based on private conversations with parties knowledgeable on the inside of the federal judiciary, justices Willis Van Devanter and George Sutherland—again both staunch conservatives—might be induced to step down and retire. In this way, Sumners proposed, an imminent confrontation between Roosevelt and the Supreme Court could be avoided. But for more than twenty months the Sumners bill had failed to muster enough support even to advance to the floor of the House of Representatives. [3]

Could an impatient FDR now be prepared to force the issue in some dramatic way? Could the beleaguered president be looking to reduce the influence of the aging, conservative majority of the court? Could this be the real purpose of the called meeting?

Soon Sumners and his colleagues from Capitol Hill would find out. At the pre-appointed time a smiling President Roosevelt wheeled into the room and positioned himself at the head of the long table. To his anxious observers, eager with anticipation, Franklin D. Roosevelt appeared as an image of optimism. A strong torso sitting erect upon a pair of withered legs, his chin remained uplifted, symbolic of the characteristic optimism so well known to an American public, long besieged by the battering effects of the Great Depression. His disarming humor, his glowing smile, his garrulous nature and air of confidence filled the room as he greeted all in attendance.

Behind the façade of president's amiable demeanor, however, there was a fierce determination, a formidable resolve, an unforgiving sense of self-righteousness. Those sitting closest to him could plainly see the furrowed lines in his face and a look of concern. The past four years wore heavily upon him. He was tired, even weary of the political battles. Yet today, as he began to address the cabinet and leaders of Congress, Roosevelt would begin by reminding all present of his sweeping mandate the previous November. After all, he had carried forty-six of forty-eight states, he reassured himself—all but Maine and Vermont; it was a stunning landslide victory over Kansas Governor Alf Landon and the Republican Party. The Democratic majority—more than sixty percent of the popular vote—had thus invested him with much political capital. Now was the time to spend it. "The people are with me," he liked to boast. [4]

And until now, the Texas congressional delegation had been as well. But that was soon to change. The ensuing meeting lasted only an hour, but it must have seemed much longer for the triumvirate from the Lone Star State. Throughout the presentation "Cactus Jack" Garner shifted uncomfortably in his chair as the "Boss" outlined his legislative proposal to add an additional member to the Supreme Court for each justice over seventy who refused to retire.

For the first time during his four years of attending cabinet meetings, Garner did not speak—not a single word. When he thought to himself how divisive this measure would be, and how the president had chosen not to consult him, or even inform him in advance, the vice president's naturally ruddy complexion became even more pronounced as his face became flush with embarrassment and anger. Listening to Roosevelt explain in unsparing candor how expanding the court to as many as fifteen members would increase the "efficiency" of the tribunal and expediency in the judicial process, Congressman Sumners displayed no emotion. Roosevelt even went on to frame his proposal in the context of a larger measure of expanding and reorganizing the federal court system—all to make the judiciary better staffed and suited to handle the backlog of cases before it. At least that was how the president explained it. Only when FDR endorsed the idea of allowing aging justices to retire with full pay for life did the legislator from Dallas show a measured look of some relief.

Across the table from Sumners, the newly-elected House Majority Leader, Mr. Rayburn, pondered how the court plan would place him in a particularly awkward position. He must have first thought of the ramifications for Democratic Party unity, the solidarity of support for FDR that had, to date, carried a tidal wave of historic legislation to passage. The great framework of the New Deal may have been inspired by the strong personage of the president, Rayburn understood, but it was the Congress that had translated FDR's ideas into action, his optimism and hopes into reality. Over the past four years the unpretentious Sam Rayburn had risen in party ranks to become one of Roosevelt's most consistent supporters and trusted allies. Now, as majority leader, he stood as a stalwart, a facilitator, a mediator, a voice of reason and compromise. Others looked to him for guidance and counsel. But the reserved "Mr. Sam" also looked to his mentor, Jack Garner, for direction.[5]

So did Congressman Sumners. Surprising to Sumners and the others from Capitol Hill, the meeting ended rather abruptly without the president asking for anyone's advice. As the gathering dispersed, with little or no exchange among the participants, Garner walked ahead of his two fellow Texans. Together the three men exited the White House and stepped back into the vice president's car. During the slow ride down Pennsylvania Avenue no one spoke for several agonizing minutes. The three men seemed so shocked by the magnitude and meaning of the president's announcement that no one yet knew what to say. "We were so stunned we hardly spoke," Garner later recalled. Then Sumners broke the silence. "Boys, here's where I cash in," he grumbled, otherwise showing no sign of emotion.[6]

This terse declaration was the first indication that Sumners was already prepared to take a stand on the issue. Preferring not to play political poker with the hand Roosevelt had dealt him, Sumners knew full well that he and his Judiciary Committee stood in the way. Any bill to "reform" and "reorganize" the federal judiciary would have to pass through *his* committee. In sum, as an experienced poker player who knew that he held the strong hand, he wanted no mistake about the fact that he never bluffed with so many chips on the table. When the three Texans thus pulled up in front of the Capitol and stepped again into the morning chill, it must have seemed to Sumners that the winter had just gotten longer, colder, and surely more bitter.

When Speaker Bankhead's gavel fell at noon that day in the House of Representatives, while the clerk read the Court bill from the well of the chamber, members began aligning on the measure almost immediately. The combative and colorful New Deal champion, Congressman Maury Maverick of San Antonio, was the first to step forward. Almost before the clerk completed the first reading of the measure, he scribbled his signature on a copy of it, signifying his support, then marched down the center aisle, held it aloft and placed it in the hopper. True to his famous name, he needed no one's approval or encouragement to stray from the herd.[7]

Meanwhile, in the north wing of the Capitol, Vice President Garner expressed different sentiments. Standing outside the Senate chamber, he responded after being asked by one trusted reporter what he thought of the president's proposal by simply holding his nose with one hand and giving a vigorous, Roman-like thumbs down with the other. This symbolic gesture was the closest expression yet of his impending public break with the president.[8]

Later that day, when Roosevelt learned of the Garner's reaction, he merely smiled. But what happened next was no laughing matter for FDR. Both the senior and junior senators from Texas foreshadowed a deep schism in Democratic ranks. On February 9 Senator Morris Sheppard, longtime veteran of the political wars, told reporters that he supported Roosevelt's court plan "in its entirety." That same afternoon his fellow New Deal supporter, Senator Tom Connally of Marlin, also of the Senate Judiciary Committee, broke ranks with the majority party by announcing that he opposed the measure "in the method and under the circumstances proposed."[9]

In sustaining the Roosevelt judicial "reorganization" plan, Sheppard, himself sixty-two years of age, upheld the contention that perhaps some justices were too old to dispose of overcrowded court dockets efficiently. Ironically, earlier in his career, when some members of Congress made a similar attempt to force aged civil service employees into retirement, he had spoken out in their defense. "The world needs the ripened wisdom of the mellow years," he had stated philosophically. Just because a man had grown old, he had maintained, did not necessarily mean that he no longer remained competent and capable. "There is no old age of the soul," he had reflected. Vision and wisdom, the type of wisdom gained only through experience, remained the only restraining influence that prevented each generation from repeating the mistakes of the past. The "fire of genius," he had added, typically burned "beneath gray locks." Apparently now, to Sheppard, the same truth did not hold for the "Nine Old Men" of the nation's highest court.[10]

What some termed FDR's "Court-packing" plan actually lay concealed and camouflaged within an omnibus bill that covered mostly procedural reforms and semantics to streamline the functions of the federal judiciary and expedite the processes of justice. In reality, the core of the measure was a thinly veiled proposal to invest in the president the authority to expand the Supreme Court from nine to fifteen justices. Under the terms of the bill, the president would also enjoy another fifty new appointments to the lower federal courts. The office of "procter," proposed within the measure, would also be created to oversee circuit and district court litigation. All the while, during the early stages of the congressional debate, Roosevelt threw his support behind other proposals already before the House Judiciary Committee, such as the Sumners retirement plan and pending legislation to provide for direct and expeditious Department of Justice appeal to the Supreme Court in cases where lower courts had rendered "adverse" decisions (those decisions that went against administration programs).[11]

President Roosevelt probably never really considered that the first real obstacle in his path to "reform" the federal judiciary would be a largely unknown congressman from Dallas, Texas, who for the past four years had consistently supported New Deal initiatives. Considering the strong character and long career of Hatton W. Sumners, however, neither FDR nor anyone else should have been surprised when the Texan stepped forward to thwart the plan. Not only had Roosevelt launched it in secret, informing none of the principles in Congress who would be relied upon to pass the bill, but he had also breeched custom and protocol in so doing. In sum, all who knew Sumners understood that, despite his public reticence and unpretentious nature, he could be a worthy adversary and formidable opponent.

Anyone who knew Congressman Sumners—truly knew him—should not have been the least surprised at his stand. After all, he had entered life in humble circumstances, and he bore all the hallmarks and traits of the quintessential self-made man. Born on May 30, 1875, on a farm just outside Fayetteville, Tennessee, he grew to understand what it meant to scratch out a living from the rocky, hard scribble country of Lincoln County, located in the south central part of the Volunteer State. At the age of eighteen he moved to Garland, Texas, and within two years began his journey toward becoming a man of the law.

After the Dallas District Attorney allowed him to read law books and study for the state bar examination in his office, young Sumners was successfully admitted to the state bar in 1893. For the next seven years Sumners enjoyed his own private law practice. Then, in 1900 he won election as Dallas County Prosecuting Attorney, serving two non-consecutive terms. During this time he gained the reputation of a tough prosecutor, determined to clean up the county by bringing to justice habitual criminals charged with a wide range of felony crimes from gambling, prostitution, and bootlegging to murder, theft, election fraud and tax evasion. Then, in 1912, the successful lawyer from Dallas emerged from a crowded field of Democrats by winning election to Congress in the newly-formed "at-large" district. Thus, in March, 1913 he became one of the famed class of 132 freshmen, including Sam Rayburn, to arrive in Washington alongside the newly-elected President Woodrow Wilson. With congressional redistricting in 1914, Sumners was elected to the seat representing the Fifth Congressional District of Texas, which included Dallas, Rockwall, Ellis, Hill and Bosque counties.

For the next quarter of a century, his stature and influence in the Texas delegation only grew, as did his reputation as a principled man of integrity and a foremost authority on constitutional law. While serving on the House Judiciary Committee, he had participated as a member of the impeachment sub-committee in proceedings against three federal judges charged with corruption and conflict of interests, the most notable of these cases involving the recent trial and removal of controversial United States District Judge Halsted Ritter in 1936.[12]

From the outset of the Court fight in 1937, Sumners positioned himself as the first and foremost obstruction for a president expecting speedy approval of the legislation. He even privately termed the proposal "infamous," and he pledged to give it "hell, specifically and generally." As Washington correspondent Mark Goodwin wrote, Sumners quickly "emerged as the key general in the fight behind the lines." No matter that events of the past four years had proved that FDR usually got his way, Sumners stated privately. Now the president had gone too far, he insisted, and it was time to *get in* his way.[13]

Over the past quarter century, Sumners had become a familiar figure in the halls of the Capitol. Since his election to Congress in 1912, he had gradually risen to be one of the nation's foremost legal authorities, more specifically a widely recognized expert on the United States Constitution. As recently as 1935 he had accepted the appointment as chief legal counsel for the international tribunal drafting a national constitution for the new Philippine government. Former president and Chief Justice William Howard Taft had even gone so far as to call Sumners "the best lawyer in the House of Representatives." Even Attorney General Cummings, architect of the Court-Packing plan, had once introduced the Texan as "one of the greatest constitutional lawyers in the United States." Little wonder, therefore, that by 1937 some argued that Sumners would be an obvious choice to fill the next vacancy on the Supreme Court—when one opened.[14]

After all, Sumners looked the part of a jurist of the high court. His manner of modest reassurance recommended him more as a learned scholar than a quintessential "common man." Still, despite his long, distinguished legal and political career and his many achievements, he always maintained pride in being simply a "country boy," a man of the people who ever remained true to his agrarian roots. As he liked to say, "everything I ever knew I learned on the farm." Always speaking colloquially in a slow, Texas drawl, he showed little of the fact that he was largely self-educated.

Gaining renown on Capitol Hill for his homespun humor, his folksy demeanor, and his uncommon eloquence, he seemed always poised, restrained and thoughtful. And he never forgot his simple origins, or the rural folks from his youth who represented to him the best, the most noble traits of a great nation. In that respect he seemed the embodiment of that Jeffersonian ideal and the Jacksonian ethos that stood at the center of the American experience. In short, he was—by the old definition—a real Democrat.

No one could accuse Sumners of being blind in his loyalty to party or president. If one word described him more than any other, that word was independent. This his actions during the 1937 session of Congress demonstrated. Although on the afternoon of February 5 he reassured reporters that the president's plan would be "given serious consideration by our committee," the sage Judiciary Committee chair began immediately an insurgency behind the front lines. Quickly he brought what FDR termed the court "reform" bill to a standstill. Attempting first to bottle up the measure in committee, he stalled, then delayed hearings for four days, thus giving himself and potential allies time to marshal others in opposition to the bill. Even when formal committee hearings began on February 10, he used his position as chair to slow down the process while others—Democrats and Republicans alike—moved to the front of the fight and "stir up opposition" among their colleagues. To many observers, his purpose seemed obvious, but as one frustrated newsman wrote, "What is exasperating to reporters, [when asked a question] he just smiles as though he knows something."[15]

While Sumners's tactic of delay appeared obvious to even the most disinterested of observers, his strategy seemed even more simple. Splitting the omnibus bill into its varied sections and sending each separate one through committee and on to the House individually, he opened the way for the least controversial parts of the proposal to pass. More importantly, he isolated and exposed the most divisive issue—

the proposal to expand the Supreme Court from nine to as many as fifteen members. Writing on February 13 to a friend and supporter, he admitted that he felt "like a surgeon, about to perform an operation." He even likened his dismantling of the administration's bill to the dissection of tissue in order to get at the cancer. Then days later, when asked by reporters why the Judiciary Committee had begun acting on the bill in piecemeal fashion and had delayed action on Roosevelt's plan to "pack" the Supreme Court, he glibly replied: "The visibility is not good, the barometer is low and the wind is not in the right direction, so we decided not to take off."[16]

In the meantime, Sumners attacked the Court-packing plan on another front. On February 10, after Sumners's Judicial Retirement bill was reported out of committee, he promptly requested that the House adjourn before any more related measures could be taken up. Apparently President Roosevelt then telephoned him, presumably to issue a plea for a meeting before a revised portion of the original bill moved forward for consideration. Sitting at his desk in the chamber later that day, Sumners then received an urgent message from the president himself: "I hope you will make no more in regard to the second bill relating to the Attorney General intervening in suits in the lower courts—especially because you and I did not have a chance to talk about it this morning. Frankly, I do not know what the bill provides."[17]

Thus during the opening days of the debate over the president's plans for the judiciary, Sumners moved out in front of FDR with preemptive proposals of his own. In sum, he was taking matters into his own hands—and that is precisely what Roosevelt justly feared. Just three days after the president's first note to Sumners, a second message, this one anonymous, appeared on his desk. The typed note listed the various federal judgeships soon to be vacant, and a scribbled message at the bottom of the page read: "I think this confidential memorandum will interest you." This cryptic note, written in pencil, and reminding the congressman of the president's power of patronage might have been an attempt to influence Sumners during his deliberations of the judiciary proposals. If so, it did not work. Subtle or otherwise, no reminder, not for a man like Sumner—known to have long held ambitions for the federal bench—would have swayed his position.[18]

As the controversy over FDR's Court-Packing Plan heated up, Sumners worked feverishly for passage of his own Judicial Retirement

Bill, which most agreed seemed a reasonable proposal, and one which might prevent an historic constitutional and political battle. Firmly believing that this legislation would effectively address the need to infuse "new blood" into the Supreme Court, he offered an attractive incentive to any justice over the age of seventy who would be willing to step down: continued full pay and benefits—for life. By retiring and not resigning, under the current provisions of the Judiciary Act of 1919, a Supreme Court justice could remain on "inactive" status indefinitely, presumably for the remainder of his life, with Congress being able to reduce his salary. Such had been the case with Justice Oliver Wendell Holmes, Jr., who left the court in 1933. In practical terms, Sumners's bill would allow justices of the nation's highest court to *retire* and still retain their pay—and their dignity. Thus the measure sought nothing more than to extend the same advantages and privileges to members of the Supreme Court as those already enjoyed by members of the lower courts of the federal judiciary. "The public ought to know," he went on record, explaining to his colleagues in the House, "that if any of these gentlemen of the Supreme Court retire they do it voluntarily. They do it," he continued, "because they feel it is fair to themselves and to the Government which gives them the privilege."[19]

His more personal feelings he revealed to longtime friend, supporter and Democratic party stalwart, Thomas B. Love of Dallas: "I am still trying to do something to get the situation straightened out without doing permanent injury to the Court as an institution." Later that year he again unburdened himself to Love. "I was determined to go in and . . . not to count the cost to myself. . . . But as I saw the situation somebody had . . . to try . . . [to stop the bill]. As I further saw it the person who did go in would probably not come out politically alive." Then he summarized his stand: "I said 'cash in' and I meant 'cash in' as we know the expression in the Southwest."[20]

For Hatton Sumners the fight to stop FDR's Court-Packing plan assumed the moral equivalent of a guerrilla insurgency. Being an individual of deep conviction and lofty principle, he refused to endorse or even assist the court proposal that, in his view, relegated the Supreme Court to a "lesser" branch of government—and the rendered the bedrock belief of the separation of constitutional powers to a mere rubble of platitudes. As a lawyer, he greatly respected the principle of an independent judiciary. The fragile system of checks and balances among the three branches of the federal government rested upon the foundation of a robust court system unfettered and unthreatened by the vicissitudes of politics and public opinion. Just as Madison, Jefferson V. Hamilton, Washington and other founders of the Republic one hundred and fifty years earlier, he viewed the American system of jurisprudence to be the best, and perhaps only, guardian against the tyranny of one, or the tyranny of many. In other words, an independent system of federal courts, he believed, remained the anchor of a nation of laws and not of men.

In so doing, Sumners was willing to sacrifice his own career in Washington, and walk away from any hopes of ever receiving an appointment to the federal bench, perhaps someday even the Supreme Court. Sumner privately admitted that, by conducting a holding action against President Roosevelt, especially on this issue, he might well be committing political suicide. By his actions during the crucial opening hours and days of the debate, however, he still disregarded the consequences of his actions. Or as he again firmly stated his decision—and his act of conscience—to block the president's proposal, no matter the cost: "I am perfectly willing to cash in if I can be useful to my country in this great emergency."[21]

While Sumners proved a towering obstacle for President Roosevelt in the House, Congressman Maury Maverick of San Antonio, a consistent New Dealer during the past four years, came forth as a leading champion of court "reform." He even emerged as perhaps the administration's principal mouthpiece for the legislation. Speaking out on the House floor and on national radio, the pudgy, curly-haired Maverick, whose appearance one colleague likened to that of an agitated bullfrog, led a special House Judiciary Reform Group, a twenty-three man steering committee formed to advance the president's plan. In his own flamboyant, combative style, he aggressively campaigned for Roosevelt's court plan, even going so far as to lend his name to it as a co-sponsor. A true paladin of the liberal wing of his Democratic party, he was not concerned with precedent, or custom, but rather results. Terming the conservative justices of the Supreme Court the "Battalion of Death," he argued that their view of the constitution was at best arcane, "looking backward instead of forward." At worst, he argued, the high court had "distorted" the constitution with their own political ideology. Maverick stood, in fact, as one of the few in Washington who still expressed

the opinion that the federal courts even lacked the expressed constitutional authority to void or strike down laws of Congress. Thus the
long-established doctrine of Judicial Review—which had reigned since
the days of John Marshall—was, in principle, an extra legal reach by
the Supreme Court to *make law*, not merely interpret it. Congressman
Sumners could not have disagreed more. For him, that authority was
both *implied* and *necessary*.

Maury Maverick turned out to be little more than a sideshow in
the carnival that was the ongoing debate over court reform. He never
reconciled his consistent loose constructionist view of congressional
authority with a strict constructionist stand on judicial power. He
saw no need to. Instead, he continued his relentless attacks upon the
"Nine Old Men," and even declared that, if Congress had the explicit
authority to create courts, it could surely "expand" them at will. More
specifically, he also argued that in recent years the courts had applied
an overly narrow view of congressional authority to regulate interstate
commerce. In time of grave national economic crisis, he asserted, the
country needed jurists who would "stick to their own knitting." Simply
stated, the will of the people and the practical urgency of the Great
Depression overrode and superceded any lofty notions of dogma or
doctrine. Too much was at stake, he insisted, for academic arguments.[22]

Speaking less than a week after the president unveiled his plan to
"pack" the Supreme Court, Maverick leveled one of the most sting-
ing attacks yet against the aging justices. "Times change," he affirmed,
"views change, and the people should have the right to adjust their
own government to their own will." Speaking on NBC's nationally
broadcast "Town Meeting on the Air" on February 11, he argued that
during the past four years the president and Congress had no reasonable choice but to act in response to the staggering economic crisis that
had paralyzed the nation. FDR and his supporters in Congress had little time to worry about stepping into some nebulous "No Man's Land"
of constitutional nuances. Then a handful of jurists on the high court
had turned their collective backs on the American people by nullifying
a series of recovery and reform initiatives. From the establishment of
minimum wage standards, child labor restraints, protections for wom-
en working in "sweatshop" in the garment industry, the eight-hour day,
to the relief of embattled farmers facing ruinous crop prices, advancing flood control and preventing soil erosion, the court had thwarted

the "will of the people." Maverick even went so far as to speculate that social security and tax reform would be next.[23]

Maverick continued to lash out at the conservative jurists of the Supreme Court for not having an "enlightened" view of the constitution. "Obstructionists" he called them. Writing to his son, Maury Jr., he explained his disgust with the situation. "There is no reason why every good thing that we do should be knocked out because five out of nine justices are prejudiced." So he concluded "there should be some new blood" on the bench.[24]

All the while Congressman Sumners remained quiet. Seemingly aloof of the political clamor and crowd noise, he would let others do all the talking. As his friend and colleague Sam Rayburn liked to say, he remained a "work horse," not a "show horse." Following Rayburn's example of leadership, he stayed behind the scenes, worked quietly, avoided interviews, and issued few public statements—and those were terse and to the point.

By February 28, however, all that mattered little. That afternoon, after consulting with Speaker Bankhead, Majority Leader Rayburn and Judiciary Committee Chair Sumners, Roosevelt made the fateful decision to shift the battle front to the Senate. In large part, because of Sumners's trench warfare against the proposal, the plan to increase the membership of the Supreme Court by as many as six new appointees would remain stalled in the House. All three leaders explained to the president that, if the Senate were to act on the measure first, pressure would be removed from the House, a chamber full of members who would stand for reelection the following year. In just three weeks, therefore, Sumners and his allies had forced the fight to move to the other end of the Capitol. In large part, Sumners had contributed mightily—mostly behind the scenes, first in committee and then in the House—to the insurgency that stopped the Roosevelt steamroller and brought the court bill to a screeching halt.[25]

Three days later, on March 1, Roosevelt signed the Sumners-McCarran Judicial Retirement Act into law. Many members of Congress, among them the bill's principal author and co-sponsor from Texas, hoped that the generous terms of the law would entice one or more of the "Four Horsemen" of the Supreme Court into stepping down. So as the Senate now prepared to sit in judgment of the divisive proposal, the need to alter the composition of the high court seemed to subside. The sense of urgency that had been placed on the plan, therefore, quickly diminished, and the shrill harangue in the halls of Congress appeared more muffled and subdued. While the president had not yet given up hope for the most controversial of his proposals for court "reform," the plan to expand the membership of the Supreme Court, the provision had been stripped from the original bill. The Court-Packing Plan stood alone now, exposed. Surely Roosevelt knew that the deck was stacked against him—thanks to a little heralded congressman from Dallas, a member of the president's own Democratic party—who had vowed a mere four weeks earlier to "cash in" his chips, but not yet fold the strong hand he had to play. That was language that FDR, leader and champion of sweeping "New Deal" reforms, fully understood.[26]

At the time, many observers believed that the real battle over the Court "reorganization" and "reform" proposal had only begun. While the ensuing fight in the Senate turned out to be a prolonged and protracted process, the proposal appeared already doomed. Sumners's holding action, bottling up the provision of the bill containing the proposed expansion of the Supreme Court justices, all but made certain of that. That action led to the rapid and complete diminution of the Texan's influence within the administration and the more liberal wing of the Democratic Party.

On June 2 news came that Associate Justice Willis Van Devanter of Wyoming, one of the conservative "Four Horsemen," had decided to step down, changing the dynamic of the debate. Simply stated, his retirement with full pay and benefits opened the way for Roosevelt's first appointment to the high tribunal. Then on July 14 Arkansas Senator Joe T. Robinson was found dead of an apparent heart attack at his home. Losing his chief legislative advocate for court reform in the Senate no doubt dealt a severe blow to the president.

Roosevelt needed a new general to guide his court reform proposal through the Senate. He needed another old sage who could influence his colleagues to support the president, someone with the experience and proven record of legislative leadership, someone like John Nance Garner. But the vice president was vacationing in Uvalde, Texas. More importantly, he stood by eager to see the bill buried.

On the morning when news of Senator Robinson's death spread through the halls on Capitol Hill, Congressman Sumners rose from

his seat in the House chamber and delivered a few comments eulogiz-
ing the gentleman from Arkansas. Clad in a cream-colored line suit,
speaking in soft, almost reverential tones, he delivered his most impas-
sioned plea yet. For almost an hour he captivated the attention of his
colleagues with a call simply to abandon, once and for all, any consideration of "stacking" the Supreme Court. He termed the speech the
"most important" of his entire public career, and he was right. Pausing
periodically and punctuating his remarks with a tomblike silence, he
implored his fellow representatives to use "good, old fashioned horse
sense." He reminded them that to continue the fight would "split the
House from top to bottom." Knowing too that deep scars would long
remain as a result of the fight, he spoke eloquently of the importance of
the nation maintaining strength and unity in time of gathering world
crises. "There is not enough left in this controversy to justify the hurt
which is being done by its continuance," he declared. Occasionally
accenting his oration with humorous stories that brought bursts of
laughter from the floor and gallery, he exchanged what seemed to be
good-natured verbal barbs with several of his colleagues, including W.
D. "Mac" McFarland of Texas.[27]

When alluding to the president of the United States, however,
Sumners voiced only respect. Reaffirming his belief that FDR had been
"imposed upon" by advisers and elements of the party who, he mentioned his past loyalty to the president, though he used the opportunity to express an unrelated concern over government deficit spending.
He then predicted that "as soon as we remove the lash from above the
heads of these judges over there, some more of them will retire. I mean
that as a fact." As Sumners concluded with a summary that stressed
the importance of the constitutional balance of powers among the
three branches of the federal government, most of his colleagues broke
into spontaneous applause. Among those moved by Sumners's simple
eloquence and precise logic was Congressman George H. Mahon of
Texas, who later recalled the speech to be his most vivid memory of
the entire Court fight. Senator Connally, who sat in the gallery looking
down that morning, later wrote that the speech "added strength to the
anti-Court packing forces" at a most critical moment during the crisis.
Representative Poage of Texas agreed that Sumners's actions "pretty
well killed it" in the House. Columnist Thomas L. Stokes likewise reported that, although formal debate over the Court matter had long

since been suspended, the address nevertheless proved "effective" and "influential" in silencing the argument of the bill's proponents. More than anything, the event provided an apt punctuation to Sumners's five-month battle to defeat the Court-Packing provision.[28]

On the afternoon of August 7, at the conclusion of a stormy fifty-nine minute session in the Senate, Garner slammed his gavel on a watered down version of judicial reorganization that made no reference to the composition of the Supreme Court. Some scholars have argued that Roosevelt's Court proposal died with Senator Robinson. In fact, the original bill, perhaps stillborn in the beginning, had already been buried beneath a mound of amendments in the chamber of the House Judiciary Committee. In the end, FDR tried desperately to salvage a compromise by proposing a substitute bill that would have allowed the president to nominate a maximum of one justice per year for each one over the age of seventy-five. But even that proposal failed to gain any traction in the Senate, much less the House. As Garner had bluntly explained the bottom line to Roosevelt at a private meeting in the White House on July 20, "you haven't got the votes." Already, FDR suspected that his self-styled "silent partner" had played a key role as silent saboteur. It had been an unseasonably hot summer in Washington, as hot as the previous winter had proved bitterly cold.

As for Hatton W. Sumners, he gained reelection the following year and continued his service in the House until 1947, ably representing the people of the Fifth Congressional District of Texas. But his influence in the counsels of the administration and the Democratic Party soon evaporated. Following his retirement from public life, he continued to offer his private legal services to various civic organizations and eleemosynary institutions in Dallas County. He became director of Research for the Southwestern Legal Foundation and a benefactor of Southern Methodist University. An aging bachelor ever devoted to the legal profession, he established the Hatton W. Sumners Foundation in 1949, which still exists to encourage and support aspiring young men and women to complete their studies in the law. In 1959 he completed for publication *The Private Citizen and his Democracy*, in which he explained the importance of civic virtue and public service in a free society. He died on April 19, 1962, and was laid to rest in the historic Knights of Pythias Cemetery in Garland, Texas. To the end, he remained an active servant of his community, and always he expressed the hope that his opposition to President Franklin D. Roosevelt's Court-Packing Plan would be remembered as an act of personal conscience and political courage.

Endnotes

1   *New York Times,* February 13, 1934.

2   Bascom N. Timmons, *Garner of Texas: A Personal History* (New York: Harper and Row, 1948), 209; George F. Sparks, ed., *A Many Colored Toga: The Diary of Henry Fountain Ashurst* (Tucson: University of Arizona Press, 1962), 37; Leonard Baker, *Back to Back: The Duel Between FDR and the Supreme Court* (New York: MacMillan, 1967), 3; Joseph Alsop and Turner Catledge, *The 168 Days* (New York: Doubleday, Doran, and Co., 1938), 64.

3   Anthony Champagne, "Hatton Sumners and the 1937 Court-Packing Plan," *East Texas Historical Journal, 26* (Spring, 1988): 46-49.

4   Ibid.; Alsop and Catledge, *The 168 Days,* 64.

5   Harold L. Ickes, *The Secret Diary of Harold L. Ickes,* vol. II: *The Inside Struggle* (New York: Simon and Schuster, 1954), 66; Raymond Moley, *After Seven Years* (New York: Harper and Row, 1939), 360.

6   Hatton W. Sumners to Thomas B. Love, October 23, 1937, General Correspondence, Hatton Sumners Papers, Dolph Briscoe Center for American History, the University of Texas, Austin. Hereafter cited as HSP; Timmons, *Garner of Texas,* 223; Alsop and Catledge, *The 168 Days,* 67.

7   Charles Michaelson, *The Ghost Talks* (New York: Putnam and Sons, 1944), 171; James McGregor Burns, *Roosevelt: the Lion and the Fox* (New York: Harcourt, Brace and World, 1956), 294; *New York Times,* February 7, 1937.

8   Ibid.

9   *New York Times,* February 10, 1937.

10   Ibid.; John T. Flynn, "Other People's Money: Senator Sheppard Turns on the Aged," *New Republic,* March 3, 1937, 110-111.

11   See Homer Cummings to Hatton Sumners, in Carl Swisher, ed. *The Selected Papers of Homer Cummings* (New York: Da Capo Press, 1972), 215; Samuel I. Rosenman, ed., *The Public Papers and Addresses of Franklin D. Roosevelt,* vol. VI, *The Constitution Prevails* (New York: MacMillan Company, 1941), 63.

12   Champagne, "Hatton Sumners and the 1937 Court-Packing Fight," 46-49.

13 Typed transcript, February 23, 1937, Mark Goodwin Papers, Dolph
    Briscoe Center for American History, University of Texas, Austin.
    Hereafter cited as MGP.Baker, *Back to Back*, 8.

14 Ibid.; *Washington Post*, February 21, 1937, 2; D. A. Frank to Sumners,
    March 8, 1937, HSP.

15 *Washington Post*, February 6, February 10, February 21, 1937; *Fort
    Worth Star Telegram*, February 10, 1937; Alsop and Catledge, *The 168
    Days*, 88; Lionel V. Patenaude, "Garner, Sumners, and Connally: The
    Defeat of the Roosevelt Court Bill in 1937," *Southwestern Historical
    Quarterly* , LXXIV (June, 1970), 39; Typed manuscript, February 23,
    1937, MGP.

16 Sumners to Robert J. Potts, February 15, 1937, HSP; Patenaude,
    "Garner, Sumners, and Rayburn," 41; *Washington Post*, February 10,
    1937.

17 Franklin D. Roosevelt to Sumners, February 10, 1937, HSP; *Time*,
    February 22, 1937, 11-12.

18 Anonymous memo to Sumners, February 13, 1937, HSP; Congressman
    W. R. Poage to Michael Collins, October 15, 1974, in possession of
    author, Wichita Falls, Texas; see also Emanuel Cellar, *You Never Leave
    Brooklyn: The Autobiography of Emanuel Cellar* (New York: J. Day
    Co., 1953, 17-19. Cellar served on the House Judiciary Committee
    alongside Sumners.

19 Alsop and Catledge, *The 168 Days*, 41, 77; *Austin Statesman*, February
    18, 1937; Franklyn Waltman, "The Sumners Judicial Retirement Act,"
    Congressional Digest, March, 1937, 79; Timmons, *Garner of Texas*, 219;
    U. S. Congress, House, *Congressional Record*, 75th Cong., 1st sess., 1757.

20 Sumners to Love, March 8, October 23, 1937, HSP.

21 Sumners to W. B. Mosher, March 8, 1937, HSP.

22 Maury Maverick, *A Maverick American* (New York: Covici Friede
    Press, 1937), 292-299, 337-342; Maury Maverick to Maury Maverick,
    Jr., March 4, 1937, Maury Maverick Papers, General Correspondence,
    Dolph Briscoe Center for American History, University of Texas,
    Austin. Hereafter cited as MMP; U. S. Congress, House, 75th Cong., 1st
    sess., 3247-3250, Appendix, 244-245.

23 Ibid.; Richard B. Henderson, *Maverick: A Political Biography* (Austin:
    University of Texas Press, 1970), 135.

24 Maverick to Maverick, Jr., March 4, 1947, MMP.

25 *Austin Statesman*, February 23, 1937; *Forth Worth Star-Telegram*, February 27, 1937; James T. Patterson, *Congressional Conservatism and the New Deal: the Growth of the Conservative Coalition in Congress, 1933-1939* (Lexington: University of Kentucky Press, 1967), 93; Baker, *Back to Back: FDR and the Supreme Court* (New York: Macmillan, 1967), 66.

26 Ibid.

27 U. S. Congress, House, *Congressional Record*, 75th Cong., 1st sess., 7141-7147; *Washington Post*, July 14, 1937.

28 Ibid.; Tom Connally and Alfred Steinberg, *My Name is Tom Connally* (New York: Thomas W. Crowell Company, 1954), 191; Thomas L. Stokes, *Chip Off My Shoulder* (Princeton: University of Princeton Press, 1940), 507.

CHAPTER 5

JIM WRIGHT

THE FIFTIETH LEGISLATURE AND THE EDUCATION OF A TEXAS
POLITICIAN

By Mark Beasley

At noon on Tuesday, January 14, 1947, freshman State Representative Jim Wright of Parker County took his seat at Desk No. 50 as
Secretary of State Claude Isbell called to order the House of Representatives of the Texas Fiftieth Legislature. Youthfully confident and
politically ambitious, the twenty-four-year-old Wright began his only
term in the state legislature, one that proved both challenging and educational. Two years earlier Wright had returned, after serving in World
War II, to a politically divided Texas where he soon eagerly immersed
himself in local politics, at times finding himself also involved in controversy. During his subsequent election campaign and in the carnival-
like atmosphere of the ensuing 144-day assembly, Wright received an
extraordinary tutorial in politics. He came to understand the legislative process and the necessity of building alliances. By the end of the
session he had won significant victories as well as experiencing disap-
pointing defeats. And in the process he gained self-confidence and the
respect of colleagues. Though his 1948 reelection bid fell short, Wright
still learned valuable lessons that aided his political education. During
this formative period Wright thus began to master the necessary skills
that led to a successful thirty-four year career as a congressman, culminating in his 1987 election as the forty-eighth Speaker of the United
States House of Representatives. Later he recalled his brief tenure in
Austin as the "most exciting, the most disillusioning and the most . . .
rewarding I had known."[1]

Late in the 1940s, Austin—a bustling city dominated by the twin
businesses of education and government—differed dramatically from
the district that Jim Wright represented. Unlike the state capital, Park-

er County was almost exclusively Anglo and predominately rural, in many ways typifying the North Central Texas area. Weatherford, the county seat, served as the market and shipping hub of a highly diversified local economy, dominated by the dairy, beef cattle, and poultry industries. Major crops included corn, oats, and peanuts, although the surrounding region produced watermelons, peaches, and pecans. Residents boasted of a flour mill and a grain elevator, a cottonseed oil plant and a clothing factory, a junior college and a local hospital—all rather provincial as compared to Austin.[2]

Wright, although having resided in the county for only a few years, had strong local ties. His father was born in Parker County and his mother grew up in Weatherford. They had met at a regional fair, his father owning a small business in town at the time as well as commanding an area National Guard unit. Soon after the birth of young Jim on December 22, 1922, the family moved from town to town as his father pursued a sales career. Because of his transient early life, Wright seized upon Parker County as his home base; at age nine he spent a memorable year in Weatherford, later revealing that "the little town had become part of me." He returned again in 1939 to attend the local junior college, where he excelled in debate and journalism. And after serving as an Army Air Corps bombardier and trainer during World War II, he came back "home" to pursue a business career and raise a family.[3]

Yet something in his life was missing; ambition for political office propelled Wright. To become better known, he volunteered for "every free job in town," helping organize a local Veterans of Foreign Wars post, recruiting over 100 new members for the district American Legion, teaching a Sunday School class at the Presbyterian church, speaking to service clubs, and promoting the Junior Chamber of Commerce. He also served as president of the Ex-Student Association of Weatherford College and occasionally guest-lectured there. In 1945, at the age of twenty-two, he was already a year beyond the minimum legal age to serve in the Texas Legislature and he decided to seek the office the following year. He felt "somewhat cheated" that long-time Congressman Fritz Lanham (having announced his retirement after twenty-eight years) had not waited "just two more years" until Wright would have been old enough to replace him. In June, 1945, Wright encountered influential newspaper publisher and Fort Worth "king-maker" Amon

G. Carter at a Weatherford celebration honoring native son Lieutenant General William Hood Simpson. Suspecting that Carter could be the key to his political future, he introduced himself to the prominent man only to be promptly snubbed. An embarrassed Wright realized immediately that any of his political achievements would be without help from Carter, especially since his pride would prevent "a second dose of that treatment."[4]

By the mid-1940s a variety of factors confirmed Texas both as culturally distinctive and increasingly conservative. While many Americans boasted of a history that sustained an "illusion" of national omnipotence, Texans, according to historian George Norris Green, magnified such beliefs; they had won their independence by shedding their own blood, had repelled "foreign" invaders, had stood as a viable republic, and had long been "the largest state in the Union." Texans reverently instructed children in their legends and history, even regarding their institutions as sacred. Jim Wright recalled that many in his state were "inordinately proud" of their contributions to the war effort; Texas had contributed a "higher percentage of volunteers" than any other state and Texas A & M had provided "more junior and middle grade commissioned officers . . . than any other college in the country." This excessive pride, according to Green, combined with a number of other ingredients to produce a "more virulent and entrenched . . . type of conservatism" in Texas. The "unique convergence of southern, western, and Mexican traditions" promoted such extremism; for decades, "unscrupulous" Anglo political bosses in South Texas had manipulated thousands of Mexican Americans steeped in largely feudal traditions. The "traditional" southern "legacy of ignorance, racism, fundamentalism, states' rights at all costs, and a streak of violence" also contributed to nurturing reactionary views. And beginning early in the 1940s two factions within the Democratic party, bitterly divided over the New Deal, dominated state politics. Although New Deal legislation encouraged liberalism, monied interests in Texas (and throughout the South), according to Green, responded with a "tremendous counter reaction." As a result conservative, corporate interests "took over the state" and inaugurated the "Establishment, a loosely knit plutocracy" controlled by "Anglo businessmen, oil men, bankers, and lawyers." By the mid-1940s these interests, increasingly dominated by the oil industry, exercised considerable influence over the state by "successfully financing campaigns for conservative candidates, lobbying, and controlling the press."[5]

During World War II, Texas, with such a unique political heritage, provided the site for an ideological battle which raged for several years. Early in the 1940s an increasingly reactionary Board of Regents of the University of Texas, appointed by Governors W. Lee O'Daniel and Coke Stevenson, sought to assert more control over higher education in Texas. They aimed to eliminate "subversive" professors, limit academic freedom, and restrict the teaching of "radical" subjects as well as the use of "immoral" materials. Dissension arose between several board members and university president Dr. Homer P. Rainey, who increasingly regarded their actions as unwarranted interference in academic administration; "certain regents," prominent historian and university professor J. Frank Dobie asserted, were "out after Rainey's scalp." A series of incidents beginning in 1942 exacerbated the strained relationship between president and board, culminating in the firing of Rainey on November 1, 1944. Students responded with torchlit protests. Faculty members rallied around the deposed president. The Texas Senate investigated. The Southern Association of College and Secondary Schools placed the University on probation for nine months. And propaganda utilized during the 1944 national political campaigns by the Texas Regulars (ultraconservative Democrats obsessed with an "alleged Negro-New Deal-labor union-communist conspiracy") helped sharpen voter awareness of the "troubles" at the University. Texans took sides, passionately defending "academic freedom" or vowing "no daughter of theirs . . . [would] ever set foot on that contaminated campus." During most of 1945 emotions throughout the state remained high as Rainey and groups of his backers campaigned for his reinstatement. Jim Wright later recalled that the controversy "was the most divisive issue" in Texas during the early postwar period, one which left "long-lasting scars."[6]

In such a rancorous political environment, Wright supported Rainey, having been impressed with him during his brief tenure at the University of Texas in 1941. After the war he still believed that such accusations that Rainey had been "coddling Communists or seeking to undermine the morals of young Texans" were unwarranted. He deplored the suspicions cast upon such outstanding professors as J. Frank Dobie, simply because they had publicly supported Homer

Rainey. And a series of radio broadcasts by the ex-president, beginning late in the summer of 1945, deeply affected Wright. He fervently embraced the educator's views on academic freedom and the role of the university; to Wright, the basic issues involved "a simple defense of the freedom of speech," a principle for which he believed Americans had recently fought a war to preserve.[7]

Wright welcomed the opportunity to perform a more active political role. During the fall of 1945 Margaret and Jack Carter, both progressive partisan stalwarts in Tarrant County, invited Wright to a strategy session devoted to reviving the Young Democratic Clubs of Texas--an organization that had lapsed during the war. He zealously joined the effort, organizing a chapter in Parker County as well as contacting "friends, wartime buddies, and former college classmates" throughout the state to establish clubs. Early in December, 1945, at the state convention in Fort Worth, the group led by Jack Carter (loyal to the New Deal and including Jim Wright) dominated the state convention consisting of twenty-three clubs by skillfully overcoming a conservative challenge. They dropped Lieutenant Governor John Lee Smith from the invitation list (because he was "an active Texas Regular and not a Democrat") and selected Dr. Homer P. Rainey to deliver the final luncheon address.

Wright played a prominent role at the controversial state convention. As a member of the Program Committee, he promoted Rainey's appearance while publicly denying sponsorship of any particular gubernatorial candidate, thus disputing claims by conservative dissidents that such a choice would split the organization. Wright, however, later admitted that his faction "wanted to encourage" the former educator to take his crusade "directly to the people by running for Governor." He also delivered a memorial speech honoring the war dead at the meeting. And as chairman of the Resolutions Committee, he reported the idealistic goals of the platform which included an antilynching law, abolition of the poll tax, lowering the voting age to eighteen, federal aid to education, and medical care for the elderly. Wright later recalled that such concepts, in 1945, were viewed as "radical," and that conservative interests throughout the state responded with a firestorm of protest. They contemptuously labeled convention participants "liberals, often hurled as an epithet." Of the "twenty or more" Young Democrats who sought public office after the convention, Wright alone won election during the following year.[8]

Early in January, 1946, Jim Wright, at age twenty-three, announced as a Democratic candidate for representative in the Texas Legislature. In his initial announcement he promised "only one thing," to work hard and use all of his abilities "in the sole interest of my county and state." During an unopposed campaign, however, he unwittingly displayed a lack of political acumen. He defied conventional wisdom by advocating controversial reforms, attacked "sacred cows" within the state, and alienated key Texas leaders. He later agreed with a friend who stated: "If there was a mistake you didn't make, it was only because you didn't think of it."[9]

Arrogant in his idealism, Wright was determined to "educate" his constituents on behalf of certain necessary reforms. He advocated a number of crucial programs--additional funding for local schools, increased teacher pay, a better public welfare program, more paved farm-to-market roads, and a statewide water system to aid agriculture and industry. His concepts were sound, his manners abrasive, and his financing plans proved extremely controversial. He even proposed levying severance taxes on the oil and gas and sulphur industries--"the untouchables" of Texas. And as a final expression of his desire for change, Wright also promoted such reforms--long opposed by many Texans--as a revised and modernized state constitution, tough lobby-registration laws, and annual salaries for legislators.[10]

In the midst of his campaign Wright waded into the "academic freedom" controversy with mixed results. Wright, outspoken and impetuous, publicly defended both Rainey and the University. During speaking engagements at various Parker County service clubs, he evoked Thomas Jefferson, Sam Houston, and even the Bible ("Ye shall know the truth and the truth shall make you free") to champion "academic freedom." Wright, while possibly converting a few people, aroused considerable animosity. Friends approached Wright, warning him to "soft pedal" this controversial theme. Upon learning that two leading citizens had murmured that he was "beginning to sound . . . like those Commies down at The University," Wright exploded: "How the hell do they equate Commies with a defense of free speech?" An astonished Wright had anticipated disagreement, but not "a whispering campaign" aimed at him personally. In his ardent defense of academic freedom, he now began to understand the risks of such a stand.[11]

Wright sought guidance from his father—and received sound advice. Wright, Sr. pointed out that, although the fiery speeches were often effective, some people were "menaced" by new ideas. He encouraged his son to speak out, but not to expect immunity from name-calling. Make "friends" out of enemies, he urged, and try to "convince them that you're a solid citizen and a man to be trusted." Then he added: "You cannot expect them to like you unless you can learn to like them." Wright, although unenthusiastic at first, "doggedly" pursued his father's counsel, later acknowledging that this paternal advice became a "fundamental part" of his belief system. As a consequence he learned to appreciate two local antagonistic "old curmudgeons long before either learned to like" him. But he eventually won them over.[12]

During this 1946 campaign, however, Wright struggled to counter both open antagonism and hidden opposition. At one veteran's gathering a drunken participant accused him of being "a Commie sonofabitch" and threw a punch. Wright, an experienced boxer, responded with a devastating display which left his unlucky adversary "crumpled in a heap like a sack of wet laundry." He later wrote that the incident was possibly "the best thing that happened in my race." Wright won a "begrudging acceptance" from many people who held misgivings about his views on academic freedom. Others, unhappy with his open support of Homer Rainey for Governor, promoted a write-in campaign against Wright—their effort failing dismally. And on the eve of the primary election in July, Wright challenged those individuals who were promoting a "whispering campaign" against him to discuss with him publicly (at the town square) any charges they had been expressing privately; no one showed up. Antagonism continued after the primary as opponents prevented him from being named to the county delegation to the September Democratic state convention, but he managed to attend the partisan conclave anyway.[13]

Wright capped his mistake-laden 1946 campaign by alienating key state leaders. For governor he actively endorsed ex-president Homer Rainey who would lose to Beauford Jester of Corsicana. He compounded his error by opposing the Governor-elect at the Democratic state convention in September, 1946. On two occasions during the fall he supported "reform" challengers in neighboring Dallas County, too politically naive to realize that the entrenched incumbents were "the most influential single delegation in the Legislature." And thus Wright's "gratuitous forays" did not go "unnoted by the members of the powerful Dallas County delegation," especially future Speaker of the Texas House of Representatives W. O. Reed.[14]

Wright, even after his election, continued to solidify his image as a liberal. In November, 1946, he played a prominent role at the contentious Houston convention of the Young Democratic Clubs of Texas, a gathering dominated by a battle between liberals and so-called "middle-of-the-roaders" for control of the organization. Wright and other liberals believed that conservatives had recently inflated their club memberships in order to gain convention votes and seize control. As chairman of the Credentials Committee, Wright consequently ruled against two dozen contested conservative delegations, trimming "their estimated 600 convention votes to 80, a weak minority"; in response the dissident Democrats bolted from the state meeting and formed a rival "junior party organ." After this tumult Wright became temporary chairman of the convention, later delivering the keynote address. In his speech Wright advocated world disarmament and the establishment of a world police force, urged an international language and a "world brotherhood," and predicted a repudiation of Senator W. Lee O'Daniel by the voters in 1948. The liberals passed a number of resolutions which mirrored many of Wright's campaign themes. Wright gained further recognition with his election as National Committeeman, not realizing that battles between rival Young Democrat groups would erupt while he served in the Legislature.[15]

As the legislative session opened, numerous issues divided Texas lawmakers. Public school teachers and state employees needed salary relief. Increased college attendance, particularly with the influx of veterans, necessitated a massive campus building program. Higher education for blacks, prodded by court action, contested—according to Governor Jester—the "wise and time-tested" policy of segregation. Growing public hostility toward organized labor foreshadowed the introduction of restrictive legislation. And lawmakers targeted veteran affairs, public health, and old-age pensions as additional areas of concern. Despite the excellent shape of state finances (the General Fund held a surplus of $35 million), Wright publicly—and correctly—asserted that the major problem confronting the Legislature was the all-important question: "where [was] the money coming from . . . to take care of the things we have all promised our constituents?"[16]

State legislators soon began the arduous task of lawmaking. But early on, Wright had his own ideas which were, in turn, scrutinized, questioned, and then opposed by many of his peers. On January 7 he suggested to Austin-area Young Democrats that the state government should unify and coordinate 109 commissions, special agencies, and bureaus, thereby providing $40 million in savings as well as eliminating the "endless criss-crossing cowpaths of duplicated efforts." After the session began on January 14, he immediately drafted two bills for government reorganization and lobbyist control. Wright also headed a group of mostly freshman representatives, who tried to raise oil, natural gas, and sulphur production taxes sufficiently to pay for increases in teachers' salaries, old-age pensions, and farm-to-market roads.[17]

Before tackling the problem of taxation, Wright joined other opinion makers to address pressure tactics in Austin that needed reform; meaningful change, however, met resistance. Lobbyists, often called the "Third House," were prominent and influential in the halls of the Capitol. In fact, Wright later recalled that they, in many cases, were "simply overpowering." Some legislators represented clients before the state's various administrative boards, while others remained privately employed by special interest groups that did business before the Legislature; both arrangements were legal under Texas statute. Wright believed that the low pay scale both for state senators and representatives—$10 per day for the first 120 days of the regular session, dropping to only $5 per day thereafter, or if in special session—encouraged some members to misuse their position for private gain. He united with kindred reformers to support pay raises and annual sessions for legislators. With more "zeal than prudence" he suggested keeping lawmakers in committees year round, prohibiting their acceptance of money or anything of value from any individual or organization trying to influence legislation, and disallowing their representation of clients before any state agency, commission, or board. Even lame-duck Governor Coke Stevenson, in a farewell address, admonished legislators to "refrain from running errands to, or practicing their professions [for pay] before other departments of government." And an Austin newspaper columnist reported that some previously skeptical lawmakers now believed that annual salaries "might be a good idea." Yet, even with such a flurry of proposals, legislative reform wilted. House committees "pigeonholed" all such bills, or the Senate simply ignored them; therefore, once again those in power, comfortable with the status quo, prevented any action.[18]

Wright's effort at lobbyist control met a similar fate. Supported by a number of freshman colleagues, his bill "with teeth" required members of the "Third House" to register, reveal the amount of their retainers, and annually list all expenses incurred, including money for the entertainment of members. In turn, the Wright proposal compelled lawmakers to document yearly all sources of income over $50. Causing "a mild furor" and facing opposition from the leadership, the bill remained bottled up in the State Affairs Committee, known as the "Speaker's private reserve" or "the deep freeze." But in mid-April, 1947, Wright and his allies, unable to gain a public hearing, were successful in transferring the bill to a friendlier committee, which, within two weeks, set a hearing. Wright, although surprised that "nobody offered any argument against it," began to understand more clearly the legislative maneuvering process. Soon opponents of the measure orchestrated a House vote to send it to still another committee, where it eventually died; the members, Wright later recalled, forwarded the bill to a "slow subcommittee with instructions to study it very carefully."[19]

Throughout the session, Wright retained his earlier "liberal" label. In a dispute over control of the Young Democratic Clubs of Texas organization Wright consistently supported the liberal faction; late in January, 1947, he failed in an attempt to forestall a House resolution commending the more conservative contingent for their "politically minded efforts." Two weeks later he willingly introduced the controversial Congresswoman Helen Gahagan Douglas (an outspoken advocate for FDR and the New Deal) at a Fort Worth Young Democrat meeting. Early in February several conservative Tarrant County state legislators, in a prepared statement released to the capitol press corps, expressed surprise that the "liberal" Wright had addressed local teachers, warning that he was "a leader of the Young Democratic group" that had been recently "repudiated" by the state Democratic party. Again in March, he invited Charles Bolte, national chairman of the American Veterans Committee, to speak before the Legislature, but opponents rejected Bolte as "too liberal," a charge Wright angrily denounced as "character assassination." And his refusal to back every piece of restrictive antilabor legislation led to unfair charges that Wright was "under the thumb of the union bosses"—not a compliment in an increasingly conservative political environment.[20]

At the same time Wright experienced the satisfaction of victory—yet again learning about the intricacies of lawmaking. The House passed two of his sponsored bills. One, the so-called State Finance Control Act, created a centralized budget agency that would audit the services provided by state agencies, develop long-range capital improvement plans, report on the condition of the State Treasury and anticipated revenue, examine agency expenditures, and suggest possible savings—all directed by a professional manager answerable to a joint-legislative committee. It also included Wright's earlier proposal to study the many overlapping and duplicitous state agencies, while recommending measures to streamline and consolidate administration. The Senate, however, failed to bring the bill up for consideration. His other measure (Wright served as a co-author) authorized funds ($1.5 million) for local soil and water conservation districts. It created a source for interest-free loans to groups of neighboring farmers, allowed for acquiring equipment to plant cover crops, and provided for building farm ponds to capture and conserve scarce rainwater. The Senate passed the bill, but on the last day of the session—June 6—it and six other measures were returned to the House by the State Comptroller because of insufficient availability of funds. With the adjournment of the Legislature, the disputed bills were abandoned.[21]

The issue of taxation also provided "fireworks" during the session, and Wright immediately declared himself a willing combatant in the fight. Early in January, 1947, he hoped to cure the problems of low teacher salaries, bad rural roads, and inadequate welfare funding in one broad stroke. He joined with five other representatives (all young war veterans from rural areas) to propose taxing the "big boys"—the oil, gas, and sulphur industries. To minimize the burden on local consumers, they intended to target natural resources currently transported tax-free to other states; using this tax-plan formula, Texas could easily gain an additional $38 million. Wright also sought to shift much of the state tax burden onto the oil industry, while attempting to protect the smaller producer. They devised a graduated severance tax so that "the bigger the producing company, the more taxes it would pay on each barrel." They reasoned that these huge companies could afford additional taxation; of the 3,300 oil producers registered in Texas, the top eight companies in 1946 had extracted more than 50 percent of the state oil.[22]

Wright and his fellow tax advocates aggressively argued on behalf of the controversial bill. At the end of January, in light of Governor Jester's no-tax campaign, they collectively denounced his program and built their case for increased revenue. They called for a *minimum* year-ly salary of $2,000 for teachers rather than the $2,000 *average* that the Governor proposed. They also regarded a Jester recommendation for 7,500 miles of new farm roads as insufficient; they wanted "to go fur-ther," insisting that "more than 10,000 miles of impassable dirt roads" existed in the agricultural areas of the state. And they argued that only two alternatives were available. Lawmakers could pay for urgent state needs and "keep the state solvent by levying fair and equitable taxes." Or they could deplete the present surplus of $35 million--while not solving any pressing problems--and force the next Legislature to assess new taxes "in a period in which . . . tax money will be still harder to find than it is today," a course Wright predicted the Legislature would "live to regret . . . bitterly."[23]

Throughout the tax debate, Wright—with his natural propen-sity for salesmanship—continued to promote his position, encourage public support, and educate his constituents. On the House floor he fought to distinguish his tax plan from a similar proposal advocated by former University of Texas President Homer P. Rainey in his recent unsuccessful gubernatorial campaign; yet some members remained unconvinced, believing that the voters had repudiated any tax increase in Beauford Jester's overwhelming victory. In his regular Weatherford newspaper column, Wright called his own measure the "Teachers' Pay Support Bill" and emphasized its fairness to Texas consumers. He also noted that the volume of mail on the subject of a natural resources tax "positively convinced [him] beyond the remotest doubt that the vast majority of Texas people are overwhelmingly in favor of the measure." Wright reasoned that raising state educational standards was worthy of funding because "every dollar spent on education is an investment in the future of freedom." At the same time he opposed a sales tax because he believed an assessment on natural resources "to be the least burdensome tax on the vast majority of the people of our state." And Wright, along with three other representatives at an Austin town meeting, urged the public to pressure the Legislature to pass additional taxes.[24]

Wright, however, faced early obstacles in pursuit of his objectives; his 1946 campaign blunders haunted him. In the last week of January, 1947, when committee assignments were finally announced, Wright failed to gain a seat on the House Tax Committee, where ten of twenty-one members had already pledged to follow Governor Jester's "no new taxes" program. His earlier campaigning against House Speaker Reed (who controlled all committee assignments) backfired, negatively affecting his own appointments. Sam Hanna, another Dallasite with a good memory, was equally antagonistic; during the announcements of committee assignments, he urged that the membership of the Tax Committee be read first "so we can get busy" and then targeted Wright, sarcastically advising him to "revise his bill to include a tax on Parker County watermelons."[25]

Although Wright and his colleagues surely faced an uphill battle, an embarrassing dilemma soon confronted them. In using their tax-plan formula, they had determined that Texas could easily gain an additional $38 million. But within a few weeks they learned that their calculations were grossly underestimated; a group of University of Texas graduate students, in researching realistic projections, had computed that the bill would actually create revenue of almost $500 million a year. Wright and his fellow legislators, hating to reveal their poor draftsmanship, "jointly preserved the myth of a $38 million a year tax bill," privately agreeing to scale down the bill upon reaching the House floor—if it ever got there.[26]

Wright and his co-sponsors of the tax bill encountered delaying tactics and obstacles by conservative opponents. The chairman of the Tax and Revenue Committee opined that no bills should be considered until someone definitely proved the need for additional funds to operate the government. In mid-February, the main committee refused to schedule hearings, deciding instead to await a subcommittee analysis of pending bills and possible needs for new levies. Wright and his associates continued to badger the committee; every few days one of them would attain recognition on the House floor and "blast the committee" for not taking any action. Wright even sought repeatedly to re-enter the bill before a friendlier committee, but every effort was blocked. He later wrote that "we tried our best to build a fire under the committee."[27]

The badgering eventually paid off. On March 18, 1947, the Revenue and Taxation Committee finally conducted a hearing on the Wright tax bill. Wright, along with five other proponents of the legislation, outlined the benefits and answered their critics during one of the longest hearings of the session--nearly four hours. He launched an initial salvo by attacking Governor Jester's opposition to new taxes, claiming that "it is meaningless to talk of raising teachers' salaries and building rural roads and at the same time say no new taxes." He echoed his earlier statements, declaring that it was irresponsible to deplete the $35 million surplus "we inherited as war savings," while emphasizing that the Wright measure was a "pay-as-you-go" plan. He also claimed that industry or consumers outside of Texas would pay the most because "80 percent of Texas production is consumed outside" the state. One proponent testified that the levy on oil production would actually reduce the tax burden for approximately 70 percent of the state's 3,300 oil-producing companies, while another deplored the fact that local exported gas was selling cheaper in Chicago than in Texas—with little benefit for the people of Texas.[28]

Despite such arguments, Wright and his allies faced considerable resistance. The "big boys," who had previously kept a low profile despite the submission of several natural resources tax proposals, spoke up forcefully for the first time. Oil industry spokespersons opposed the bill for a variety of reasons: Texas needed low-cost fuel to attract new industrial development, the income of royalty owners would shrink by half, and "a few cents tax would result in plugging thousands of small wells." They countered charges of huge industry-wide profits and argued that the gas and oil industries already contributed 52 percent of total tax revenues of the state. And they pointedly raised the issue of excessive spending, urging the Legislature to pursue more effective means to raise teachers' salaries—by collecting delinquent taxes (estimated at $90 million) and limiting the loss of "millions of dollars each year through the evasion of gasoline taxes." Other witnesses continued this well-orchestrated assault, complaining about an already heavy tax burden and diminished profit margins.[29]

Fourteen opposition witnesses from across the state testified before the Committee—and sixteen more were awaiting their turn when the hearings ended four hours later. What an incredible display of political steamrolling! Wright and his fellow legislators were simply overwhelmed; the Committee killed the measure by a vote of 12 to 2 (with one present and not voting). One Austin newspaper columnist suggested that the Revenue and Taxation Committee "was stacked" against the Wright tax bill, as "advocates argued to no avail." The writer commented that, although both sides contradicted each other, the representatives "sat in a coma," seemingly uninterested in ascertaining the facts. Natural resources industries "ran small operator after small operator" in front of the Committee until "they sounded like a bunch of bantam chickens at a cock fight." Any slim hope of passage faded when Wright failed to persuade four members to sign a minority report, hence a total victory for the "no-new-taxes" bloc as well as the "big boys."[30]

Despite this bruising defeat Wright redoubled his efforts to attain additional revenue for needed public services; in the process he learned valuable political lessons. As co-sponsor of a House measure (HB 44) to tax natural gas that would raise $35 million annually for teachers' salaries and rural roads, Wright was determined to succeed. He now knew, after his own bill had been killed, that opponents would be out in force. He had carefully identified the parliamentary maneuvers that had stalled the measure from reaching a vote over a three-week span. So on April 3 Wright, Charles McClellan of Eagle Lake (the primary sponsor), and Woodrow Bean of El Paso (author of another natural resources tax bill), quietly circulated among the members, securing promises not to adjourn for the coming Easter holiday before HB 44 came to a vote. The tactic worked; the bill passed by a comfortable majority that same day. A week later Wright, in his weekly Weatherford newspaper column, reflected on two lessons learned and remembered. He noted that "you can't always tell by a member's vote just what he may have been doing to help or hurt a bill"; the behind-the-scenes maneuvering might prove just as important. And he warned that a small, well-organized, and alert group could often "thwart the will of the majority for weeks, and by filibustering tactics . . . sometimes defeat a bill."[31]

As the fight over taxes continued to escalate, Wright waded into the fray. Late in April, 1947, after Governor Jester had called upon the Legislature to reduce or omit current spending bills because of "the mandate of the people that there shall be no new taxes," Wright challenged the Governor on the floor of the House. He argued that Jester did "not have a mandate from the people to protect" from taxation those who exploited the state's natural resources and "should stop this inane talk about cutting appropriations." He also maintained that the treasury would need an additional "$27 million to carry out our necessary appropriations," and he insisted that promises made for improvements during the campaign were not for Texas oil and gas companies. To Wright it was clear, if members voted for teacher pay raises or rural roads without adequate funds to back them up, then the House would be "indulging in the most base and hypocritical sham in the world." He also cited several errors in Jester's estimates of financial revenue for the state. "Can we depend upon this [information]," he asserted, "or is it inclined toward wishful thinking?"

Opponents immediately retorted. One accused Wright of making the same statements that defeated candidate Homer P. Rainey made during the previous summer and under those circumstances "wouldn't believe Jester regardless of what he said." Loud boos rose from the assembly when Wright retorted, "You flatter me by putting me in the same class with that great man."[32]

The rhetoric escalated and Wright remained near the center of the battle. During a May 9 radio interview, Jester replied to his critics, castigating the "demagogic smoke screens" created by natural resource tax advocates in the Legislature. A storm of protest ensued. Wright joined other lawmakers on the House floor who chided Jester for his "name-calling." He responded to the Governor on several radio stations as well as in the next issue of the left-of-center *Texas Spectator*. While insisting that he did not have a "private vendetta" against Jester, Wright nevertheless characterized himself as someone "who does not like being called a demagogue." Point by point, he countered the Governor's assertions that any taxes on natural resources would be passed on to Texas consumers or that his election demonstrated a "solemn mandate" for no additional taxes. He asserted that state polls had "repeatedly shown a resounding majority of Texans approve this form of taxation." He also demonstrated the legitimate need for additional revenue to meet pressing state problems. And thus, he concluded: "Who, then, is a 'demagogue'? Is it the lawmaker who tries to keep his state solvent by raising revenues sufficient to do the things he promised his constituents? Or is it someone else?"[33]

Early in May, 1947, the tax and economy blocs neared stalemate in the House, but Wright and other natural resources tax advocates ultimately faced defeat and disappointment. The choices to break the impasse remained clear—either cut dramatically projected expenditures (causing major distress to state departments) or pass new tax bills or return to deficit spending (only allowed under the state constitution if four-fifths of both houses concurred). Late in May, 1947, the state comptroller "solved" the dilemma by revising the revenue estimates upward for the next two years by $32 million and by refusing to authorize funds beyond the seven pending major appropriations bills. The state could squeak by until the next legislative session, thus allowing the Legislature to move swiftly toward adjournment. A disappointed Wright realized that many one-shot expenditures, including soil conservation and hospital construction, faced certain abandonment. He was especially unhappy about the Senate's repeated refusal to follow the House lead and adopt a farm-to-market road program. He lamented that promises made to constituents prior to the legislative session were cast aside and that the state had "spent all of our wartime savings and done nothing to replace them." Wright also predicted that the "big-overpowering issue" of the next session would be over taxation because additional revenue would be "absolutely necessary."[34]

With the adjournment of the Fiftieth Legislature in June, 1947, Wright had every reason to feel optimistic about his future despite a mixed performance. According to one Austin newspaper columnist, he would not be "overlooked by the 50th's historians." Conservatives had labeled him early as a "dangerous character" and had successfully blocked many of his "uninhibited ideas," adopting a saying in the process: "If it's Wright's, it's wrong." But Wright, the commentator concluded, was "bright . . . and soon caught on and let others take the lead." Wright had indeed mastered valuable lessons in just a few months; he had absorbed a great deal of knowledge about politics, the legislative process, parliamentary procedure, and the importance of alliances. Small victories tempered discouraging defeats. He had fought hard and "finished stronger" than he had begun. And he made mistakes, but had profited from them. Wright later recalled that he had "learned the ropes . . . made lots of friends and earned respect from some of those who'd first held me in contempt." At least, he recollected, "they could no longer ignore me."[35]

Wright returned home to Weatherford, only to be confronted with an issue which disturbed a number of his constituents. Dairy farmers, representing several hundred families in the county, complained to Wright that large-scale milk distributors (mostly located in Fort Worth and Dallas) had recently begun a troubling practice. They had imposed, collectively and arbitrarily, a new pricing scheme which alienated county milk producers. The big companies had established a "quota" for each dairyman, paying them approximately 40 percent less for all milk over a certain fixed amount; the standard price of $5.30 per hundred pounds dropped to $3.20. Although profits diminished for area farmers (Wright estimated their loss as "more than $25,000 a week"), the creameries failed to pass on any savings to consumers. Wright, who had been "fascinated" with antitrust law since his tenure in the service, believed this situation represented a "flagrant" case of powerful interests conspiring "in restraint of trade" and thus was illegal under Texas statute. He publicly asked Attorney General Price Daniel to investigate. The state consequently filed suit against these companies who soon abandoned their questionable practices. As a result, local dairy producers regarded Wright as somewhat of a "prairie populist and trust buster," and, he later recalled, they became his "fast friends and staunch supporters."[36]

During the next eight months Wright remained enthusiastic about his future. His family business continued to prosper; by the end of 1947 its sales force had expanded to twenty-four (up from one just two years earlier). He also had acquired many new friends. Farmers appreciated his legislative efforts on behalf of soil and water conservation as well as farm-to-market roads. County dairymen lauded his advocacy in their recent dispute with large creameries. Local teachers recognized Wright as one of the "outstanding advocates of higher pay" for educators during the last session. Requests for speaking engagements proliferated. As a result, early in January, 1948, Jim Wright declared his candidacy for a second term in the state legislature, promising to "continue to fight for the average, ordinary people and not for the special interests." At age twenty-five, he considered himself "politically invincible."[37]

But in the spring of 1948 a bizarre event changed this optimistic picture. A postcard addressed to "Mr. Jim Wright, c/o The Town Marshall, Weatherford, Texas," arrived, praising his recent San Antonio speech for his support ("like Mrs. Roosevelt") of communism and interracial marriage. Of course, Wright had never uttered such statements in his speech; the mystery writer had deliberately slandered him, knowing such views were reprehensible in post-World War II Texas. Initial confusion over delivery of the card (Weatherford lacked a town marshall) had guaranteed that several people had read its inflammatory contents. An exasperated and angry Wright wanted to find the sender, to do something, but friends advised him to "just forget it." But others certainly remembered; Wright later learned that "nagging suspicions" about him had begun to circulate.[38]

A local labor dispute compounded his problems. The Weatherford Spring Company, the community's largest single employer, faced a crisis. While workers wanted to organize a labor union to bargain collectively for higher wages, the plant owner threatened to fire anyone who joined such a union. Employees then threatened to walk off the job. Representatives from both management and labor looked to Wright for guidance; he was the only person in town to possess copies of the new labor restrictions passed during the most recent legislative session. Wright, eager to help, convinced the "hot-headed" owner's son not to harm physically the union organizers because the National Labor Relations Board would certainly frown upon such action. But when the two union representatives visited him to discuss the situation, Wright blundered politically by inviting them to lunch. Within hours, news had spread that he had been seen socializing with the "out-of-town labor agitators." And within a few weeks pamphlets appeared, branding Wright as a "pro-labor lawmaker" and a "tool of the labor bosses" as well as recommending his defeat.[39]

Opposition to Wright surfaced, but seemingly, was not too formidable. In February, 1948, Eugene Miller announced his candidacy for Representative. During the 1920s he had served two terms in both the state house and senate, afterwards becoming an attorney and lobbyist in Austin. In more recent years he had entered several Parker County races for the Texas Legislature and Senate, gaining a reputation for negative campaigning rather than winning. Late in 1946 he had been charged with criminal libel by a state senatorial candidate who had traced a scurrilous circular about him to Miller.[40]

Wright was still confident about his reelection chances, but wisely heeded warnings by political friends. To Wright, the choice for voters was simple; he represented the new politics, Miller the old. Town-square pundits and country commentators alike confirmed his optimistic assessment. But some savvy observers remained cautious, one, noting Miller's usual tactics of goading his opponent until he became angry, advised Wright to "keep . . . [his] head, plow a straight furrow, watch [his] temper," and not to "get down in the gutter with" Miller. Another urged him to conduct "a decent campaign" and people would draw their own conclusions. Still another remarked that Miller rarely ran to win, but ran instead "to get somebody else defeated," and his target was obviously Wright. He predicted an additional candidate, a "clean-cut fellow" without any political scars or enemies would enter the race and stand to benefit if Wright engaged Miller in a "mud-slinging" contest.

Such prophecy proved accurate. Early in June, shortly before the filing deadline, Floyd Bradshaw announced his candidacy, promising (with a jab at Wright) "no radical platform of increased taxes, or, any other revolutionary plan of 'cure-all' legislation." A teacher and principal at Dennis (a small country town on the Brazos River) as well as a life-long Parker County resident, he was a political neophyte, enjoying a "generally good reputation." As an educator and a ruralist, he could draw support from two of Wright's bases of support. And he fit the pattern prescribed by a Wright advisor; he was "the man recruited to catch the apples while Eugene Miller shook the tree."[41]

But Wright refused to play their game. He determined to pursue his reelection by emphasizing his record. And he continued to be in demand as a speaker throughout the county, receiving encouragement wherever he went. On July 3, his appearance at Spring Creek only confirmed this optimism. Refusing to respond to Miller's deliberate goading and fabricated statements, Wright promised the crowd not to "insult . . . [their] intelligence with cheap name-calling but honor" them with an honest and thoughtful discussion of relevant issues. He then noted that someone could not assault "another's character without soiling his own character" and further observed that the public was surely "plain sick and tired of that kind of low level campaigning." The crowd approved, as more applause followed his succinct examination of his record. Wright, "with a giddy sense of triumph," realized that the crowd was on his side, later recalling, "round one was mine."[42]

The next day a local political odds-maker predicted a Wright victory without a runoff. But then tragedy intervened. Late in the evening of July 7, unknown assailants shot Eugene Miller outside his adoptive Bethesda home (located ten miles northwest of Weatherford). The mortally wounded Miller, remaining conscious throughout the night at the area hospital, expressed surprise at the assault as well as ignorance of his attacker's identity or motive. He speculated to several witnesses that "left wing Communists" might have targeted him because of his consistent denunciation of them as well as civil rights programs and labor groups. Despite three blood transfusions, Miller died the next morning. His assailants were never found, the paucity of clues perplexing authorities.[43]

Wright, "visibly upset" upon hearing of the shooting, had quickly volunteered to give blood, his growing enmity toward his combative opponent now forgotten. He even offered a reward for the arrest and conviction of those responsible for Miller's murder. Despite such actions, ugly stories and wild rumors began to surface, alarming Wright; Miller had claimed to possess a secret recording of a Wright speech before a communist gathering, and had promised to produce a photograph of Wright together with an unnamed communist woman "at the proper time."

But how could Wright respond to a dead man? He became increasingly sullen and frustrated. His sister tearfully told him of overhearing comments speculating that he must have been aware of the murder in advance. How else would he have known to show up at the hospital to offer a blood transfusion? Tales of his brief fight with a drunken veteran two years earlier were resurrected and talk about his "red-headed temper" circulated. One farmer claimed that he had seen Wright practicing with a pistol out in the country. Another person tried to bribe a family employee to steal Wright, Sr.'s old World War I pistol for a ballistics test; the Texas Rangers assured an angry Wright that his father was not a suspect. Local gossips, fueled by earlier Miller insinuations, also questioned Wright's patriotism, adherence to Southern tradition, and Democratic party loyalty.[44]

During the last week of the political race the "whispering campaign" against Wright became public. One political ad blasted his legislative record on labor issues, accusing him of voting "in accordance with the demands of the union lobbyists." It also condemned his prior support for Dallas individuals currently associated with the "liberal" Henry Wallace presidential campaign. Another advertisement cited his meeting with CIO organizers as evidence of labor union backing and charged him with political evasion. And a front-page Floyd Bradshaw ad implied that Wright was not opposed to "Communism."[45]

In the aftermath of the Miller murder Wright continued to follow his speaking itineraries but with little enthusiasm, obviously frustrated about the rumors and seemingly hesitant to respond publicly. But he finally fought back; the Bradshaw ad "was too much." Refusing to engage in negative attacks, Wright forcefully defended both his character and record in the newspapers and on the stump during the remaining four days before the election. To counter "irresponsible gossip" he stated his positions on the major issues; he was a patriotic American, a defender of free enterprise, states' rights, and segregation, as well as an opponent of the Henry A. Wallace candidacy and CIO leader John L. Lewis. As for his labor record, he insisted that he had voted on the merits of each bill, siding with "working men" when they were correct and with "management" when they were right. He implored voters not to be deceived by "last-minute propaganda" against him. And during the last two nights of the campaign, Wright declared his "manifesto," fervently swearing his allegiance to the nation and its form of government, fiercely denouncing "those who'd seek political advantage from a tragedy, or impugn the patriotism of their fellow Americans." The old fire had returned, the crowds were with him once again. On the last night in Weatherford, the audience punctuated his speech with applause and "gave a standing ovation at the end."[46]

But Wright had waited too long. A last minute change in the site for the Weatherford candidate speeches resulted in a smaller-than-usual crowd. Thus, his fiery response to the "whispering campaign" failed to reach enough people. The slanderous rumors had accomplished their purpose; some constituents surely believed Wright was a communist, others suspected him of being an accessory to murder. After the ballots were counted, Wright lost the July 24 primary election by thirty-eight votes.[47]

The defeat disillusioned Wright, leaving scars. The previous few months had produced "the most traumatic experience" of his life. In his published "thanks" to supporters he expressed appreciation for their "faithfulness" in "the face of all slanderous and false things" spoken about him, his personal pain almost palpable. His wife wanted to move away, unwilling to live among individuals who could believe such vicious rumors and unsubstantiated allegations. But Wright refused, vowing "to show them by the way we live that they were wrong."

Despite such bravado, he suffered long-term psychic effects. The realization that some people had embraced such slander led to bouts of self-doubt. Recurrent feelings of remorse plagued him as well; he could not shake the idea that his campaign oratory might have unwittingly incited someone to violence. As a result, in the future, whenever a crowd began to respond excessively to his rhetoric, he would instinctively ease off, fearful of provoking an incendiary reaction. In July, 1948, Jim Wright, at the age of twenty-five, firmly believed that his political "future was behind" him.[48]

But Wright was wrong. For a period of time he submerged himself in the family business, but he could not stay away from politics. In 1950 he became Mayor of Weatherford, Texas, serving for four years. Subsequently, he ran for a seat in Congress as an underdog in 1954, surprising many who believed a small town politician could not win in a district dominated by the larger city of Fort Worth. Nevertheless, his constituents reelected him as their U. S. congressman seventeen times; Wright served from 1955 to 1989, rising to become Majority Leader (1977-1987) before his election as Speaker of the House of Representatives in 1987. Certainly he had learned much in those early formative political years, lessons that would stay with him throughout his long legislative career. Later Wright recognized the value of the political education he had received during his lone term in the Texas legislature, recalling his brief tenure in Austin as the "most exciting, the most disillusioning and the most . . . rewarding I had known."[49]

Endnotes

1 *Dallas Morning News*, January 14, 1947, 1; June 8, 1947, 2; Jim
   Wright, "Unfinished Autobiography," MSS, chapter 8, p. 17, Jim
   Wright Collection, Mary Couts Burnett Library, Texas Christian
   University, Fort Worth Texas (hereafter cited as JWC); *Roster and
   Standing Committees, Fiftieth Legislature, The Senate and the House of
   Representatives of the State of Texas* (n.p.: Texas Prison System, 1947)
   found in binder entitled *Roster and Committees: 43rd-52nd (1933-1951)*
   (Austin: Texas Legislative Reference Library, n.d.).

2 Wright, "Unfinished Autobiography," ch. 9, p. 1; *Weatherford, Parker
   County, Texas Fruit & Dairy Center: A Pictorial of Weatherford, Texas*
   (Weatherford: Weatherford Chamber of Commerce, 1946), 5, 7, 13,
   22-23, 26-29, 34-35, 45; *Texas Almanac and State Industrial Guide:
   The Encyclopedia of Texas, 1949-1950* (Dallas: A. H. Belo Corporation,
   1949), 574.

3 *Weatherford Democrat*, May 30, 1993, 1; June 1, 1993, 1, 10; June 2,
   1993, 1-2; Ben Procter, "Jim Wright," in *Profiles in Power: Twentieth-
   Century Texans in Washington*, ed. by Kenneth E. Hendrickson, Jr.,
   and Michael L. Collins, (Arlington Heights, Illinois: Harlan Davidson,
   1993), 229-239ff.

4 *Weatherford Democrat*, June 21, 1945, 1; June 28, 1945, 1; October 4,
   1945, 2; November 1, 1945, 1; January 17, 1946, 1; March 21, 1946,
   1; April 4, 1946, 7; *Daily Herald* (Weatherford), January 16, 1946, 4;
   April 29, 1946, 4; October 24, 1946, 4; interview with Jim Wright by
   Ben Procter, Houston, Texas, February 18, 1992; Wright, "Unfinished
   Autobiography," ch. 7, 6-9, 17, 20-21, JWC; Procter, "Jim Wright," 238.

5 Wright, "Unfinished Autobiography," ch.7, 10-11, JWC; George
   Norris Green, *The Establishment in Texas Politics; The Primitive Years,
   1938-1957*, Contributions in Political Science, Number 21 (Westport,
   Conn.: Greenwood Press, 1979), 3-7, 15, 17-18, 45-57ff. Professor
   Green noted that the Establishment "leaders--especially in the 1940s
   and 1950s--were dedicated to a regressive tax structure, low corporate
   taxes, antilabor laws, political, social, and economic oppression of
   blacks and Mexican-Americans, alleged states' rights, and extreme
   reluctance to expand state services. On federal matters they demanded
   tax reduction, a balanced budget, and the relaxation of federal controls
   over oil, gas, water, and other resources."

6 In 1942, after the physicians at the Galveston medical school had
   successfully resisted administrative changes sought by Rainey, the

regents relieved the president of any responsibility over the medical branch. In the spring three economics professors appeared at a Dallas anti-labor meeting. After being denied an opportunity to speak, they gave a public statement challenging the fairness of the meeting. Despite positive recommendations by their department, their dean, and Rainey, the astonished men were fired (or "not rehired") by the University of Texas Board of Regents. Then in 1943 this same board of regents explored ways "to abolish the tenure rules" so they could easily dismiss any undesirable professors, but only managed to weaken the procedures. They also refused to approve funds for social science research which Rainey supported. And their efforts to ban John Dos Passos' *The Big Money* (the third novel in the trilogy *U.S.A.*, filled with "filth and obscenity" according to one regent) from university use as well as "fire" the person responsible for placing such a book on the reading list of one sophomore course particularly alarmed Rainey. After further tensions developed, Rainey dramatically summarized his grievances during a meeting with the faculty in October, 1944. The regents, using such an overt act of "insubordination," fired Dr. Rainey on November 1, 1944. Board members then made additional charges against Rainey to support his firing. The resulting controversy continued unabated throughout the political campaigns of 1946 in which Rainey (as a gubernatorial candidate) and the University were major issues. Green, *The Establishment in Texas Politics*, 83-100ff; Seth S. McKay, *Texas and the Fair Deal, 1945-1952* (San Antonio: Naylor, 1954), 47-61, 69, 75; Wright, "Unfinished Autobiography," ch. 7, 11-14, 16, JWC; J. Frank Dobie, "For Your Careful Consideration," [reprint of article from after June, 1943?], in File 1: "Rainey, Homer P., 1944-1947," Box 16, Margaret B. Carter Papers, 1926-1976 (AR 239), University of Texas at Arlington Libraries [hereafter cited as MCP (AR 239)]; J. R. Parten, *The University of Texas Controversy*, statement before the Texas State Senate Educational Committee on November 28, 1944, in File 1: "Rainey, Homer P., 1944-1947," Box 16, ibid; Henry Nash Smith, Horace Busby, and Rex D. Hopper, *The Controversy at the University of Texas, 1939-1946: A Documentary History*, 3d ed. (Austin: Student Committee for Academic Freedom, Students' Association, University of Texas, 1946), 3-33ff.

7   Wright, "Unfinished Autobiography," ch. 7, 14, 16-17, JWC; *Daily Herald* (Weatherford) September 4, 1945, 1; Green, *The Establishment in Texas Politics*, 89; McKay, *Texas and the Fair Deal, 1945-1952*, 69; Dobie, "For Your Careful Consideration"; Alice Carol Cox, "The Rainey Controversy at the University of Texas, 1938-1946," Ph.D. dissertation, University of Denver, Denver, Colorado, 1970, 127.

8   The platform adopted at the December, 1945, Young Democrats

Convention also included a call to vest control of atomic weapons in
a world security council which could also outlaw war, continuation of
price controls to prevent inflation, a redrafting of the state constitution
"based on more liberal principles of government," and (in a pointed jab
at Texas Regulars and past gubernatorial administrations) requested
that the Governor "refrain from appointing to positions of honor and
importance members of the Texas Regulars and Republican parties."
Wright, "Unfinished Autobiography," ch. 7, 24-27; ch. 8, 6-7, JWC;
Wright interview, February 18, 1992; *Daily Herald* (Weatherford),
October 23, 1945, 2; December 5, 1945, 4; *Fort Worth Star-Telegram*
(A.M.), December 1, 1945, 1-2; December 5, 1945, 16; December
6, 1945, 18; December 7, 1945, 2; December 8, 1945, 3; "The Young
Democratic Clubs of Texas State Convention, December 6-7, 1945,
Hotel Texas, Fort Worth, Texas," program, in file 4: "Young Democratic
Clubs of America, 1945-1946," Box 22, MCP (AR 239); Margaret Carter
to Mrs. Cunningham, March 15, 1947, in file 1: "Young Democratic
Club of Tarrant County, 1945-1948, n.d.," Box 22, MCP (AR 239).
Wright denied any advocacy of a Rainey candidacy chiefly because
the association constitution required no endorsements for candidates
and neutrality in political races; *Fort Worth Star-Telegram* (A.M.),
November 28, 1945, 8.

9   *Daily Herald* (Weatherford), January 1, 1946, n.p.; *Weatherford
     Democrat*, January 3, 1946 n.p.; Wright interview, February 18, 1992;
     Wright, "Unfinished Autobiography," ch. 8, p. 1, JWC.

10   Wright, "Unfinished Autobiography," ch. 7, 6, 26-27; ch. 8, 1-7, JWC;
     Procter, "Jim Wright," 235-236, 239; Wright interview, February 18,
     1992.

11   Wright, "Unfinished Autobiography," ch. 7, 16-18, JWC.

12   *Ibid.*, 19-20, JWC; Wright interview, February 18, 1992, Procter, "Jim
     Wright," 238-239.

13   *Daily Herald* (Weatherford), July 24, 1946, 3; August 3, 1946, 3;
     Weatherford Democrat, July 25, 1946, 4; August 8, 1946, 1; Wright
     interview, February 18, 1992; Wright, "Unfinished Autobiography," ch.
     7, 22-24, JWC.

14   *Ibid.*, 1, 4-6, JWC; *Fort Worth Star-Telegram*, September 11, 1947, 1;
     Procter, "Jim Wright," 239; Wright interview, February 18, 1992.

15   Resolutions passed during the November, 1946 convention included
     calls for legislation against lobbying, annual salaries for legislators,
     redistricting of state legislative districts, upholding labor's right to
     collective bargaining and a closed shop, a stronger United Nations,

and support for the legislative agenda of Governor-elect Jester while opposing a sales tax as a method of financing improvements. *Fort Worth Star-Telegram* (A.M.), November 15, 1946, 2; November 16, 1946, 1, 12; November 17, 1946, 1, 8; Margaret Carter to Mrs. Cunningham, March 15, 1947, MCP (AR 239).

16 *Austin American*, January 5, 1947, 1-2; January 8, 1947, 1, 5; January 9, 1947, 1-2; January 10, 1947, 1, 3; January 14, 1947, 1, 3; *Dallas Morning News*, January 5, 1947, 1, 20; January 14, 1947, 1; *Weatherford Democrat*, January 16, 1947, 8. See McKay, *Texas and the New Deal, 1945-1952*, 134-153, for an account of the Fiftieth Legislature (primarily based on newspaper sources).

17 *Austin American*, January 8, 1947, 2; January 14, 1947, 1, 3; January 28, 1947, 1, 12; *Sunday American-Statesman* (Austin), January 26, 1947, 1; Procter, "Jim Wright," 239-240. The legislative history of the bills is found in Texas, *Journal of the House of Representatives of the Regular Session of the Fiftieth Legislature of the State of Texas Begun and Held at the City of Austin January 14, 1947* (Austin: A. C. Baldwin & Sons, 1947). The government reorganization bill was House Bill (HB) 106, *House Journal, 50th Legis.*, 161; the lobbyist control bill was HB 68, *House Journal, 50th Legis.*, 150; and the natural resources bill was HB 15, *House Journal, 50th Legis.*, 134.

18 Wright, "Unfinished Autobiography," ch. 9, 2-11ff, JWC; *Dallas Morning News*, February 11, 1947, 2; March 12, 1947, 3; *Austin American*, January 16, 1947, 1, 4; January 28, 1947, 6; February 11, 1947, 3; *Sunday American-Statesman* (Austin), January 26, 1947, 1; Procter, "Jim Wright," 239; *Weatherford Democrat*, February 13, 1947, 8. On various proposed constitutional amendments, see *House Journal, 50th Legis.*, 190, 706, 3325, for information on House Joint Resolution (HJR) 3 to increase compensation of legislators sponsored by Vernon McDaniel (Wright supported); 192, 515-516, 707-708 on HJR 10 to provide additional sessions of legislature sponsored by John L. Crosthwait (Wright supported); 1840, 2191-2192 on HJR 26 to increase compensation for legislators sponsored by Grady Moore (Wright supported); 206 on HJR 15 to increase legislator pay sponsored by Jimmy P. Horany and 214 on HJR 19 to provide for annual sessions and increased salaries sponsored by M. K. Thomas--the last two bills never came up for consideration. For Senate action on various House proposals, see Texas, *Journal of the Senate of the State of Texas; Regular Session of the Fiftieth Legislature, Convened January 14, 1947 Adjourned June 6, 1947* (Austin: Von Boeckmann-Jones Co., [1947]), 1482-1483 on HJR 3 which failed to pass on third reading; 369, 618 on HJR 10 which passed committee but was never brought up for a vote; 892,

1023, 1472 on HJR 26 which never was brought up for a vote.

19   Wright, "Unfinished Autobiography," ch. 9, 11-14, JWC; *Dallas Morning News*, April 20, 1947, 2; *Austin Statesman*, April 22, 1947, 3; *Austin American*, January 28, 1947, 5; February 4, 1947, 3; *House Journal, 50th Legis.*, 150, 1516, 1810; Procter, "Jim Wright," 239. Charlie Conner of Haskell was the co-sponsor of HB 68. The bill was re-referred to the Committee on Privileges, Suffrage, and Elections and then to the Committee on Representation Before the Legislature.

20   *Austin Statesman*, January 30, 1947, 1; *Dallas Morning News*, February 12, 1947, 16; *Austin American*, February 11, 1947, 4; March 20, 1947, 9; *Daily Herald* (Weatherford), March 19, 1947, 1; *Fort Worth Star-Telegram*, February 5, 1947, 10; February 8, 1947, 3; *The Texas Spectator*, February 17, 1947, 9; *House Journal, 50th Legis.*, 828-830, 1114-1116, 1119, 1146-1149, 1811-1812; Wright, "Unfinished Autobiography," ch. 10, 1-8ff, JWC. For background on the Young Democrats of Texas split, see *Dallas Morning News*, January 12, 1947, Sec. 2, 1; January 16, 1947, Sec. 2, 1; *Sunday American-Statesman* (Austin), January 12, 1947, 1; *Austin American*, January 11, 1947, 1, 6.

21   Wright, "Unfinished Autobiography," ch. 9, p. 17, JWC; *Austin American*, April 15, 1947, 2; *Austin Statesman*, June 5, 1947, 1-2; June 17, 1947, 1; June 26, 1947, 1; *Dallas Morning News*, June 7, 1947, 1, 14; June 27, 1947, 18; Procter, "Jim Wright," 239-240. HB 106, the government reorganization bill, was co-sponsored by W. K. Tippen of Abilene, Phillip L. Willis of Kaufman, Frank C. Oltorf of Marlin, Gus M. Lanier of Marquez, I. B. Holt of Olton, C. M. McFarland of Wichita Falls, Davis Clifton of McKinney, Sid Gregory, Jr., of Gatesville and J. B. Sallas of Crockett; see *House Journal, 50th Legis.*, 161, 1480-1481. For Senate action on HB 106, see *Senate Journal, 50th Legis.*, 635. The soil and water conservation district bill, HB 455, was originally sponsored by J. A. Luedemann of Brenham and Lamar Zivley of Temple; Wright signed as co-author later in the session; see *House Journal, 50th Legis.*, 462, 2167, 2721-2725, 3349. HB 455 originally called for $3 million in funding, but the Senate halved the amount in the waning days of the session. On June 6, 1947, the State Comptroller returned seven bills, including HB 455; only $9,103 of projected state revenue over the next two years remained unallocated. At the end of June the Attorney General, asked by Speaker Reed for guidance, ruled that the "ghost bills" (so-called because of their uncertain existence) were dead unless four-fifths of each house agreed to deficit spending. With the Legislature already adjourned, the bills were dead.

22   *House Journal, 50th Legis.*, 134-136ff; Wright, "Unfinished

Autobiography," ch. 10, 1, 8-12, JWC; *Dallas Morning News*, January
30, 1947, 3; *Sunday American-Statesman* (Austin), January 26, 1947, 1;
Austin American, February 7, 1947, 4. The natural resources tax bill,
sponsored by Wright, was House Bill (or HB) 15; the other sponsors of
the bill included James C. Spencer of Athens, Edward P. Hughes, Jr., of
Newton, Davis Clifton of McKinney, Paul Wilson of Geneva, and Sid
Gregory, Jr., of Gatesville. They estimated that their proposal would
create an additional $38 million in revenue: $26 million for schools,
$10 million for farm-to-market roads, and the remaining $2 million to
supplement the pension fund. Sulphur, produced by using a patented
process by the largest companies for $3.50 per ton, sold for at least
$18 per ton but yielded Texas only $1.28 in taxes. The bill's framers
proposed raising the levy to $5.00 per ton, but promised to exempt
small-time producers not utilizing the patented process. Natural gas
sold at the wellhead for nearly ten cents per thousand cubic feet and
was distributed to out-of-state consumers for fifty-to-sixty cents per
thousand. The bill would raise the natural gas duty from 5.2 percent of
market value to a severance tax of one-and-one-half cents a thousand
cubic feet at the well. But it also would repeal a gas utility gross receipts
tax that Wright later recalled "would keep the cost the same for Texas
industrial and residential consumers." Wright and his associates, with
the assistance of Austin attorney Bob Eckhardt, devised a scheme to
change the current 4.5 percent tax on oil to a graduated severance tax
ranging from 3 to 15 percent.

23 *Dallas Morning News*, January 30, 1947, 3; *Austin American*, January 30,
1947, 9.

24 *Austin Statesman*, April 30, 1947, 12; *Austin American*, January 28,
1947, 1, 12; May 3, 1947, 11; *Weatherford Democrat*, February 6, 1947,
6; February 27, 1947, 8; April 24, 1947, 11; May 15, 1947, 5.

25 Wright, "Unfinished Autobiography," ch. 8, 1, 4-6, JWC; *Austin
American*, January 29, 1947, 1-2; June 5, 1947, 4.

26 Wright, "Unfinished Autobiography," ch. 10, 12-13, JWC.

27 Wright, "Unfinished Autobiography," ch. 10, p. 13, JWC; *Dallas
Morning News*, February 12, 1947, 4; February 18, 1947, 4; *Austin
Statesman*, February 27, 1947, 1; *Austin American*, February 28, 1947,
1-2; *Sunday American-Statesman* (Austin), March 2, 1947, 8; *House
Journal, 50th Legis.*, 556-562ff.

28 *Austin American*, February 28, 1947, 12; March 19, 1947, 1-2; *Austin
Statesman*, March 17, 1947, 1; March 19, 1947, 1-2; *Dallas Morning
News*, March 19, 1947, 3; *Fort Worth Star-Telegram*, March 19, 1947, 7.

29 *Austin American*, March 19, 1947, 1-2; *Austin Statesman*, March 19, 1947, 1-2.

30 *Austin American*, March 19, 1947, 1-2; March 28, 1947, 4; *Austin Statesman*, March 19, 1947, 1-2; *Dallas Morning News*, March 19, 1947, 3; *Fort Worth Star-Telegram*, March 19, 1947, 7. See Eugene Miller, "The Big Boys: A Lobby Awakens," in *The Texas Spectator*, March 24, 1947, 3-4 and "The Same Old Song--the Same Refrain," in *The Texas Spectator*, April 14, 1947, 4-6, for a former legislator's jaundiced view of the "big boys" and the Wright bill; a year later Miller ironically ran against Wright who sought a second term in the Texas Legislature.

31 *Dallas Morning News*, March 26, 1947, 1; April 4, 1947, 3; *Weatherford Democrat*, April 10, 1947, 8. HB 44 passed the House but never came up in the Senate, effectively buried in a subcommittee.

32 *Dallas Morning News*, April 22, 1947, 1, 12; April 25, 1947, 3; *Austin American*, April 25, 1947, 1, 9; *Austin Statesman*, April 23, 1947, 1; April 24, 1947, 1, 5; April 25, 1947, 5.

33 Jim Wright, "Unfinished Autobiography," ch. 10, 14-16, JWC; *Dallas Morning News*, May 10, 1947, 1; *Austin American*, May 10, 1947, 1; May 14, 1947, 1, 11; *Austin Statesman*, May 13, 1947, 1, 13; *Texas Spectator*, May 19, 1947, 8-9.

34 *Austin Statesman*, May 24, 1947, 1; *Dallas Morning News*, May 11, 1947, 5; May 22, 1947, 2; May 25, 1947, 2; *Fort Worth Star-Telegram*, May 11, 1947, 8; *Weatherford Democrat*, May 29, 1947, 8; June 5, 1947, 7.

35 Wright, "Unfinished Autobiography," ch. 10, 17-18, JWC; *Austin American*, June 5, 1947, 4; Procter, "Jim Wright," 240.

36 In his letter to Attorney General Price Daniel (published in *The Texas Spectator*) Wright concluded that the milk distributors entered into an agreement to discourage and restrict production, limit free competition among themselves, and maintain "an actual shortage by talking of an imaginary 'surplus' and thus" uphold "the prices for which they market and sell the product at artificially high levels." Interview with Jim Wright by Ben Procter, Houston, Texas, February 20, 1992; *Weatherford Democrat*, June 26, 1947, 2; July 22, 1948, 4; *The Texas Spectator*, June 30, 1947, 8.

37 Wright, "Unfinished Autobiography," ch. 12, p. 1, JWC; *Weatherford Democrat*, July 24, 1947, 1; September 11, 1947, 1; October 23, 1947, 2; January 1, 1948, 8; February 5, 1948, 1; July 22, 1948, 4; *Daily Herald* (Weatherford), January 1, 1948, 2; April 9, 1948, 4.

38 Wright, "Unfinished Autobiography," ch. 12, 1-4, JWC.

39 The Weatherford Spring Company was later renamed the Weatherford Oil Tool Company. *Ibid.*, 7-8, JWC; *Daily Herald* (Weatherford), July 23, 1948, 3.

40 Wright, "Unfinished Autobiography," ch. 12, p. 4, JWC; *Weatherford Democrat*, October 10, 1946, 1; December 26, 1946, 1; March 11, 1948, 5; July 8, 1948, 1; *Daily Herald* (Weatherford), February 20, 1948, 3; July 8, 1948, 1. For Wright's observations on Eugene Miller's tactics in the 1946 election and his resulting libel trial (which ended with a hung jury), see Wright, "Unfinished Autobiography," ch. 8, 7-11, JWC.

41 Wright, "Unfinished Autobiography," ch. 12, 4-6, 8, JWC; *Weatherford Democrat*, June 3, 1948, 11; *Daily Herald* (Weatherford), June 1, 1948, 2.

42 Wright, "Unfinished Autobiography," ch. 12, 9, 11-16, JWC; *Weatherford Democrat*, May 13, 1948, 5, 11; June 10, 1948, 3; June 17, 1948, 8; June 24, 1948, 2, 4; July 1, 1948, 2, 4; July 18, 1948, 11; July 15, 1948, 3; *Daily Herald* (Weatherford), June 11, 1948, 4; June 18, 1948, 4; June 25, 1948, 4; July 2, 1948, 3; July 9, 1948, 4; July 16, 1948, 3.

43 Wright, "Unfinished Autobiography," ch. 12, 17-20, JWC; *Fort Worth Star-Telegram* (A.M.), July 9, 1948, 1-2; *Weatherford Democrat*, July 8, 1948, 1; July 15, 1948, 1; July 22, 1948, 1; *Daily Herald* (Weatherford), July 9, 1948, 4; July 10, 1948, 2.

44 Wright, "Unfinished Autobiography," ch. 12, 17-18, 21-24, JWC; *Daily Herald* (Weatherford), July 3, 1948, 4; July 12, 1948, 4; July 20, 1948, 2; *Weatherford Democrat*, July 1, 1948, 9; July 22, 1948, 3; *Fort Worth Star-Telegram* (A.M.), July 9, 1948, 1-2.

45 *Weatherford Democrat*, July 22, 1948, 6, 12; *Daily Herald* (Weatherford), July 21, 1948, 1, 4; July 23, 1948, 3.

46 Wright, "Unfinished Autobiography," ch. 12, 24-26, JWC; *Weatherford Democrat*, July 22, 1948, 3, 7; *Daily Herald* (Weatherford), July 20, 1948, 2; July 22, 1948, 5; July 23, 1948, 2, 4.

47 Bradshaw defeated Wright—2120 to 2082 (a thirty-eight vote majority). Wright, "Unfinished Autobiography," ch. 12, 25-26, JWC; *Weatherford Democrat*, July 1, 1948, 2; July 8, 1948, 1; July 29, 1948, 1; *Daily Herald* (Weatherford), July 23, 1948, 4, 5; July 26, 1948, 4.

48 Wright, "Unfinished Autobiography," ch. 12, 1, 26-27, JWC; *Weatherford Democrat*, July 29, 1948, 4; *Daily Herald* (Weatherford), July 28, 1948, 4.

49 Wright, "Unfinished Autobiography," ch. 8, p. 17, JWC.

CHAPTER 6

MARY ELIZABETH HOLDSWORTH BUTT

SOCIAL ACTIVIST AND ADVOCATE FOR THE MENTALLY ILL

By Mary Kelley Scheer

On February 22, 1954, the civic leadership of South Texas assembled in Laredo to recognize "the citizen who has contributed most to the development and progress of Southwest Texas during the past five years." Previous recipients of the award included *San Antonio Express* publisher Frank Huntress and Lon C. Hill, president of the Central Power and Light Company of Corpus Christi. But on this occasion the presentation ceremony at the 57th annual Washington Birthday Celebration luncheon was different. Superintendent of Schools J. W. Nixon presented a silver loving cup to Mary Elizabeth Holdsworth Butt, the first female recipient of the prize. Introduced as one "who is loved, admired, [and] respected by those who have had the privilege of working with her," he praised her "untiring work in the fields of child welfare, youth development, education, hospitals and other activities." Butt, a petite, soft spoken, fifty-one year old mother of three, accepted the title of "Mrs. South Texas, 1954" with characteristic modesty. Shy and retiring, she observed that she was only a representative for others who "worked as diligently as she in educational and welfare work." Unbeknownst to her audience at the time, Butt's greatest contribution would lay in the future. For the next twenty-five years Butt would become the foremost authority and advocate for the humane treatment of the state's mentally ill.[1]

Born on February 4, 1903, on a ranch near Loma Vista, Texas, Mary Elizabeth was the fourth of seven children born to Thomas and Rosa Holdsworth. Her father, the son of an English school master, immigrated to Texas in 1882 and spent his early years working the family homestead in Zavala County and then running an irrigation pump near Eagle Pass. Following his marriage to Rosa Ross in 1896, Thomas moved his growing family to northern Mexico where he worked as a mining engineer. But the volatile conditions and political instability of the Mexican Revolution necessitated a return to Texas in 1912. Thus, at age nine Mary Elizabeth, along with her other siblings, moved to Kerrville where her father purchased the Light and Ice Company. In the Texas hill country she inherited from her father his guiding philosophy to "do the thing you feel you must do," as well as his desire for her to complete her education, graduating from the University of Texas at Austin with a degree in English.[2]

Prospects for young Texas women in the first half of the twentieth century, however, were limited. Constrained by law and custom within a private sphere of the home, few women had the power or wealth to effect real change. Although gaining the right to vote in 1920, they still could not serve on juries (until 1955). While single women enjoyed greater latitude, married women could not sue, make contracts, or establish a credit rating without their husband's signature. Few attended college, secured professional jobs, or served in statewide offices. Rather, their ambitions for careers were modest, training to be teachers, secretaries, social workers, or nurses. For example, in 1930 Texas women comprised over 80 percent of its teachers, 90 percent of its nurses and librarians—but less than 2 percent of its doctors and lawyers. Similar to many others like herself, Butt accepted the likelihood that she would become a teacher and thereby secured positions at schools in Center Point and then in Kerrville.[3]

Several factors, however, intervened to alter the direction of Butt's life. Growing up within the Methodist Church, she absorbed the Christian obligation "to create Christ's kingdom on earth." The women's missionary movement that appeared in the 1880s invested women with the social and religious responsibility of expanding the community of believers. This opportunity to do God's work outside the home fostered a greater degree of autonomy as Methodist women established their own societies, funded parsonages, and founded city missions. Grafted onto their evangelicalism was the language of the social Gospel, which expressed Christian concerns about the social and economic problems of urban life. As Texas transitioned from a rural, agrarian state to a modern, industrialized society by 1940, Methodists reacted to the loss of traditional values and morals by supporting temperance, prohibition, and other social reforms. The adoption of the 1918 Social Creed by the Methodist Episcopal Church South General Conference recognized "the social disorder of our day" by laying out a progressive agenda, including the abolition of child labor, the elimination of poverty, and the shortening of the 6-day work week. The Women's Society of Christian Service (WSCS), renamed in 1939 to better reflect their expanded roles, gave Methodist women such as Mary Elizabeth Butt and others "a means of influencing the community." Consequently, in many Texas towns and cities they were instrumental in a wide variety of reforms, such as removing offensive tent shows, eliminating disagreeable vaudeville acts, and reporting on conditions in city jails and poor farms.[4]

As Methodist women took on ever-widening roles, they inevitably confronted the question of race. As a southern state Texans imposed discrimination and segregation on most aspects of public and private life, denying African Americans and Hispanics any meaningful political or economic power. Within the Methodist Church attended by Butt, blacks and whites were separated into sectional churches. Although the Northern and Southern branches joined together in 1939, they utilized the "separate but equal" doctrine legally established in 1896 to maintain racial segregation within its "jurisdictions." While the newly-reorganized Methodist Church brought together the largest number of black members of any predominately white Protestant church, it also created a mechanism for keeping the two races separate within the Jim Crow structure. At the same time, a separate Southwest Mexican Conference, which included all Texas Spanish-speaking Methodists, was also formed, thereby maintaining de facto segregation of the Hispanic population as well.[5]

Along with her strong religious and reformist beliefs, her marriage in 1924 to Howard E. Butt, Sr., a young, ambitious entrepreneur who worked in the family grocery business (the C.C. Butt Cash and Carry, later the H.E. Butt Grocery Co.), also proved transformational. As the family grew with the births of sons Howard, Jr., Charles, and daughter Eleanor, the H.E.B. empire also expanded, necessitating a move to the Rio Grande Valley in 1929. There Butt, a young woman of twenty-six, confronted the deplorable living conditions of families in the region. "The social needs in the Valley back then made a very big impression on her," son Charles later recalled. Moved by the extreme poverty, inadequate health facilities, and substandard schools of a segregated society, Butt believed that such injustice existed only "at the sufferance of its citizens." A devout Christian who often quoted the New Testament directive to serve "the least of these," she therefore vowed to do something positive for Valley residents when time and resources allowed.[6]

As the wife of a prosperous businessman in the 1920s and 1930s, Mary Elizabeth Butt was soon able to leverage her wealth and position to attack social injustice and alleviate suffering. Acknowledging that she could not live in a "state of affluence" without helping others, she sought a wider expression of her benevolence and piety. Her privileged condition, combined with a sense of *noblesse oblige* and religious commitment, allowed her to satisfy a "compelling force" within her to improve society. Access to secretarial and household help, as well as to financial assets, gave her the time and resources to attend meetings, serve on numerous boards, lobby lawmakers, and tour the state without neglecting her family. While her husband applauded her gains, he also occasionally begrudged the time her work took away from him. Yet he never asked her to stop. "He sputtered," she reminisced, "but he wanted me to go on." So while Howard was "occupied in multiple ways" managing the H.E.B. food store chain, Butt spent a portion of the family income and countless hours on civic and charitable endeavors. As Howard Butt succinctly stated: "I make the money and Mary spends it on worthy causes—and I'm glad she does."[7]

The Progressive Era agenda to improve society, although somewhat diminished during the interwar decades (1920-1940), also influenced Mary Elizabeth Butt. This ideology, which sought to perfect the human condition through government intervention and private activism, replaced the old nineteenth-century philosophy of *laissez-faire* individualism. In short, there was a strong impulse to do good. For example, Texas Progressives sought to reform politics and prisons, eliminate slums and child labor, and improve public health and education. Women in particular, through their clubs and associations, volunteered their various talents and reforming zeal to those endeavors that would improve the community. Specifically, by the 1930s Texas women could claim credit for establishing kindergartens and YWCAs, building playgrounds and libraries, and eliminating child labor and juvenile detention among hardened criminals.[8]

Within the Progressive and Methodist traditions, Butt expressed concern both for the spiritual and physical well being of "God's children." She believed that if a problem could be recognized and studied, then she should do her best to solve it. As Mental Health and Mental Retardation (MHMR) Commissioner John J. Kavanagh observed in 1974: "She does her homework and in a scientific manner. She identifies the problem, does her research and reaches her conclusions based upon her research and analysis." Beginning in the 1930s she therefore launched a series of projects targeting some of the health and educational needs of South Texas families. Completely unschooled in social service theory or practice, she utilized her dining room table to plan and organize her many projects. Her whirl of voluntary interests ranged from programs for disabled children and facilities for tuberculosis victims to vision and hearing screenings for elementary school children. In fact, Butt introduced the use of the first audiometer in the area, an instrument to gauge hearing acuity. The State Crippled Children's Program officed out of her home, providing over 100 children with corrective surgery in medical centers outside the Valley. Additionally, she served on the Community Chest Board and chaired the Cameron County Child Welfare Board, as well as worked for the expansion of libraries, organization of a YWCA, creation of an old age facility, and establishment of a district American Cancer Society.[9]

As a resident of South Texas, Mary Elizabeth Butt especially wanted to awaken the state to the acute health needs of the region. Often viewed as "the end of the world," the Rio Grande Valley was devoid of governmental agencies to relieve the suffering, poverty, and crippling deformities of its largely Mexican-American population. Of particular concern to her was the lack of treatment facilities for tuberculosis victims, of which 45 percent resided in South Texas. An infectious disease that had once afflicted her father-in-law and several uncles, it was indigenous to the area. Spread by air born particles, the bacterium lived in "nests" such as crowded quarters. "One could think of little else when entering a home," Butt recalled, "where the breadwinner was stricken with tuberculosis, the children were hungry, [and] a club footed child hobbled about the little *jacal*." Government, schools, and social organizations neglected them, while private resources were inadequate in the depressed conditions of the 1930s. Believing that "one solitary life can make a difference," she decided to try and alleviate the human suffering she witnessed. Butt therefore was instrumental in establishing TB hospitals such as Hilltop Sanitarium (1953) near Corpus Christi and securing the needed drugs to treat the disease.[10]

Gradually, however, Butt's activities took on a statewide scope. In 1933, along with husband Howard, she helped found the H. E. Butt Foundation, one of the earliest, private foundations in the state. Its mission was both charitable and religious with an emphasis on Christian leadership and service, especially through the establishment of youth camps and ecumenical retreats in the Texas hill country. Thereafter, Mary Elizabeth Butt served as its president for over 40 years. Then, in 1949 she also was responsible for helping organize the Conference of Texas Foundations and Trust Funds, later renamed the Conference of Southwest Foundations. As the first such organization in the nation, its purpose was to provide better communication and efficiency among private foundations in the allocation of charitable dollars.[11]

Despite a full calendar of social and philanthropic activities, in 1955 Mary Elizabeth Butt accepted a new challenge. Governor Allan Shivers appointed her to the governing board of the Texas State Hospitals and Special Schools (TSHSS), supplanted in 1965 by the Texas Department of Mental Health and Mental Retardation (MHMR). Initially, the governor offered the post to husband Howard Butt, a successful and prominent member of the business community, because "he had been making himself obnoxious about the conditions in the mental hospitals." If he was on the board, Shivers reasoned, he would then have to "put up or shut up." But due to his busy schedule and health concerns, he reluctantly declined. Howard recommended, however, that his wife Mary Elizabeth be appointed to one of the three available positions. Although hesitant at first to name a woman to a board with a large biennial budget, Shivers yielded due to the political and financial influence of the Butt name. But her appointment caused "many a deep furrow in many a male brow," recalled Josephine Sparks of the Driscoll Foundation. Few females at the time had held important appointive posts. Besides, in the post W.W. II era, a woman's place was in the home making bread—not in the boardroom making policy. The ideal 1950s suburban housewife, according to author Betty Friedan, was "young and frivolous, almost childlike; fluffy and feminine, passive; gaily content in a world of the bedroom and kitchen, sex, babies, and home." Nevertheless, despite the "automatic resistance of hard-headed men on the board" and threats to resign rather than serve with "some society matron," Butt soon joined the all-male club. Over the next twenty-five years, five succeeding governors reappointed her. Then, upon her retirement in 1981, she was named an emeritus MHMR board member, the first person so honored by any state board.[12]

By the time Butt joined the MHMR board, the treatment of mental illness in the United States and Texas had been characterized by cycles of neglect and reform. Initially, mentally ill individuals were hidden away at home or placed in private custodial care. Some were even confined to poorhouses or jails since insanity was once considered a "sin" and subject to punishment. In the mid-nineteenth century, before the writings of Sigmund Freud and the revolution in psychiatric practice, reformers such as Dorothea Dix and others began lobbying for the more humane treatment of the mentally ill and the establishment of state-supported hospitals and asylums, or places of safety, that would "prevent injury to themselves and to others." As a result in 1856, in keeping with the Texas Constitution of 1845 that committed the state to provide hospital treatment for the insane, the Texas legislature appropriated $50,000 to establish the State Lunatic Asylum (now Austin State Hospital). As the first such institution in the state, it was soon followed by three more state asylums in Terrell, San Antonio, and Abilene. These facilities removed mental inmates from the state prisons to primarily custodial institutions, which emphasized detention, economy, and management. In short, from before the Civil War until well after the turn of the century, the mentally ill or insane in Texas were simply separated from society and "warehoused."[13]

With the advent of the twentieth century, the Progressive Era marked a change in the attitudes and practices toward the mentally ill. Progressives emphasized the capacity for people to recognize and solve problems using "the application of science to social life." Behavior patterns, they contended, could be identified, modified, and taught. Practitioners of this new approach therefore launched a broad-based crusade known as "mental hygiene" that wedded private initiative with public authority to prevent disease and other social ills. Initiated by Clifford Beers, a Connecticut man who had personally experienced brutality and neglect in several mental hospitals, the movement called for improved treatment and heightened public awareness of mental illness. Many medical doctors and psychiatrists such as B. M. Worsham and F. S. White of the Austin State Hospital subscribed to this ideology, advocating more humane, non-institutional alternatives to mental hospitals with an emphasis on "scientific investigation and treatment of the insane." But mental hygienists did not limit their activities to the problems of the mentally ill. They also addressed issues of improved education, child guidance, and juvenile delinquency, arguing that early intervention was essential to counteract the growing social maladaptation rates. Well-adjusted children, reformers believed, would be "the best guarantors of a stable, productive adult population."[14]

Despite a more enlightened, scientific approach to mental health care, Texas lagged behind in substantive reform. A 1916 survey of the Texas state hospital system uncovered the widespread use of jails and almshouses for inmates due to an urgent need for space. Furthermore, according to asylum superintendent Dr. John Preston, the system was "a part of the political spoils of the party in power." Hospital superintendents, like the governors who appointed them, came and went, resulting in scant continuity, accountability, or improvements in the wards throughout the decades. As a result, the study recommended the creation of a centralized Board of Control to establish formal accounting practices and coordinate financial budgets within the hospital system. To meet the growing population needs of the state, it also called for the creation of two additional hospitals, one at Rusk and another at Wichita Falls for the mentally ill. Nine years later, as a result of a second investigation, the Texas legislature removed the words *lunatic* and *insane* from the names of its institutions and provided for two psychopathic hospitals; however, the one in Dallas was never built and the one in Galveston was delayed until 1931 due to a lack of appropriations. A mandated mental hygiene program to educate the public on health issues was also never funded. Then, with the onset of the Great Depression, which increased the emotional and mental anguish of many Texans and, in turn, overtaxed the existing hospitals, the state system further deteriorated. With the overwhelming immediate needs of unemployment, homelessness, and hunger, state hospitals could do little more than serve as "human warehouses." Consequently, these meager reforms were mostly cosmetic and budgetary. Tangible improvements in the prevention and treatment of the mentally ill, as well as the conditions within the state hospital system, were not substantially altered.[15]

While the Texas legislature failed to meet adequately the needs of the state's mental patients, private philanthropic foundations stepped in to provide support where government funding fell short. At the national level the Rockefeller Foundation helped make possible the establishment of the Bureau of Social Hygiene in 1911 to study mental illness, prostitution, venereal disease, and delinquency. At the state level, Mary Elizabeth Butt utilized the resources and facilities of the H. E. Butt Foundation outside Kerrville to house mentally ill patients during summer camping trips. More significantly, however, was the creation by Ima Hogg, a Houston philanthropist, of the Hogg Foundation for Mental Health (1940), which adopted "a broad mental health program" as its mission. Influenced by the principles of the mental hygiene movement and the ideas of psychologists Austin Rigg and Will Menninger, Hogg envisioned a statewide program of prevention and education. Having experienced her own bouts of depression and insomnia, she also believed that no one was perfectly balanced and at some time or another "everyone needs help." Thus, in the face of government budgetary constraints and overwhelming needs, wealthy philanthropists and humanitarians such as Mary Elizabeth Butt, Ima Hogg, and others were able to leverage their private wealth for the improvement of Texans' mental health.[16]

Despite new public and private funding, many of the same problems that plagued the state mental hospitals since the post-Civil War period continued to exist into the 1940s. Overcrowding was particularly problematic. In 1866 Superintendent W. P. Bell observed: "The asylum at present [Austin State Hospital] seems crowded to its limit of accommodation." Bell then listed others concerns as well, such as the lack of early intervention, failure to pay by non-indigent patients, and inadequate state funding. Similarly, in the 1940s terrible conditions persisted due to the backlog of problems that had accumulated during the depression and war years. In 1941 the Texas Committee on Eleemosynary Institutions uncovered "shortages of food, inefficiency in management, [and] cruelty beyond belief." Many persons declared insane languished on waiting lists due to a lack of beds. Some were temporarily housed in county jails until space was available. In 1942 the Board of Control attempted to alleviate the problem by shoving beds "closer together and pallets were placed in hallways and on screened porches." During World War II conditions only worsened as Texas soldiers returned home, many with mental disorders classified as "shell shock." The 1942 Texas legislature tried to relieve the demand for space by creating one new facility, the State Dairy and Hog Farm (later the Texas Leander Rehabilitation Center), and converting the Confederate Home for Men into a state hospital the next year. Emphasis then shifted from treatment to productivity as patients became employees in wartime food production. One observer described the system as a network of "vast farms and armies of serfs," performing labor for the state at little or no expense. Those who could not work sat on the wards in idleness.[17]

Reform of the Texas state hospital system languished until late in the 1940s. Depression, war, ignorance, and a lack of sustained public interest postponed any real improvement. Then in 1948 Albert Deutsch, a writer, journalist, and social scientist, published *The Shame of the States*, which gave a failing grade to the nation's care and treatment of the mentally ill. Not one state mental hospital met even "the minimum standards" set by the American Psychiatric Association (APA), which in 1946 called for no "less than one psychiatrist for every 150 patients." Substandard care, he contended, afflicted the entire nation, both in the North where conditions were generally considered "the best" and in the South, which historically placed near the bottom of the list.[18]

In 1949 Governor Shivers, the forty-one year old lieutenant governor who assumed the office after the sudden death of Governor Beauford H. Jester on July 11, urged capitol correspondents to investigate the situation in Texas. Sponsored by Sigma Delta Chi, a journalism fraternity, newspaper reporters made a 1,000 mile swing through Texas that resulted in a two-page expose by the *Daily Texan* of the "sordid conditions which existed throughout the Texas hospital system." Timed to coincide with the opening of the 51st legislative session, the newspaper article urged the governor to launch a "full-scale investigation of Texas mental hospitals." To meet the public outcry the Texas legislature acted. In 1949 it removed the state hospitals from the Board of Control, which was overburdened and unable to give adequate attention to the state's eleemosynary institutions. In its place, the legislature created a nine member Board for Texas State Hospitals and Special Schools (TSHSS), appointed by the governor. Immediately, the TSHSS board conducted a comprehensive tour of all the state institutions, confirming what Deutsch and a U. S. Public Health Service report discovered: Texas fell far below the standards of care set by the American Psychiatric Association. With a national average of $638.02

per patient, Texas spent only $516.14. According to Dr. L. P. Ristine, superintendent at the Austin State Hospital, Texas was "fifty years behind the times." These shocking revelations and negative publicity, which embarrassed state and health officials, led to reorganization efforts to correct some of the worst abuses within the prevailing asylum model of care.[19]

By 1950 mental health reform had an advocate in the statehouse. Governor Shivers recognized the urgent need to upgrade state hospitals and expand facilities. Moreover, without immediate government intervention, state funds for the TSHSS system would run out by August 31, 1950. At the same time Shivers needed a campaign issue to rally the voters. He was facing a tough reelection challenge from liberal Democrat Ralph Yarborough and, according to public relations advisor Jake Pickle, Shivers needed to "take the lead for one or two liberal things," such as the long overdue appropriations for eleemosynary institutions. But the state faced a $26 million revenue shortfall and the only avenue to expanding programs and balancing the budget was a tax increase— always a risky political position. Since hospital funding would soon expire, Shivers decided to call a special 30-day legislative session--one that had been planned by Jester until his untimely death. It would be devoted to a single issue--the state hospital emergency.[20]

On February 1, 1950, Governor Shivers addressed the state legislature and recommended the "urgent consideration" for funds to operate and expand the state hospital system. Having visited most of the state hospitals in the previous months, he described the facilities and conditions as "pitifully inadequate." "We have 24,000 people crowded into space that properly should house only 14,000," he stated. Furthermore, Shivers added, at the Austin State Hospital, "a mere stone's throw from the Capitol," there were only ten doctors and four registered nurses for 3,200 mental patients. He also produced three articles, which had been published in Texas weeklies, to support his position that the hospital system had been neglected for years and was "a disgrace to Texas." Immediate measures were needed, he urged, to remedy the scandalous conditions. Concluding his speech, Shivers cleverly crafted his closing argument: "Texas, the proud Lone Star State—first in oil—forty-eighth in mental hospitals. First in cotton—worst in tuberculosis. First in raising goats—last in caring for its state wards." [21]

To fund his long-overdue reforms Shivers asked for—and received--additional revenue. Without a tax increase, he warned, "the only alternative is to close our state hospitals and turn out the helpless, the needy seniles, the epileptics and the feeble-minded to fend for themselves...." But the state needed to overcome its deficit first before any new spending. "If we are going to appropriate in the spring," he said, "we must tax in the winter." Despite a "no new taxes" environment, Shivers, according to historian George Norris Green, became the first governor to call together all the major industry lobbyists to the Governor's Mansion and outline his ideas. He proposed a broad-based "special additional tax" on such items as oil, gas, whiskey, cosmetics, insurance companies, and utilities. Additionally, a special "penny-a-pack" levy on cigarettes would provide a $5 million building fund for the next seven years. At a time when oil and gas companies enjoyed record profits, critics charged Shivers with letting "the big interests off scot-free" by funding most of his reforms using consumer sales taxes. Other opponents argued that the new tax on cigarettes was not "equal and uniform." Nevertheless, the Texas legislature agreed to the new taxation and passed the first significant state hospital funding bill in over ten years, providing $21 million in operating costs and additional money for new construction of state mental institutions.[22]

Initially, improvements to the care of the mentally ill addressed non-treatment issues such as "brick and mortar" funding and institutional operation. In 1951 two new hospitals were added to the TSHSS—the Kerrville State Home (later the Kerrville State Hospital) and the Vernon State Home (now the Vernon Center). The conversion of abandoned military installations for use by patients also increased the physical inventory. But with expanded facilities came "a tidal wave of admissions" without the necessary doctors to diagnose and treat patients. Furthermore, many of the physicians who worked in the state hospital system did not have psychiatric training and were "the misfits, the derelicts, the sick men, the old, retired men, [and] a few good men who finally quit in disgust." Budgetary items also did not address low salaries, untrained attendants, and high employee turnover. Despite funding for new physical plants, the treatment of the mentally ill in Texas rarely rose above the level of basic custodial care.[23]

By the time Mary Elizabeth Butt attended her first MHMR board meeting on December 12, 1955, the state hospital system, especially its treatment and care of the mentally ill, was approaching a crisis. In the spring of 1955 the *Austin American-Statesman* ran a series of articles asserting that conditions at state hospitals continued to be "in bad shape." Despite six years of corrective measures, Texas still ranked "among the worst in the nation." Facilities remained "outmoded and inadequate;" patient and staff morale was low; and administrative machinery was "bogged down in a morass of outdated laws, dead ends, apathy, and stopgap planning." At the 100-year-old Austin State Hospital, 16,500 inmates occupied a space designed for 9,800. Patients slept on floors, ate in toilets, and lived in "firetraps." Several wards, according to a released inmate, "smelled like a zoo." At the Rusk State Hospital 104 patients were crowded into buildings intended for 50, sometimes sleeping two to a bed. There was no privacy, no recreation, and "nothing to do but wait." Furthermore, the aged and disabled mixed with mental patients and children and adults resided side-by-side. And to make matters worse, 20 percent of all patients had never been diagnosed, while others had resided in the hospital system for more than fifteen years![24]

As the only female member on an all-male MHMR board, Butt, now an attractively-attired fifty-seven-year-old woman, exhibited a demure, yet determined demeanor. She not only had to prove her competence, but maintain her femininity as well. Always fashionably dressed in designer suits with hat and gloves, she understood that it was a man's world and "you have to look good to do good." Butt recalled that her early days on the board were akin to being "adrift on a sea of ignorance." With characteristic resoluteness of purpose, she immediately embarked on a program of self-education into the controversial and little-understood arena of mental health. She acquired an extensive library of books on the topic. She visited at her own expense the Menniger Foundation in Topeka, Kansas, a leader in the mental health field, and the Bruno Bettleheim program for children with emotional problems in Chicago to learn about the diagnosis, treatment, and prevention of the illness. Furthermore, Butt traveled to every mental health hospital and special school throughout the state--something no other board member did—inspecting not only the physical structures, but everything from the food and utensils to the furniture and wards. "Not a lay person in the state knew more on mental health care," daughter Eleanor asserted. At the same time, she unfailingly attended MHMR meetings six times a year in Austin to report her findings, raise issues, and suggest reforms.[25]

As her expertise increased, Butt developed the necessary organizational and leadership skills to challenge the status quo. "She was an expert at getting others to help her in her quests," mental health official Marion Shira wrote. Butt frequently made phone calls and wrote letters to individuals soliciting their help. Convinced that a particular project depended on their participation, many who came under her persuasive sway quickly enlisted. "I've long had a habit of having bright ideas," she recalled, "then talking other people into doing the work." Realizing that no individual or institution could work alone, she also brought together teachers, doctors, nurses, businessmen, and community leaders, many times without remuneration, to work in cooperative partnerships. Her command of the written and spoken language, as well as her commitment to "do the right thing," allowed her to move seamlessly and effectively from the home to the community and then to the MHMR board.[26]

Butt's interest in mental health care was genuine and long-standing. As a student of the human condition and an advocate for those less fortunate, Mary Elizabeth Butt developed a vision for the humane treatment of the mentally ill with an emphasis on prevention. She advocated a holistic approach, first mending the physical ills of patients such as the tuberculosis victims she encountered in the Valley, then concentrating on their mental problems. In an era when individuals often sought help only after illness struck, Butt advocated childhood education and counseling programs to prevent mental illness and reduce social problems. In a 1962 speech "The Conquest of Mental Illness," she pointed out that "the problem begins long before the illness starts and can be counteracted in Christian homes, the church and the school." More importantly, Butt was one of the first MHMR board members to envision and then champion a shift from custodial to community-based care, insisting that "the retarded, the mentally ill, [and] the emotionally disturbed child" have access to treatment near their homes, not in remote isolated facilities. "It's immeasurably better for the child if he can be kept in his home community," she asserted. "A state hospital traumatizes him and stigmatizes him for life."[27]

The U.S. Public Health Service and the Texas Research League, a non-profit corporation engaged in nonpartisan research, had long advocated a plan similar to the one Butt supported. Both agencies had stressed the need for extensive outpatient programs, specifically the establishment of mental health clinics for those with early symptoms of mental illness or for those recently released from state hospitals. Such centers, which would not became a reality in Texas until 1958, would be particularly important since the Texas population was expected to increase 56.7 percent in the next twenty-five years (1950-1975). In a 1950 report "The Mental Health Programs of the 48 States," the Council of State Governments stated that while the general population had increased 2.6 times, the mental hospital population had increased 12.6 times. Without reform Texas, with a population of 7,711,194 in 1950, could conservatively expect its mental patients to increase from approximately 15,000 to over 180,000 inmates by the 1970s.[28]

During her first year on the MHMR board, Mary Elizabeth Butt became aware of the wretched conditions that existed in the state mental health facilities. In one year she interviewed doctors and administrators at all the state institutions. What she learned was shocking. There was no treatment program in the mental hospitals because "hospital budgets did not allow for drugs." Furthermore, overcrowding, inhumane treatment, and understaffing characterized the entire system. Describing the state institutions as "warehouses of human misery," Butt observed BDOs--blind, deaf, and orphaned children--packed into "the worst fire trap in Austin." Juvenile delinquents were "kept under lock and key," while the mentally ill were placed into "awful old fortresses." Their food, furnishings, and cleanliness were substandard. In fact, she was known "to get down and scrub the floors herself," if necessary, to improve sanitation. Medical care in those facilities was inadequate as well. In 1955 the state operated six mental health hospitals with only 16 physicians (medical doctors and psychiatrists) for 2,978 patients, a ratio of about 1:186. Conditions improved only slightly the next year, with nine institutions housing 4,316 inmates. Only 31 physicians and 274 nurses (full and part-time) attended the population. The ratio of physician to patient was 1:139 and full-time nurse to patient was 1:148; however, these statistics did not take into account those living at home or in the community requiring out-patient treatment, numbering an additional 15,000 persons. Furthermore, many facilities were scattered throughout the state, a good distance from a patient's home and family, and many of the humane aspects of in-house care such as recreation and gardening had been eliminated in favor of "warehousing," which was more cost-effective. As a result, according to longtime Butt family friend and Episcopal minister Clifford S. Waller of San Antonio: "The vast majority never got out."[29]

While Mary Elizabeth Butt did not initially seek to expand her social activism to encompass mental health, it quickly became the issue where she would have the most impact. At board meetings she raised embarrassing questions and according to son Howard, Jr., became "a thorn in their side." Typically, she saw her role as an advocate for the mentally ill, a generally inarticulate group without a vote or a voice. While most MHMR members seemed interested only in budgetary concerns or "bricks and mortar" issues, Butt focused on the immediate needs of improving treatment and upgrading conditions for residents. She believed that more state funds should be allocated to hire professionals. "We particularly need more money for training doctors and paying doctors," she insisted. Texas, with a population of over 9.5 million in 1960, spent less than other less populous states, ranking forty-ninth among the fifty states. Its per-patient expenditure was approximately $4-6 per day compared to a national standard of $10. She also supported a cohesive system of upgraded facilities, especially the creation of community-based centers, including out-patient day care for the mentally ill and drug abuse counseling. Providing nutritious meals, better kitchen facilities, and cheerful dining halls were also urgent needs that concerned her. In short, Butt refused to accept "second-best care" for patients committed to the Texas mental hospital system.[30]

Undaunted, Mary Elizabeth Butt launched a determined campaign to force the MHMR board to provide a more humane, community-based mental health system in Texas. One year after her appointment, Butt initiated a camping project for the mentally ill. She brought hundreds of patients to the H. E. Butt Foundation camp outside Kerrville without charge to the state. There they enjoyed outdoor activities such as swimming, hiking, and sports, without "locked doors or windows." No inmate ran away or attempted suicide. She also upgraded hospital kitchens and dining rooms, often inspecting them at 6 a.m. "to insure patients were getting the right kind of food." Butt knew about "genteel ways of living and knew that you could not teach someone to be genteel unless you were genteel to them." So she divided the institutional dining halls into smaller ones, adding curtains and family-style dining tables. Butt chased the birds and insects out of them by installing screen doors. With the aid of dietitian Cynthia Bishop she tried to improve the quality of the food by adding enriched soy products and more fresh vegetables. Then, she insisted that the metal plates, cups, and spoons be replaced by traditional dishes with knives and forks. And to drive home her point on one occasion she served visiting MHMR board members their meals and coffee using the existing institutional utensils. Within a month the policy was changed.[31]

In the Austin legislature Mary Elizabeth Butt was also an effective lobbyist. At a time when few housewives entered into public spaces, Butt regularly testified before congressional committees and single-mindedly lobbied state officials. She doggedly reminded them to do what was morally right, rather than politically advantageous. As a result of a 14-month study of 23 state institutions conducted by the Texas Research League, of which she was an advisory member, Butt urged the state legislature to address outdated procedural and commitment practices. The result was the adoption of a new Mental Health Code (H.B.6), which became effective January 1, 1958. Considered at the time as a model for other states, the law, drafted by the University of Texas School of Law with advice from the Hogg Foundation for Mental Health, defined mental illness as "a person whose mental health is substantially impaired." It specifically excluded those suffering from epilepsy, senility, alcoholism, or mental deficiency, transferring those state patients instead to private nursing facilities. It also changed "criminal-like" admission procedures to facilitate patient hospitalization with "the least possible trouble, expense and embarrassment to themselves and their families." At the same time another law (H.B. 906) reversed earlier practices by providing that individuals who committed acts while "criminally insane" were not responsible for their behavior.[32]

By the 1960s the movement to deinstitutionalize the nation's mentally ill population gathered momentum. After decades of reform, the old asylum model was still broken. Decentralization, community alternatives, and prevention were seen as desirable replacements for institutional care. At the national level in 1961 the prestigious Joint Commission on Mental Illness and Health issued its final report, proposing that no new mental hospitals be constructed. Instead, the report recommended that all existing state hospitals with more than 1,000 beds should be "gradually and progressively" converted into long term care centers only for the chronically ill. Accordingly, in 1963 President John F. Kennedy signed the Community Mental Health Centers Act, the last piece of legislation he approved before his death. This law provided $4.2 million of federal matching funds to the states and local governments for community mental health centers. To take advantage of this new federal program, Texas formed a seven member Inter-agency Committee on Mental Retardation and citizens' task forces to develop a statewide plan to meet the guidelines for obtaining funding. The result was the adoption of a major portion of the Texas Plan, which recommended the discarding of the custodial asylum model, except for the most severely-retarded, and the near unanimous passage (139 to 1 in the House, and 30 to 0 in the Senate) of the 1965 Texas Mental Health and Mental Retardation Act (H.B. 3).[33]

Effective September 1, 1965, the new legislation (H.B. 3) created the Texas Department of Mental Health and Mental Retardation (MHMR), replacing the old Board for Texas State Hospitals and Special Schools created in 1949. This new governing body corrected the confused lines of authority under the former dual-headed agency (TSHSS) by separating special schools and Confederate homes from the state mental hospitals. The MHMR board would only supervise mental health care facilities, while expanding its services to include vocational training, recreational programs, and outpatient care. More importantly, the act created approximately 30 community-based health centers with matching federal funds to deinstitutionalize patients, making treatment available closer to their homes.[34]

The development of community mental health and retardation centers fulfilled the vision of Mary Elizabeth Butt for the mentally ill in Texas. As part of the larger public debate in the 1960s to create the Great Society, it provided a new, innovative approach to their care and treatment near their homes and families. Texas Governor John Connally described this shift as a "new departure" that was "a brighter promise for effective treatment and prevention, as compared with results obtained from relying on institutional care alone." The newly-created regional mental health treatment centers would be administered by local boards of trustees, thereby shifting control for the sick back to the community. They would provide comprehensive diagnosis, evaluation, rehabilitation, and recreation on an out-patient basis. Several sites would also offer day care programs for the retarded

and short-term residential care. Early intervention through education and counseling programs were also available. As a consequence,
the state hospital population dropped from 16,000 in 1966 to below
8,000 by 1975, allowing more persons to live outside an institutional
setting. With a smaller number of inmates, hospitals could maintain
more effective staff-to-patient ratios. As Butt observed, the concept of
community-based centers for the mentally ill and retarded had placed
mental health on "good footing in Texas from El Paso to Beaumont
and Laredo to the Panhandle."[35]

The strength of her character and the courage of her convictions
allowed Mary Elizabeth Butt to help reform the mental health care system in Texas. Those who knew her applied numerous descriptives: in-
trepid, the embodiment of absolute determination, intelligent, tough,
but always compassionate. Even into her sixties she did not shrink
from conflict and was not afraid to challenge the status quo. Her views,
always firmly stated, sometimes startled or alienated others. Yet, she
was never intimidated by powerful men. "Set upon an objective,"
MHMR Commissioner John J. Kavanagh observed that "Mrs. Butt
pursues it with the doggedness that would disgrace a marine sergeant."
Convinced of the righteousness of her position and buttressed by her
deep-seated spiritual beliefs, she was an indefatigable worker for positive change. "You may think what you want about me," she famously
stated, "but you are going to do the right thing . . . or I'll embarrass
you in the board meeting by bringing it up." As the only woman on
the MHMR board for over 18 years (until joined by Lynn Darden), she
was its moral compass, its champion of the downtrodden. According
to board chairman Horace Cromer, Mary Elizabeth Butt was "the best
man on the board."[36]

The source of Butt's social activism and mental health advocacy
always puzzled her family and friends. "My mother cared passionately
about others," recalled son Charles. "It's always astounded us that she
developed such a social conscience. She didn't grow up in a home with
a big social service component." Nevertheless, like many young, educated women who were products of the Progressive Era, she absorbed
a social awareness and commitment to find some form of meaningful
work for herself. Improving mental health care resources for all Texans brought a sense of purpose, allowing her to share her vision of a
stable home and family life that she had personally enjoyed. She also

drew considerable spiritual support from her husband, a devout Baptist, who credited his own mother for instilling in him "the importance of public service." Christians, he believed, should be good stewards of their wealth and serve others. But Mary Elizabeth Butt also possessed a deep religious faith and social consciousness, stemming in part from her Methodist training and the teachings of John Wesley. Determined to always "do what was right," she acknowledged a "compelling force" within to improve the well-being of others who were less fortunate. As she later wrote: "It is a strange thing . . . with me there has always been this urge to build—to leave in this world some tangible evidence of having been there."[37]

Although Mary Elizabeth Butt never seriously challenged the existing race relations of the Jim Crow era, she did defy the social conventions of the day by championing ethnic unity. Recalling the early years of Butt's activism, former *Caller-Times* reporter Chauncey Cox, observed: "Some of those women were doing things their husbands didn't approve of." For example, Butt frequently tutored black students in her home who had been labeled "unteachable" by the school system so they "could keep up with [their] peers at school." After moving to Corpus Christi in 1940 she became troubled by the lack of day care facilities for African American children and helped found the Mary Bethune Day Nursery. Then in 1945, a decade before court-mandated segregation, she formed a coalition of women, including Bernice Leonard from the black community and Rosa Garza from the Mexican-American community, to establish an interracial YWCA in Corpus Christi. Its location and services were chosen "so that people of all races could be brought together to work for the good of the community." Later, she startled citizens when she, along with several supporters, helped integrate the YWCA swimming pool and open the H. E. Butt foundation camps to all ethnic and racial groups. In the state hospitals and schools, which had been "segregated according to color" since the nineteenth century, dormitories and dining rooms remained separate. Whether Butt ever spoke out about racial segregation or unequal facilities is unknown, but like most public facilities in Texas, full integration of its state hospitals would have to wait until the passage of the Civil Rights Act of 1964.[38]

On October 6, 1993, Mary Elizabeth Butt died of natural causes at her home in Corpus Christi, Texas, at the age of ninety. Banner headlines across the state announced: "Mary Butt dies after a lifetime of charity work." Newspaper stories gave full accounts of her life and accomplishments. Hundreds attended her funeral at the First United Methodist Church in Corpus Christi and heard Reverend Clifford Waller deliver a eulogy. He compared her civic commitment to the Biblical mandate to "feed my sheep." Mary Elizabeth Butt, he remarked, loved to feed people and "she had a lot of sheep to feed." Friends and associates remembered her as an intelligent, energetic woman with a deep-seated concern for the welfare of others. And Lady Bird Johnson, who had known and admired her, described Butt as "a patrician women" who was "totally devoted to her family and community." But for many, Butt would be remembered as "the number one client advocate" for the mentally ill in Texas. Afterwards, her body was interred next to her husband in Glen Rest Cemetery in Kerrville.[39]

Yet, for all her social activism, history has largely overlooked this woman. While many Texans recognize the H. E. Butt name associated with the grocery chain, few are aware of the civic, charitable, and mental health work of Mary Elizabeth Butt. And why? Several answers come to mind. First, Butt was a very private person, more comfortable working behind the scenes than in the limelight. She had remarkably little ego.

Whether as chairwoman or strategist, she didn't care who got the credit, daughter Eleanor remarked, "She just wanted it done." Second, she was very shy socially, viewing herself as primarily "a homemaker and citizen." The recipient of numerous awards, Butt often sent family members to accept the many tributes and accolades. Although committed to the church, she rarely joined women's groups or clubs, preferring instead to read the *Bible* at home and personally confront injustice wherever she encountered it. Third, like many members of wealthy families Mary Elizabeth Butt, along with husband Howard, was wary of too much press coverage or publicity. She preferred to give anonymously to favorite causes and push forward on those projects she felt "she must do." As son Charles, now head of the H. E. Butt food chain, explained in 1985: "Anytime we see our name in the newspaper we figure we made a mistake." Fourth, historians' assumptions about significance and marginality eclipsed her brand of social progressivism. Eschewing traditional avenues of a professional career, club work, or elective positions, she represented what lay persons, armed with determination, compassion, and a sense of justice can accomplish in their communities. By leveraging her social position, wealth, and vision, she believed that she could have "a little impact on the delivery of services to those who need help, and on the laws of Texas."[40]

And she did. Mary Elizabeth Holdsworth Butt made a significant difference in the lives of Texans. According to MHMR board member Lynn Darden, she "touched more lives than any other living Texan who has never held an elective office." A 1982 Harlingen newspaper account concurred, noting that Butt had positively affected "over a million people in the past 50 years in one way or another." Such proclamations were not hyperbole. Realizing that "nothing creative or contributive comes from isolation," she brought together volunteers and professionals, businessmen and government officials, lay and religious leaders in cooperative partnerships to find solutions to the problems of urban Texas. In an era when government was reactive to social problems such as illness, delinquency, and poverty, Butt was proactive, confronting those issues head-on through education, prevention, and early intervention. Many of the programs and institutions she helped found, including the H. E. Butt Foundation, the YWCA, mental health centers, vision and hearing screenings, public libraries, TB hospitals, and juvenile detention centers continue to serve the needs of Texans. Living in South Texas--a region devoid of an adequate social infrastructure such as hospitals and schools—she significantly improved the prospects for residents in communities from Kerrville to Brownsville, Laredo to Corpus Christi.[41]

At the state level, Butt's most sustained influence lay in her steady interest in improving the state's mental health system. According to Josephine Lamb, director of nursing for the TSHSS, more progress in mental health reform occurred in the first five years that Butt was on the board "than in the previous hundred." As the longest serving member on the MHMR board, she brought a distinct set of moral and spiritual values to mental health issues, as well as female concerns centered on the home, nutrition, education, and health. Refusing to acquiesce to board members more interested in buildings than human beings, Butt demanded the more humane treatment of patients by focusing on better food, cheerful environments, and recreational facilities. Convinced that the asylum concept for the treatment of mental illness had failed, she championed the deinstitutionalization of as many inmates as possible. During her tenure on the MHMR board, she oversaw the transfer of the mentally ill in Texas from custodial to community care. With the establishment of 30 statewide community-based centers more patients could receive treatment at home and live independently, thereby lessening the need to isolate them from society. Committed to reform, she then acted as a watchdog so that policies and programs were properly implemented. While Governor Shivers and others claimed the political victory--"the successful revamping and tremendous new emphasis upon our State Hospitals and Special Schools,"—Mary Elizabeth Holdsworth Butt set the moral tone, serving as a spokesperson for the mentally ill and the "mental health conscience of the people of Texas."[42]

Mary Elizabeth Holdsworth Butt does not fit easily into the paradigm of politically active Texas women who joined woman's clubs, the suffrage campaign, or the feminist movements of the twentieth century. Indifferent to building a personal legacy or advancing political causes, her brand of social activism was rooted in her deep-seated spiritual faith and "compelling force" to do what was morally right. Never one to simply "throw money at a problem," Butt's style of leadership was characterized by direct, personal action. What mattered was doing "the thing you feel you must do" by doggedly confronting a problem and then indefatigably working for positive improvement. Although she did not seek or hold elective office, she nevertheless was an integral part of the reform coalition who pressed for social change. As such she helps fill in the still-emerging narrative of women's activism after achieving the vote in 1920 and the rebirth of feminism during the 1960s. Her influence on public policy and her advocacy in behalf of the mentally ill and others less fortunate for over a quarter of a century attests to her rightful place in Texas history.

Endnotes

1   The family of Mary Elizabeth Holdsworth Butt has yet to release her private papers, therefore, a complete biography of her life is unavailable. Excerpts from the Butt journal are taken from *Newsbriefs* published by the H.E. Butt Foundation. "Mary Elizabeth Holdsworth Butt," special edition, Summer, 1994, hereafter referred to as MEHB; clipping, *Austin American*, November, 18, 1954, VF: Butt-Holdsworth, Butt-Holdsworth Memorial Library, Kerrville, Texas, hereafter referred to as B-HML; clipping, "Mrs. South Texas," VF: Butt-Holdsworth, B-HML; *Citizen Advocate*, March, 1982, MEHB, p. 1.

2   Mary Elizabeth was one of six children born to Thomas and Rosa Holdsworth. "Background on the Butt Family," pp. 1-3, VF: Butt Family, B-HML; "Background on the Holdsworth Family," p.1, VF: Butt Family, B-HML; MEHB, p. 4.

3   In 1918 Texas women gained the right to vote in primaries. Annie Webb Blanton became the first woman elected to public office when she won the post of state superintendent in 1918. Other women served on local school boards or in appointive positions. Beginning in 1923 until 1970 only twenty women served in the Texas legislature and one woman, Miriam "Ma" Ferguson, was elected governor, although her independence from former governor and husband James "Pa" Ferguson is still debated. Nancy Baker Jones, *Capitol Women: Texas Female Legislators, 1923-1999* (Austin: University of Texas Press, 2000), p. 281; MEHB, p. 4.

4   Walter N. Vernon, et al., *The Methodist Excitement in Texas: A History* (Dallas: The Texas United Methodist Historical Society, 1984), pp. 160-161, 236-243, 294).

5   Peter C. Murray, *Methodists and the Crucible of Race, 1930-1975* (Columbia: University of Missouri Press, 2004), pp. 3-4; Vernon, et al., *The Methodist Excitement in Texas*, pp. 231-235, 280-281; Anthony Quiroz, "The Quest for Identity and Citizenship: Mexican Americans in Twentieth-Century Texas" in *Twentieth Century Texas: A Social and Cultural History*, John W. Storey and Mary L. Kelley, eds. (Denton: University of North Texas Press, 2008), pp. 41-68; Cary D. Wintz, "The Struggle for Dignity: African Americans in Twentieth-Century Texas," in *Twentieth-*

Century Texas, Storey and Kelley, eds., pp. 69-104.

6   Howard was a Baptist while Mary Elizabeth was a Methodist; Howard
     E. Butt, Sr., acquired stores in Del Rio, Brownsville, Harlingen, Gonza-
     les, Austin, and San Antonio. MEHB, p. 4; "Howard E. Butt, Sr., Special
     Edition," fall, 1991, VF: Butt Family, B-HML; *Texas Monthly*, April,
     1988, pp.108-109; clipping, *Kerrville Times*, vol. 85, no. 161, VF: Butt-
     Holdsworth, B-HML; clipping, "Newsmakers of the Century," VF:Butt-
     Holdsworth, B-HML; clipping, *Corpus Christi Caller-Times*, Oct 7,
     1993, VF: Butt Family," B-HML; telephone interview with Howard Butt,
     Jr., January 5, 1999, San Antonio, Texas, in possession of author; inter-
     view with Eleanor Butt Crook, January 17, 2003, San Marcos, Texas, in
     possession of author.

7   MEHB, pp. 8, 11; Crook interview.

8   For women's social activism see Elizabeth York Enstam, *Women and the
     Creation of Urban Life, 1843-1920* (College Station: Texas A&M Uni-
     versity Press, 1998); Jacquelyn M. McElhaney, *Pauline Periwinkle and
     Progressive Reform in Dallas* (College Station: Texas A&M University
     Press, 1998); Judith N. McArthur, *Creating the New Woman: The Rise
     of Southern Women's Progressive Culture in Texas, 1893-1918* (Urbana:
     University of Illinois Press, 1998); Elizabeth Hayes Turner, *Women,
     Culture, and Community: Religion and Reform in Galveston, 1880-1920*
     (New York: Oxford University Press, 1997); Judith N. McArthur, "Sav-
     ing the Children: The Women's Crusade Against Child Labor, 1902-
     1918," in *Women and Texas History*, Fane Downs and Nancy Baker
     Jones, eds. (Austin: Texas State Historical Association), pp. 57-71 and
     Anne Firor Scott, N*atural Allies: Women's Association in American His-
     tory* (Urbana: University of Illinois Press, 1991).

9   *Austin American Statesman*, October 7, 1993; *Corpus Christi Caller-
     Times*, October 7, 1993.

10   For a history of tuberculosis and its treatment see Thomas M. Daniel,
     Captain of Death: The Story of Tuberculosis (Rochester, N.Y.: Univer-
     sity of Rochester Press, 1997) and Frank Ryan, *The Forgotten Plague:
     How the Battle against Tuberculosis was Won—and Lost* (Boston: Little,
     Brown, and Co., 1993). *Impact*, January-February, 1981, p. 9; *Corpus
     Christi Caller-Times*, Oct 7, 1993; "Profile: Mary Holdsworth Butt," B-
     HML; Butt, Jr., interview; Crook interview.

11   While the H.E. Butt Foundation was a pioneer in the field, the George
      Brackenridge Foundation in San Antonio was the first in Texas, created
      in 1920. Interview with Cliff Waller, March 13, 2003, San Antonio, Tex-
      as, in possession of author; MEHB, pp. 7-8, 11; *Kerrville Mountain Sun*,
      Jan 23, 1982; Mary L. Kelley, *The Foundations of Texan Philanthropy*
      (College Station: Texas A&M University Press, 2004), pp. 70-79.

12   Butt joined eight men on the board: Durwood Manford (chairman)
      from Smiley, R.F. Higgs from Stephenville, James H. Wooten, M.D.
      from Columbus, Herbert Martin from Mexia, John Dudley from
      Houston, Raleigh Ross, M.D., from Austin, James Windham from
      Livingston, and Howard Tellepsen from Houston. Although no more
      than three members could be M.D.s, there were no qualifications for
      TSHSS board membership. They received $10 for each meeting, plus
      expenses. Mary Elizabeth Butt was appointed to her first 6 year term
      from December, 12, 1955 to February 15, 1961. She was subsequently
      reappointed by Governors Price Daniel, John Connally, Preston Smith,
      Dolph Briscoe, and William Clements. Butt to Shivers, November
      7, 1955, Box 1977/81/273, file: appointments, Hospitals and Special
      Schools, Bd. For, Texas State Archives; *Annual Report for 1954-1955*,
      Texas State Hospitals and Special Schools, Texas State Archives, Austin,
      Texas, file: T362T31r, p. 1; *Impact*, Jan-Feb, 1981, p. 9; Betty Friedan,
      The Feminine Mystique (New York: Norton, 1974), pp. 33-68; Crook in-
      terview; *San Antonio Express*, Oct 7, 1993; *Centennial Journey*, January
      23, 1983; *Daily Texan*, January 11, 1949; *Dallas Morning News*, October
      13, 1963; *Impact*, January-February 1981, p. 9.

13   For a discussion of mental health care in the United States, see Gerald
      Grob, *Mental Illness and American Society, 1875-1940* (Princeton, N.J.:
      Princeton University Press, 1983) and *From Asylum to Community:
      Mental Health Policy in Modern America* (Princeton, N.J.: Princeton
      University Press, 1991). Also see David J. Rothman, *Conscience and
      Convenience: The Asylum and its Alternatives in Progressive America*
      (Boston: Little, Brown and Co., 1980). Gary E. Miller and Ira Iscoe, "A
      State Mental Health Commissioner and the Politics of Mental Illness"
      in *Impossible Jobs in Public Management*, Erwin C. Hargrove and John
      C. Glidwell, eds. (Lawrence: University Press of Kansas, 1990), p. 104;
      Kenneth D. Gaver, "Mental Illness and Mental Retardation: The History
      of State Care in Texas," *Impact* (July-August, 1975), pp. 3-6; *Constitu-
      tion of the State of Texas*, 1845, art. 16, sec. 54.

14   For contemporary mental hygiene theories see William White, *The Mental Hygiene of Childhood* (Boston: Little, Brown, and Co., 1923), Grob, *Mental Illness and American Society, 1875-1940*, pp. 144-178, and Rothman, *Conscience and Convenience*, pp. 293-375ff. Kate S. Kirkland, "A Wholesome Life: Ima Hogg's Vision for Mental Health," *Southwestern Historical Quarterly*, CIV (January, 2001), p. 428; Dan L. Creson, "Mental Health," in *The New Handbook of Texas*, IV, Ron Tyler, et als., eds. (Austin: Texas State Historical Association, 1996), p. 624; Waller interview.

15   Sarah C. Sitton, *Life at the Texas State Lunatic Asylum, 1857-1997* (College Station: Texas A&M University Press, 1999), pp. 36-59; Gaver, "Mental Illness and Mental Retardation," pp. 7-9.

16   Grob, *Mental Illness and American Society, 1875-1940*, p. 178; Kelley, *The Foundations of Texan Philanthropy*, pp. 46-57; Kirkland, "A Wholesome Life," pp. 417-447.

17   See Committee on State Eleemosynary and Reformatory Institutions, "Report to the 48th Texas State Legislature," *House Journal* (May 6, 1943): 2882-30; *Looking to the Future: The Needs of the MHMR System* (Austin: Texas Department of Mental Health and Mental Retardation, 1980), p. B1; Gaver, "Mental Illness and Mental Retardation," pp. 5, 9-10.

18   Albert Deutsch, *The Shame of the States* (New York: Harcourt, Brace and Company, 1948), pp. 15-24, 88.

19   The first Texas Board for State Hospitals and Special Schools was composed of nine members, serving six-year terms. See also James E. Peavy, *History of Public Health in Texas* (Austin: Texas State Department of Health, 1974). Press Release, Box 1977/81/234, file: State Hospital and Special Schools, Press Releases, Shivers Papers, Texas State Archives; Report of the Board of Texas State Hospitals and Special Schools, Box T362T31r, file 1949-50, Appendix 13, Texas State Archives; Gaver, "Mental Illness and Mental Retardation," pp. 10-11; *Daily Texan*, January 11, 1949; *Austin American-Statesman*, February 10, 13, 1955; *Dallas Morning News*, October 13, 1963.

20   Although sympathetic, Governor Jester had vetoed previous hospital appropriations due to a lack of available state funds. Shivers to H. E. Dill, January 24, 1950, Shivers Papers, Box 1977/081/414, file:

Texas Board of State Hospitals and Special Schools, 1950, Texas State Archives; W. S. Bell to Shivers, February, 1950, Shivers Papers, Box 1977/081/133, file: Misc. Texas State Archives; Ricky F. Dobbs, *Yellow Dogs and Republicans: Allan Shivers and Texas Two-Party Politics* (College Station: Texas A&M University Press, 2005), pp. 54, 149; Sam Kinch and Stuart Long, *Allan Shivers: The Pied Piper of Texas Politics* (Austin: Shoal Creek Publ., Inc., 1973), pp. 73-74; George N. Green, *The Establishment in Texas Politics: The Primitive Years, 1938-1957* (Westport, Connecticut.: Greenwood Press, 1979), pp. 137-138; Gaver, "Mental Illness and Mental Retardation," p. 10.

21 Shivers' speech became known as the "Goat Speech." Message of Governor Allan Shivers, 51st legislative called session, February 1, 1950, Box 1977/81/239, file: Eleemosynary Institutions, Shivers Papers, Texas State Archives.

22 Kinch and Long, *Allan Shivers*, pp. 73-74; Green, *The Establishment in Texas Politics*, p. 138; Sitton, *Life at the Texas State Lunatic Asylum*, p. 134; *Dallas Morning News*, October 13, 1963.

23 The special session of the legislature accomplished its task in 24 days. Hart to Ben, July 10, 1950, Box 1977/81/234, file: State Hospitals and Special Schools, Correspondence, 1950, Shivers Papers, Texas State Archives; Survey Reports of Texas State Schools for Mentally Deficient, 1950, p. 6, Box aT362T3m, Texas State Archives, Austin, Texas; *Wichita Falls Record News*, 1951; Gaver, "Mental Health and Mental Retardation," pp. 11-12; "Mentally Ill and Mentally Retarded, Care of, in Texas," in *The Handbook of Texas*, III, Eldon S. Branda, ed. (Austin: Texas State Historical Association, 1976), p. 588.

24 *Austin American-Statesman,* February 10-13, 1955.

25 Crook interview; Waller interview; *Kerrville Mountain Sun*, October 13, 1993.

26 MEHB, pp. 6, 8; clipping, *Corpus Christi Caller-Times*, Oct 7, 1993; "Profile: Mary Holdsworth Butt," B-HML.

27 *San Antonio News*, May 4, 1962; *Centennial Journey*, January 23, 1983, *Corpus Christi Caller-Times*, March 7, 1975.

28 Projection of the Population of Texas, 1950-1975, p. 4, Box 86/107, file: Texas Research League, Allan Shivers Papers, Center for American His-

tory, Austin, Texas; *Austin American- Statesman*, Feb 10, 1955; Gaver," Mental Illness and Mental Retardation," pp. 17-18; Rothman, *Conscience and Convenience*, p. 374.

29 Board for Texas State Hospitals and Special Schools, 1954-55, Annual Report, pp. 4, 6, file: T362 T31r, Texas State Archives, Austin, Texas; Board for Texas State Hospitals and Special Schools, 1955-56, Annual Report, pp. 6, 8, file: T362 T31r, Texas State Archives, Austin, Texas; Waller interview, MEHB, p. 13; *Impact*, January-February, 1981, p. 9; *San Antonio Express*, January 18, 1982; *Corpus Christi Caller-Times*, April 24, 1990.

30 *San Antonio News*, May 4, 1962; Waller interview; Butt, Jr., interview; U.S. Bureau of the Census, U.S. Census of Population, *General Population Characteristics: 1960* (Washington D.C.: Government Printing Office, 1961), pp. 45-55.

31 Glenn V. Ramsey, "A Report on the Camping Project" in *A View of the State Hospital Camping Project* (Austin: Hogg Foundation for Mental Health, 1960), pp 7-19; MEHB, p. 8; Waller interview, *Corpus Christi Caller-Times*, May 4, 1994; Sitton, *Life at the Texas State Lunatic Asylum*, pp. 138-143.

32 The Mental Health Code was later revised in 1983. Department of Mental Health and Mental Retardation, pp. 1-2, file: Archival holdings II.35a, Texas State Archives, Austin, Texas; Board for Texas State Hospitals and Special Schools, 1958-59, minutes, pp. 2-3, file: H2300.2 M668, Texas State Archives, Austin, Texas; Mikel Jean Fisher Brightman, "An Historical Survey of the State of Texas' Efforts to Aid the Mentally Ill and Mentally Retarded" (M.A. thesis, University of Texas at Austin, 1971), p. 40; Sitton, *Life at the Texas State Lunatic Asylum*, p. 143; Texas Research League Report, 1954-1955, 13 vols.; H. B. 6; H.B. 906; Mental Health Code Task Force, RG 032, Records 1981-85, pp. 1-2, Texas State Archives, Austin, Texas.

33 President John F. Kennedy signed the 1963 Community Mental Health Centers Act to provide funding for "early diagnosis and continuous and comprehensive care, in the community, of those suffering from these disorders." Texas received its first allotment of $182,800 in July 1963. Minutes, July 12, 1965, pp. 19, 115, Board for Texas State Hospitals and Special Schools, Texas State Library; "Mental Health," *The New Hand-*

book of Texas, p. 626; "Care of the Mentally Ill," *The Handbook of Texas*, 1978, p. 589; H.B. 3, 59th Texas legislature, regular session, 1965; *Dallas Morning News*, October 13, 1963.

34 The new MHMR department consisted of a nine member board that set policy, several commissioners with administrative control, an executive director, and staff.

35 Community-based health centers were not without their problems, including inadequate funding, homeless patients with mental illness, and a lack of an integrated support system. Steven B. Schnee, "Asylum and Community: Friend Not Foe," in *Community Care of the Chronically Mentally Ill: Proceedings of the Sixth Robert Lee Sutherland Seminar in Mental Health* (Austin: Hogg Foundation for Mental Health, 1989), pp. 34-36, 41-42; Gaver, "Mental Illness and Mental Retardation," p. 28; Sitton, *Life at the Texas State Lunatic Asylum*, pp. 149-155.

36 Lynn Darden of Fort Worth joined the board in 1973. Minutes, June, 1973, Texas Board of Mental Health and Mental Retardation, Box 1998/147-1, Texas State Archives; *Impact*, Jan-Feb, 1981, p. 9; Waller interview, Crook interview; *San Antonio News*, May 4, 1962; MEHB, pp. 8, 13.

37 "Newsmakers of the Century," B-HML; MEHB, pp. 1, 6, 11.

38 *Corpus Christi Caller-Times*, May 4, 1994; *YWCA Annual Report*, 1993, VF: Butt-Holdsworth, B-HML; Gaver, "Mental Illness and Mental Retardation," pp. 6-7, 18, MEHB, p. 7.

39 *Corpus Christi Caller-Times*, October 7, 9, 1993; *Houston Chronicle*, October 7, 1993; *Austin American-Statesman*, October 7, 1993; *Impact*, Jan-Feb, 1981, p. 9; MEHB, pp. 8, 12-13.

40 Despite her desire for anonymity, Mary Elizabeth Butt received numerous honors during her lifetime, including Texas Woman of Distinction, Mrs. South Texas, a Meritorious Service to the Children of America award from the National Council of Juvenile and Family Court Judges, honorary doctorates from Baylor University and Paul Quinn College, and recognition from the Hogg Foundation for Mental Health, the Parent's Association for the Retarded in Texas, Alliance for the Mentally Ill, and the Texas Library Association. *Austin American-Statesman*, April 29, 1985, p. 2; *Texas Monthly*, April 1988, pp. 102-107, 144-160; Crook

interview.

41 *Corpus Christi Caller-Times*, October 21, 1971; Waller interview; MEHB, p. 8.

42 In 2003, H.B. 2292 merged 12 state health and human services agencies into five, officially abolishing the Texas Department of Mental Health and Mental Retardation (effective September 1, 2004). A new Texas Department of State Health Services took over mental health and state hospital services and the Texas Department of Aging and Disability Services took over mental retardation services, including state schools for the mentally retarded. Funding for mental health services continues to be a problem. In 2006 Texas was ranked 47 out of 50 states in per capital spending and serves only a small percentage of those needing mental health care. Shivers Papers, Box 86/107/2, file: biographical: Allan Shivers, p. 2, Center for American History, Austin, Texas; MEHB, p. 8, *San Antonio Express-News*, September 17, 2006, p. 5H.

CHAPTER 7

MARIE FLICKINGER

THE "TAR WARS" FIGHT OVER THE BRIO TOXIC WASTE SITE

By Eddie Weller

When *South Belt Leader* publisher Marie Flickinger confronted an Environmental Protection Agency official, asking him "Why would you lie about us and this community," he replied, "Marie, that's the only way we can beat you." After nearly two decades, that statement still bothered her. "Think about this. The people I pay with my payroll taxes think it's ok to lie to Congress . . . because that's the only way they can beat us." After fighting the EPA for over a decade and eventually winning in the battle, the disgust is still there. And that long fight completely changed her attitude toward the government. "In 1982, when this whole thing started, I had full faith in the government, but not anymore."[1]

Flickinger, the leader of a group the local EPA officials often referred to as the "hysterical housewives," was referring to the clean up of the Brio Super Fund site southeast of Houston overseen by the government. The toxic waste dump was the closest site on the National Priorities List to a residential community in America, with chemical pits less than 18 inches from the fences of homes in the Southbend neighborhood. Throughout the fight over how to protect the local citizens from the toxic chemicals stored nearby, the EPA contended no threat to the public safety existed—even as numerous studies showed increased health risks and birth defects, water contamination, and air pollution. [2]

But how did a problem like this begin? For over a century petroleum, and the chemicals produced from it, has been central to the growth of the Texas economy. While the wells drilled near Corsicana in 1894 may have started the process, the Texas economy did not begin its shift from cotton and cattle until the gusher at Spindletop. Then after major strikes in the Permian Basin at Big Lake (1923) and the giant East Texas field (1930s), petroleum became the centerpiece of booming business. Early on Texas companies began reaping the rewards of refining the raw crude. Whether in drilling or refining, companies normally disposed of waste materials in the cheapest manner available thus insuring greater profits.[3]

As refineries grew along Galveston Bay, a number of these in Texas City dumped their wastes nearby at what eventually became known as the Motco Site. But by the mid-1950s locals wanted the waste dumped further from their homes, leading to the opening in 1957 of the Hard-Lowe Company site about 20 miles southeast of Houston, just east of the Gulf Freeway (Interstate 45) on Choate Road. The set-up seemed advantageous to all involved. More than twenty companies would bring their sludge left over from refining to a rural area without nearby residents. Hard-Lowe was guaranteed $10,000 a month profit by the major refineries for receiving the waste. Then any oil they could reprocess to a usable material, they could sell back for increased profits. All they had to do was accept everything delivered to them by the companies, amounting to approximately 750 million pounds over 25 years. The only problem occurred when they received more than they could process, but that was not even too difficult—the company would just dump the byproducts into open pits until they were able to refine them or they seeped into the ground.[4]

While the site was active, it went through several phases which contributed to the contamination. From 1957 to 1969 the company's main operations included recovering petrochemicals from the styrene tars and other chemicals from vinyl chloride residue, as well as regenerating copper catalysts from the waste. The first chemical pits were constructed before 1960 to hold the styrene tars. Between 1969 and 1982, the control of the site changed hands several times, with Friendswood mayor Ralph Lowe selling and buying back the property more than once. By 1970 the in-ground impoundment had grown to fourteen large, uncovered pits containing many known carcinogens. As the 1970s progressed more chemical waste was dumped in the area, with the pits filling numerous times.[5] If the pits were already full, employees would dump the extra spoilage in nearby rice fields or at other times they would spray the mixture on dirt roads to hold down the dust—considered a community service by rural homeowners who had no idea the spray included carcinogens. In later years employees would spray the roads at night so that no one could blame them later. Perhaps out of concern for the health of some of their workers, as early as 1970 the company began covering one of the pits with clay, although most of the pits were not covered until toward the end of the decade; often the contaminants were still in the pits. Immediately west of the Brio site was the Dixie Oil Processing plant (DOP) which also stored toxic materials, in particular metals, in pits. Eventually both sites would be placed on the superfund list and both were owned at different times by Ralph Lowe.[6]

Nearly thirty years after the dumping began, the Environmental Protection Agency began the process to list the site on the National Priorities List—better known as superfund sites. Since 1957, however, the area had experienced enormous changes. No longer was it a rural setting; because of Interstate 45, Houston's suburbs had grown up adjacent to the site. Prospective buyers were told that the old refinery would soon be dismantled. The Southbelt area was booming. The middle and upper middle class neighborhoods of Green Tee Terrace, Kirkmont, and Sageglen were all opening up, along with Arlene Weber Elementary school. As Marie Flickinger remembered, the community was "family oriented and church oriented, a little community where people really knew each other." The area's two largest employers, still in their infancy, Southeast Memorial Hospital and San Jacinto College South were hiring people less than a mile from the old pits. Once empty rice fields now held large subdivisions filled with children, as young families moved out from Houston. Just to the west of the site, and receiving run-off from the site, were the Little League baseball fields. And immediately adjacent to the toxic waste site was Southbend, one of the most affordable subdivisions in suburban Houston; yet some of the backyards were less than two feet from the storage pits.[7]

From the moment in October, 1984, when the Environmental Protection Agency nominated the Brio site for the National Priorities List, events and issues began to unfold rapidly. The Principle Responsible Parties (PRPs) who had caused the pollution quickly formed the Brio Site Task Force (BSTF) to protect their interests. According to the superfund law, the PRPs would have to pay the cost of the clean up. It would, therefore, benefit the companies to begin planning the least expensive remediation by working with the Environmental Protection

Agency. In addition it began trying to shape public opinion to lessen outbursts from local citizens. The BSTF hired Norma "J. J." Goldman to oversee the public relations work, while also giving her great power within the task force.[8]

Almost immediately the BSTF began trying to convince people that no danger existed and that everything would be fine—with mixed results. Approximately 300 people showed up at the first public meeting at Weber Elementary, located two hundred yards from Brio, in December, 1984. The experts from EPA and the Texas Department of Water Resources asserted that the "situation at Brio had been greatly exaggerated" and that "no immediate threat to their health and homes existed." Yet the citizens questioned the studies, asking why the air quality samples were taken in January instead of the summer when "hydrocarbons vaporize more readily." People were also skeptical about the safety of the water well that the subdivision used, but the government officials assured them no danger existed. The meeting did not succeed, since nearby homeowners filed suit against the home builders less than a month later.[9]

Shortly thereafter people began noticing the many health issues for those living nearby; believing that the conditions were related to the chemicals, many people looked to leave the Southbend subdivision. In January, 1985, more than 150 home owners sued the builders, Pulte Homes, Ryland Homes, Campbell Homes, and Park Avenue Homes, for deceptive trade practices for selling homes next to a toxic waste dump. Pulte said it had no idea it was anything but an old refinery until 1983, but the residents countered that they should have known of the toxic waste dump—especially since a magazine had written about the site as early as 1979. At the same time several people began complaining of skin rashes, headaches, kidney infections and "new" allergies. "It's been like a horror movie," according to resident Penny Perez. "My son is sick at least twice a week. He goes outside to play and comes back in with a rash covering his back." Other parents complained of young children with similar issues. Andrew Glaston noted that his daughter "breaks out in rashes and has strange fevers" and has nearly daily bouts with "wheezing or coughing." After hearing this and other information district judge Frank O. White issued an injunction permitting residents of Southbend to leave their homes without fear of ruined credit or foreclosure while the lawsuits progressed. [10]

In this early phase of the Brio fight, Marie Flickinger was on the sidelines; even though she would eventually become the most influential person in the fight. Born in Iowa, the raven-haired publisher was in her forties when she began the fight. With only a high school degree, she learned journalism from a short stint at a Friendswood paper before starting her own publication with her best friend Bobby Griffin. The little league mother trusted the government and all of those in authority—hardly the norm for journalists in the post-Watergate era. Her biggest effort up until Brio had been for improved flood control measures in the area after the enormous flooding of the late 1970s.[11]

Initially Flickinger believed the neighborhoods were safe and that the government would protect the residents if necessary. Her weekly newspaper, the *South Belt Leader*, ran stories trumpeting the safety of the air, soil, and water. "I went to a meeting with EPA and heard the people who were angry and upset and thought, you know these are people after money, no big deal," she recalled. "The federal government said it was ok so it's got to be ok. They are the Environmental Protection Agency—you have to believe what they say." She reported that the site would be fully cleaned up in five years, once the work was begun, making the land usable for other activities or businesses. One area resident castigated the paper for its one-sided coverage of the issue which seemed only to give the side of the BSTF. The next week she published "An Open Letter to Southbend Residents" that attacked anyone who had abandoned their home in Southbend as either someone trying to get out from under a mortgage they could not afford or trying to make some "extra money." The following week when someone attacked the open letter in the opinion section, she added a note explaining that the "Open Letter" was actually a paid advertisement. At first no editorials or investigative stories appeared with a negative view of the clean up. In fact the paper tried to squelch the rumor that incineration was being considered after EPA assured them of it in May, 1986.[12]

The first time Flickinger began to oppose the government's efforts came when the final Record of Decision (ROD) was being prepared. Up to that point people believed that the site would be completely cleaned up. But the ROD provided for only a partial cleanup, perhaps as few as five of the twenty-one pits, leaving most of the rest untouched and the area unusable to the community. Flickinger and other local leaders formed the Brio Total Cleanup Task Force in March, 1988.

EPA site director Lou Barinka "said the term 'cleanup' may have been misunderstood" that "cleanup means reducing the risk." Flickinger was obviously beginning to have some questions about EPA's veracity when she argued elected officials must "protect the people who are not experts. The EPA is not infallible. They need checks and balances." She further complained that "85 percent of the research" on Brio was done by the PRPs, which she said was "like having the fox guard the chicken house."[13]

Flickinger quickly became the loudest critic of the EPA and the cleanup plan because of several events. "First we started catching them in lies—little lies—no big deal, but still lies." Up until this time her big crusade had been for flood control in the area. One day Jim Green, Harris County Flood Control Director came by her office and she asked him to look at some aerial photographs of the area from the 1950s through the early 1980s. She did not know that Green had interpreted aerial photographs for the federal government years earlier. "We spread them out on my desk and put them in time chronology and Jim said to me, 'somebody's been dumping crap all over this place.'" He pointed out particular areas now in the Southbend subdivision. So she began asking questions; the EPA began giving her "flippant answers that didn't mean anything." By the end of 1988 the tone in the *South Belt Leader* had changed. Articles questioned the EPA. In a story written by Flickinger, she pointed out the health risks cited by expert witnesses in a court case brought by homeowners. And in a signed editorial she attacked the government by asking, "Who's the EPA protecting?"[14]

Early in spring, 1989, two events further moved Flickinger and the *South Belt Leader* to become an outspoken critic. First former Friendswood mayor and DOP owner Ralph Lowe invited the *South Belt Leader* to attend a meeting with the BSTF and EPA. Lowe "told me there were major problems. . . . He wanted my help in getting the government to acknowledge how bad the land was." When Flickinger and reporter Trigg Gardner showed up for the meeting, EPA refused to hold the meeting. While Lowe was certainly using the meeting to his advantage at a time when the press was regularly bashing him, the fact that the EPA would not meet with the press present made Flickinger even more skeptical.[15]

The second catalyst to the changing attitude involved the little league fields adjacent to the DOP site; Flickinger had served on the little league board when the land was bought and her husband had even welded all of the back stops when the fields were created. Again Lowe was involved in this event. He invited Flickinger and other civic leaders, including County Attorney Mike Driscoll and Harris County Flood Control District Director Jim Green, to the DOP site right next to the baseball park. Earlier that week EPA had assured Flickinger that nothing dangerous existed on the DOP site. Yet Lowe had said that tar was emerging from the ground throughout the site. When they arrived, "sure enough tars are seeping up all over the place." The tar "was actually the contaminants that had been placed in the ground and they were rising up just like buried tires." But the goo was also underground. "At one point Ralph Lowe . . . took a stick and punched it into the ground and it [the thick liquid black substance] was about [eighteen inches] deep." She videotaped the trip to DOP, including Lowe pulling the stick out of the ground with it covered in tar. During that visit, Bobby Miller, who had been vice-president of United Sports Association in 1975 when the ball fields were constructed, found old drainage pipes he remembered from when USA brought in loads of soil to raise the low area in order to build the fields. The pipes drained liquid from DOP to the lower rice fields. With yet another health hazard for the children of the neighborhoods, the EPA had obviously lied again about "no possible health risks."[16]

Later that week she called the EPA to discuss what she had seen. As usual she taped the conversation for later use in her newspaper. When she brought up the fact that Lou Barinka, Brio site manager for the EPA, had said no tar was at the sight but that she had just seen some, one of the men said, "There's no more tars than would fill a couple of inches in a bucket. " Yet as the video showed they saw far more. When she asked if they had moved the straw to look for any tar, since the EPA said straw was often put over tar to try and absorb it, to look for tar, she was met with silence. They continued to say there were only minute amounts of tar. Then when she questioned about the ball fields next to the site Roger Meacham said, "Marie, that site is not only fenced it's posted." Yet the video showed that the sign was bent and on the ground and covered with dirt and had "been like that a long time." Furthermore, he said "Marie it's not our job to be guardians of the neighborhood children." She recalled later thinking "Whoa! You're the

EPA what are you supposed to do if not protect us?" From that point forward Flickinger never faltered in her battle.[17]

Even as the battle raged over baseball, the *South Belt Leader* continued its investigation, uncovering new information causing even greater concern in the area. Early in April, 1989, the paper released a story based on an affidavit by Richard Guilliams, a "25-year Monsanto employee and the Regional Manager for Monsanto," that quoted him as saying "the existence of harmful chemicals within such proximity [less than half a mile] to human habitation is identifiable and imminent." The same article cited a report by Toxcon Engineering Company, one of the EPA contractors, that said soil contaminations levels 25 feet west of a pit on in the northwest area of the DOP site and next to the ball fields was extraordinary. The Texas Water commission had set 50 parts per million (ppm) as the alert level for copper; close to the little league fields Toxcon measured the copper at 2820 ppm—nearly sixty times the acceptable level. When questioned why the public was not notified of the results, BSTF spokesperson J.J. Goldman could not give an excuse.[18]

A few weeks later the *South Belt Leader* stirred the controversy again. Flickinger and Gardner revealed that the companies operating at Brio had dumped toxic waste at night off-site. Former employee Terry Pat White recalled building an eight-feet long PVC pipe spreader bar with a nozzle attached every six to ten inches which was attached to the rear of tank trucks, allowing the driver to release the heated tars and oil by-products as they drove. Oiling dirt roads was a commonly accepted practice in rural areas to keep down the dust, so often no one complained. Yet several times in the 1970s the Texas Water Quality Board investigated "excess dumping" by Brio, requiring the company to re-grade the road and vacuum the contaminated water out of the ditches. According to the story, not only were roads "oiled" but nearby fields, including the future baseball fields, were used as dump locations. According to White "We dumped a lot of bad stuff on both the roads and the fields. We loaded the trucks with the bottoms of the bottoms. The stuff you couldn't get rid of." The employees would mix styrene and phenolic tars, motor oils, and "anything else the companies could not get rid of," then heat them to 120 degrees, and, if the substances were too thick, mix them with chemical thinners so that the trucks could dump them. Driver P. C. Vasquez remembered dumping toxic wastes in the fields that became the Southbend subdivision, gaining access to the fields by a pipeline easement. At times drivers even got stuck in the fields, in one case causing them to work "all night and most of the next day to get him out." Another driver, Henry Faulk remembered dumping "anything and everything anyplace we could. At the time we did not know . . . that it might have harmful effects. We just knew that the company couldn't use it."[19]

Another struggle for the community was just finding out the chemicals located in the sites. The EPA had developed a priorities list of chemicals to look for based on earlier sites. Most of these were used in agricultural, such as insecticides and herbicides; waste products from refineries, however, were completely different, yet just as dangerous. When tests were run, EPA would only look for the 133 priority chemicals—everything else was just "unknown." At first no one realized that most of the chemicals were not even being looked for. Yet in spring, 1989, this became a major issue. People began pushing for testing independent of EPA that would identify all of the chemicals. Over 500 toxic chemicals had been identified in Texas already. Of course the BSTF balked at this. But when Lowe took samples from the sites in a "mayonnaise" jar for testing and new chemicals, in particular the mutagen chloroprene and the known carcinogen phenylhydrazine, were found, the paper began demanding an explanation. EPA quickly called Lowe's samples invalid, but the *South Belt Leader* continued investigating—finding that no one locally at the EPA could even explain where the priorities list came from. A further example came from the EPA Health Assessment released in April, 1989, where "evidence of plant toxicity was found at the northwestern area between DOP and Brio." The "black granulated soil" in a 2000 square foot area was "devoid of plant life." But since the test did not show any of the priority chemicals in the soil everything was labeled an unknown and the "cause of the phytotoxicity is unknown." The report also noted that the water in Mud Gulley was contaminated because the ground water was contaminated with volatile organic compounds (VOCs). Anyone coming in contact with the water was at risk, although the underbrush and some fencing would make frequent contact unlikely. Mud Gulley, however, flows into Clear Creek and from there into Galveston Bay. The newspaper questioned why the government was not publicizing the dangers to the local waterways.[20]

In the midst of these revelations the EPA took a more aggressive stance toward the *South Belt Leader*. In a letter hand-delivered to Flickinger, site manager Lou Barinka requested all of the information the newspaper had uncovered including "an accounting of individuals you may have received information from, their allegations and any supporting documents." Flickinger published the letter on the front page of the paper with a detailed response—denying them the documentation. She announced that much of the information would be available by May 4 (when it appeared in the *South Belt Leader*), but that she would "honor" the requests of those who asked for anonymity; the people came to the newspaper because they "lack confidence in the EPA." She then castigated him for the close relationship between the government, the companies that polluted the area (the PRPs), and the PR representative of those companies, J.J. Goldman. As she wrote, "Many have gotten the mistaken opinion that she [Goldman] works for the EPA." Furthermore, she was "disturbed to learn" that Goldman was discussing with local citizens the letter from Barinka the day it was written, before it had even been delivered to Flickinger; obviously she had seen the letter in advance, if, in fact she had not written it. Instead of intimidating her, the letter backfired and angered the publisher even more.[21]

A few months later Flickinger hit a homerun in her battle over the ball fields. With 250 people attending a meeting at Stuchberry Elementary School of the United Sports Alliance, the little league association, she unveiled an hour long video entitled "Tar Wars." It begins with her outlining everything the *South Belt Leader* had uncovered, including where Monsanto had, in official documents, changed the listed level of the soil covering the pits "from inches to feet." It explained how pipes had drained from the DOP site to the area now occupied by the ball fields—thus showing probable contamination below the ground. While the evidence was thorough and convincing, the coup de grace was toward the end of the video when they played thirteen uncut minutes of the conversation between Flickinger and the six EPA officials she had recorded after the trip to DOP. Even as they said no tar existed or just trace amounts, the video showed many large sludge puddles and how close the tar was to the surface, with just a few inches of fill covering the pits. At the end of the meeting the little league voted unanimously to close the ball fields out of concern for the safety of the kids "just because they saw what the federal government was saying was wrong."[22]

During the summer the BSTF began dismantling the old refining towers, storage tanks and buildings while installing air monitoring equipment. Yet the community people fought on in many ways. For instance community members formed Homes, Environment, Lives in Peril (HELP) late in 1988 and the members kept up the pressure—often through letters to the editor. In addition HELP would often hold protests to keep the publicity up, which the paper always covered. The *South Belt Leader* kept up its investigations, writing in July that toxic chemicals were found at DOP, such as vinyl chloride, copper, zinc, lead and "substantial amounts of mutagens and carcinogens." In addition the paper reported for the first time the possibility of dioxins at the site, an important concern in the final settlement. And while the tests from the ball fields revealed no immediate threats, additional independent testing of the DOP site showed vinyl chloride, benzene, and other chemicals in the tar samples. The *Leader* even exposed the poor record of the company dismantling the old refinery equipment, pointing out the Chemical Waste Management and its parent company Waste Management Incorporated had been fined many times all over the country for inadequate safety measures such as turning off monitoring systems when they were about to break environmental safety regulations. The company had been fined millions of dollars by EPA over the years, making the paper question why they had been chosen to dismantle the aged equipment.[23]

Throughout the fight the leading adversary of the paper was Norma J. "J.J." Goldman, the highly-paid PR representative for the BSTF; she reputedly made hundreds of thousands of dollars each year on the Brio site alone—even though she managed the publicity for several other sites as well. She often made unsubstantiated claims—always telling or implying how safe the site was. For instance she continually stated that children were not in danger. On several occasions she announced that a 250 feet deep "dense, non-permeable clay" barrier separated the surface area from the underground drinking water the neighborhoods used. Yet the U.S. Geological Survey said the largest barrier they could find was "a 60-foot section of low permeable clay between the two aquifers," prompting County Attorney Mike Driscoll to crack that "only two places in Harris County have a 250 foot impermeable clay barrier and all they have in common is that J.J. Goldman is the chemical companies PR representative at both locations." In fact the clay barrier was semi-permeable and averaged less than fifty feet deep; in addition old oil drilling in the area allowed for the contaminants to migrate downward along the pipes. And when Flickinger confronted her about the growing number of birth defects, Goldman responded "there couldn't be birth defects out there because she was a Christian grandmother and she wouldn't work for someone like that." She would also hold public meetings, allowing everyone to come—except Marie Flickinger. To combat this, Dr. Parker Williams, San Jacinto College South President and a long-time confidante of Flickinger, appointed college biology professor Catherine O'Brien to represent the college at all formal meetings; O'Brien was a leading supporter of Flickinger and one of the most effective fighters against the EPA. So any community information flowed directly to the publisher. At one point Flickinger was banned from a meeting at Weber Elementary, so she tried to get arrested, but "Rick Holloman would not let them arrest me," she remembered. "That made me pretty mad because I wanted to get arrested; I thought I could make my point better. Here they were having a public EPA meeting and kept our group outside." But the treatment did not slow down the *Leader*; "It didn't do them any good—it just made me more determined."[24]

At times the fight became personal between the two strong-willed, well organized women. According to Flickinger "she was a real bitch. She was conniving. For the first few years when I got on the other side I was almost as obsessed with her as I was with the fight." Goldman would host coffees in the homes of local citizens to tell them "How to get Marie." Yet in fighting back, Flickinger and the "hysterical housewives" showed real flare. For instance at one public meeting they got three mannequins from the local J.C. Penney's store and a mattress. They then dressed one up as Uncle Sam, one as EPA site manager Lou Barinka, and one as J. J. Goldman. When the TV crews arrived, they found all three in bed together—a definite way to make the local newscast. In the end Flickinger surmised that "she cost the chemical companies a lot more money. The more she stirred us the more money she made." Goldman would remain the biggest opponent throughout the entire battle.[25]

The lawsuit by homeowners against Monsanto brought new and

damning information against both EPA and the BSTF, with the *South Belt Leader* trumpeting the new revelations. On October 19, 1989, it reported that nearly three years earlier when excavating for samples the Brio Technical Committee decided that "Pit Q [is] too risky, switch to Pit B for incineration samples" because of the heavy vinyl chloride emissions from Pit Q.

Yet in March, 1987, two months after the testing, the EPA said that no vinyl chlorides had been found in Pit Q. Then in January, 1990, EPA manager Barinka admitted when pressed by Flickinger that they knew that vinyl chlorides could be found in Pit Q, but could give no reason why that had been deleted from the documents. In addition the newspaper revealed that the BSTF had paid J.J. Goldman's company to shred documents that might be relevant to the case. Shortly thereafter State District Judge Alice Oliver Trevathan ordered Monsanto to pay $190,000 to the homeowners attorneys for not producing all of the documents as required in the discovery phase.

By the time the material was revealed, the plaintiffs had already rested their case, so the judge allowed them to recall witnesses and re-open their case. At the end of the trial, John Brothers, an employee of Researching Engineering Inc. (REI) which had done the remedial investigation, dropped a bomb on the court; he announced that someone had changed the numbers in the original report before it was released by EPA. For instance REI, had found only six to eighteen inches of earthen cover over Pit J, while the report listed 78 inches of covering. He saw at least eight other changes from his field notes. He also commented that he and his men all wore protective suits and air tanks when working there because the vinyl chloride far exceeded safety standards. On February 12, 1990, the jury cleared Monsanto of wrongdoing, although the case was far from over.[26]

In order to fight effectively, HELP applied for and received a Technical Assistance Grant from the EPA. These grants were meant to help community groups hire experts to advise them concerning government regulations and rules. With this money they hired Joel Hirschhorn, who had been employed in the congressional Office of Technology Assessment, to advise them about the overall remediation process. Even before being hired, he had addressed locals at the behest of Congressman Jack Brooks (D-Beaumont) who represented the area. Hirschhorn had attacked EPA and its close relationship with the PRPs in general and the Brio case specifically at a congressional hearing. Once he began working under the TAG grant, his insights proved invaluable, often providing the necessary environmental credentials for the case. His reports blistered EPA and the BSTF and how closely they had worked together against the local residents' welfare. He pointed out that the government reports often purposefully overlooked possible contaminants. He also blasted as "galling and misleading" the discussion of air standards along the Brio fence line, calling it "flagrant evidence of how the fundamental conflict of interest" existed between the chemicals companies and the BSTF.[27]

Health concerns, especially for children, were among the biggest issues in the battle. While many people knew of anecdotal instances of unusual illnesses and birth defects in the Southbend neighborhood, no one had undertaken a systematic study of the children. So once again the "hysterical housewives" began the legwork under the leadership of Cheryl Finley. They started with a few "Avon moms" but eventually went to nearly forty women who would go door-to-door to get their neighbors to fill out the questionnaire. The initial results were frightening; of the 18 babies born on South Canyon between 1982 and 1991, two had died as infants while over forty percent had birth defects. Thirteen of the remaining sixteen living children had chronic health problems. From that beginning the women spread out, finding more and more instances of illnesses and birth defects. As the women compiled the results, most of them decided to leave. Of the original forty who started taking the survey to their neighbors, thirty-six moved from the neighborhood within one year because of the startling results. After moving many of the women noted that their children had gotten better, confirming in their minds that Brio was responsible.[28]

Flickinger then led an effort to the Agency for Toxic Substances and Disease Registry (ATSDR) to conduct a formal survey, but they did not have money to fund the study. When they asked for funding from EPA, they were turned down, so Dr. Barry Johnson, ATSDR chief suggested having Dr. Waldemar "Buzz" Johanson, who was working on a Masters in Public Health at the University of Texas Medical Branch, to analyze the data the women had gathered for his thesis. Much to the surprise of those involved with the study Johanson began throwing out survey respondents for the slightest reason. To many it appeared that he was diluting the results. Since only a third of the residents who had lived in the subdivision during the years of the study completed the survey, he factored in the other two-thirds by multiplying the number of births by three. Yet he did not raise the number of birth defects. Even with this "most conservative" approach he proved that the rate for CNS (central nervous system) abnormalities such as spina bifida, anencephaly, and other conditions was nearly 3.8 times the national average. Congenital heart defects were 2.4 times the national average. After he released his report he told Flickinger, "I was so afraid you would find out some of the things I'd done. I'd been the hired gun for a number of chemical companies." He further explained his culling of the information, saying, "I had to make sure that the product I had done could not be questioned. I threw them out before they threw them out." Birth defects had finally been proven. ATSDR would then do a further study that corroborated the earlier findings and helped to change the final settlement.[29]

Even as the BSTF began building an incinerator on the property, a new wrinkle moved to the forefront—the efforts to close Weber Elementary School just two hundred yards from the Brio site. As local residents began fighting to move their children out of the school, the paper took up the fight to close it. Flickinger found aerial maps that appeared to show dumping of wastes on what became the school property. Numerous parents complained of their children, who lived outside of the Southbend neighborhood where the school was located, getting rashes and becoming ill from September through May, but becoming well during the summer and over the Christmas break. Yet the Clear Creek Independent School District (CCISD) refused to consider any student transfers, even as teachers were allowed to transfer to other schools. The efforts then became more unusual. One night Chalice Crow and Janice Johnson, two of the "hysterical housewives" called Flickinger to come to Crow's home. She had strewn the trash from the CCISD administration building across her garage floor; thus began the nightly dumpster diving to get information about any changes in policy toward Weber Elementary as well as the district's plans for fighting the efforts to close the school. For months they would take the trash from the previous night and use it to replace new trash when the cleaning personnel put it out. For the district the women proved to be an embarrassment on many fronts, even as they tried to figure out who was "leaking" information to the *Leader*. Finally some NASA contractors who were in the same building noticed the nightly trash hauls; as they discussed it in the hall, the superintendent heard them. That night they caught the women.[30]

Eventually, the efforts and pressure worked. The school paid for many "bogus" tests—getting the results they wanted, according to Flickinger. Yet when CCISD board member Roger Davis, who lived in the South Belt area, pulled his children out of the $10 million Weber Elementary School most could predict the final choice, even thought the district had "fought this tooth and nail." At first the board allowed students to transfer to other CCISD elementary schools. Then the Friday before the January 28, 1992, school board meeting, superintendent Ron McLeod called to alert Flickinger that the school board was going to vote to close the school. "After he told me that I went home and went to bed and spent the whole weekend in bed I was so depressed." The following Monday she called him and asked, "Ron are you sure?" When he said he was, she told him, "I really was looking for you to tell me why this is ok. This is what you haven't taken into consideration." According to Flickinger, he said "'I thought you'd be happy.' I said 'How can you be happy closing an elementary school.'" He then replied, "Just think of all the kids who won't be exposed in the future." That remarked helped sustain Flickinger throughout the rest of the battle. And when Arlene Weber Elementary School was rebuilt nearly a decade later, she served as one of the community advisors to the school.[31]

Over the years the BSTF tried to silence the paper or question Flickinger's ability and credibility. At one point Goldman asserted that Flickinger was fighting to make a big profit since their family owned homes in Southbend. In truth her son had bought a home there for rental property, but had boarded it up; he could not rent it to someone with Brio nearby. At meetings throughout the area Goldman would often question how someone with a high school education could challenge the EPA, the experts in their fields, over the safety of the community. Eventually she went to the paper's advertisers and told them "the only way to stop me was to cut our money and stop advertising," Flickinger recalled. One opponent even circulated a flier to local businesses saying, "if you place ads in the *Leader* you are supporting the destruction of the South Belt." This forced Flickinger to respond with an editorial pointing out the lies in the ad—including the accusation that they had been part of eight lawsuits, when they had not been a party of any of the legal action. "Our revenue went from right under 1 million ($960,000) to about $500,000 in one year." Many people cut back because they believed Flickinger was hurting their property values. The largest flight came from realtors, who had been among the largest advertisers. This led to the rumor that she was able to support the paper during these times by her success in Las Vegas at the black jack tables. While admitting that "Vegas has been good to me" and that it provided "the only break that I had," she would not say that the gambling kept the paper afloat. In fact she used savings from the good years through the rough ones. And just as the money was running out, the tide turned and advertising picked up a bit. At the worst time, her partner and best friend, Bobby Griffin asked her if she could, "do this fight a little bit." Flickinger in her characteristic straight forward manner responded, "you can't; it's just like being a little bit pregnant." She even contemplated having to go back to printing the newspaper in her garage if it went bankrupt.[32]

One of those who attacked often was J. J. "Doc" Welby, a resident of Southbend who believed everything the EPA said. He wrote many letters to the editor, which the *South Belt Leader* published, that were scathing in their attacks on Flickinger. At one point he organized a protest outside Weber Elementary where he led the people in the chant: "Close the *Leader*, not the school." Even worse was the nearly weekly newsletter he put out in the Southbend neighborhood. He called everyone opposed to the EPA's plan the weasels, reserving the moniker "head weasel" for Flickinger. He also attacked her husband and children, believing they were just out to make money on a lawsuit. In the end a number of residents came up with a way to discredit Welby and his newsletter. Lucy Peterson wrote a newsletter just like his, but she went just a bit too far, saying things like "Well what if the kids are dinking a little bit of toxins in the drinking water. No big deal." According to Flickinger, "It sounded like Welby and she blasted me in it. I'm still the head weasel. But it made him a little bit crazier." Next they had to make it physically look like his newsletter, using the same paper, type font and ink. The paper was the problem; he used a type none of them had seen before. Finally they tracked it down, allowing Flickinger to print the edition, making it, "the spitting image of his paper." The next question was how to deliver it to the homes without anyone realizing Welby had not delivered it. Southbend resident Larry Carter got men from a homeless shelter into a truck and then had them deliver it quickly throughout the neighborhood at 6:30 AM on a Saturday morning. According to Flickinger, "As luck would have it that was the first Saturday in about two months that Doc did not put a newsletter out." Later that day they gathered at a Southbend residence as they did whenever the newsletter came out. When Welby came out, Flickinger recalled that "We played the game fine. I said, 'God Welby you've kinda gone over it this time.'" No one believed him when he denied writing the newsletter, since it looked just like his. And no one took his newsletter seriously again.[33]

One of Flickinger's strengths was working with local politicians and getting them on her side in the Brio fight. The County Attorney Mike Driscoll was one of the earliest to join the cause; he eventually urged the Commissioner's Court to oppose incineration. At a county hearing organized by Commissioner El Franco Lee, South Belt residents delivered a petition with over 10,000 signatures of people against burning the waste. One of the most raucous changes was with long-term Democratic Congressman Jack Brooks of Beaumont whose district barely included the South Belt area. When he growled at Flickinger over the phone about the issue and was about to hang up, she called his hand with some high-pitched, colorful language aimed at his old age and bad attitude which caused him to laugh and apologize. From that point on he became one of the best proponents for oversight of EPA, even sending Joel Hirschhorn to study the area. She even got Republican Congressman Tom Delay, a known friend of the chemical companies, to agree to fund a health study, which he assumed would vindicate the companies since that is what they had told him. And when she had a "Brio Summit" in March, 1993, most of the elected officials showed. The EPA representatives had announced they would not attend, but then had to change their mind and speak at the meeting because of all the dignitaries present.[34]

Eventually, the residents began succeeding with their lawsuits and moving out. Famous Houston attorney Joe Jamail won a $39 million dollar out-of-court settlement from Monsanto for the 1,700 plaintiffs on June 15, 1992. Then less than a week later Farm and Home Savings Association, the original developer, agreed to a $128 million settlement to buy out all of the homeowners; they would be required to move within a year. That same week other chemical companies added $8.5 million to the settlement. When added to the earlier payout by Farm and Home it totaled more than $200 million dollars to the 1,700 plaintiffs. After paying the cost of the homes, and one-third to the four law firms, most of the money went to trusts set up for the children. By mid-1993 Southbend would be a ghost town.[35]

Yet the BSTF was still proceeding with plans to open the pits and incinerate the toxic material. As the crews prepared the site for the incinerator and began erecting it in 1993, problems arose with the volatile chemicals which easily vaporize, going into the air. Shortly after work began, benzene, a highly toxic chemical, began showing up at air monitors. At the same time vinyl chloride, 1.2 –di-chloroethane and other chemicals were found in Mud Gulley, which drains the site, at 75-122 times the state standard for safety. Then further downstream the toxins were showing up in Clear Creek, a feeder to both Clear Lake and Galveston Bay, causing the state to warn against eating fish from Clear Creek. After denying for years any offsite toxins, the EPA and the state air quality agency finally admitted in July, 1993, that chemicals were leaching off site and into the air. It appeared that whenever work was done on the Brio site, it would set off the air monitors. For instance on August 25 a chemical release of vinyl chloride, a known carcinogen, caused a shutdown of the site and brought about multiple investigations; a young safety officer at the site resigned his $4,500-a-month job because of the lax safety standards. The EPA then required offsite air monitoring and an alert siren whenever a toxic release occurred. Another release prompted a second shut down in March, 1994. Two more releases occurred during the first week in April. And the *South Belt Leader* highlighted each incident with in-depth coverage. Still the EPA was moving ahead with the planned incineration.[36]

With incineration fast approaching, several things happened that finally pointed to victory. One of the most important was a change in presidential administrations. With Bill Clinton's defeat of George Bush and the return of the Democrats to the executive branch, the leadership of EPA was changing; the chemical companies were not automatically correct. This did not mean everything was tilted in favor of the community—only that they would receive a balanced hearing. Even before the election, however, a change came to the office of the ombudsman; Bob Martin would now be working with the public over

Brio. Even that relationship started roughly, however. When he decided to visit Houston to see first-hand what was happening at Brio, his superiors refused to fund the trip. When Flickinger arranged to use frequent flier miles from a community member to buy a ticket and to put him up in donated rooms at the Hilton, his bosses forbid him to travel to Houston. When Flickinger heard of a meeting in Dallas for Region 6 of the EPA which Martin would be attending, she prepared him a notebook, drove to Dallas and met him in a bar after one of the meetings. As she went over the material, she realized that many of the leaders of EPA were sitting at a table next to theirs, listening. "I told them, 'you don't have to eavesdrop, come on over and I'll show you, too,' but they wouldn't sit with us."[37]

After that meeting things began to progress rapidly. According to Flickinger, "Bob's boss said 'I am going to have Bob look at this and he will get back to you in a couple of weeks.' Two weeks turned into five or six months." Working with Martin over long distance—the phone bill often topping $500-600 per month—she realized that when the Ombudsman's report came out in April, 1994, it would be supporting the public efforts to stop incineration. Yet even then Goldman and the BSTF still believed that they would win, especially since the incinerator was already built. Before the final report came out in April, "she told me I didn't understand how it worked," Flickinger remembered. She explained that the EPA would listen, "to everyone but now calmer heads will prevail and they will water it down. You won't even recognize that report." But by that time Flickinger already knew the outcome that Martin had shared with her.[38]

The final report slammed the incineration plan in numerous areas—ending it as an alternative. What was the "biggest bunch of nails in the coffin," according to Flickinger, was the presence of dioxins at the site. The BSTF knew the dioxins were there and planned to burn them, but they had downplayed it throughout the fight. The EPA required an incinerator to burn dioxins to 99.9999%, but the incinerator the BSTF had built would only burn them to 99.99%. Thus it would violate EPA regulations. "I didn't care about those last two nines," remembered Flickinger, "but it mattered to the government. They built a four-nine incinerator, not a six-nine incinerator." And with that oversight, the decision to burn the chemicals was over.[39]

After that decision, the EPA changed radically, becoming more concerned about the desires of the community. In a short time the government decided to dismantle the incinerator without ever firing it up. Instead they acquiesced to the community activists' views, deciding to stabilize the site with a "cap and cover" plan. Rather than digging up the chemicals and allowing some to escape into the air, they placed a thick clay cap over the site, put in deep walls around the site to stop further migration of the chemicals underground, and fenced off the abandoned former Southbend neighborhood. This would stop the toxic chemical releases that threatened other nearby subdivisions and would allow the college and the hospital to continue to expand in the area.

In retrospect Marie Flickinger played the crucial role in changing the plans of the chemical companies, the Brio Site Task Force, and the EPA. By studying and reporting on the activities of the BSTF through the *South Belt Leader*, she was able to inform her friends and neighbors of an enormous public health risk. She kept the issue in front of the public and eventually changed public opinion through continual, weekly crusading over nearly a decade. She even triumphed over the BSTF at the last minute when the EPA closed the incinerator without using it, after it had been erected; never before had the EPA stopped a planned remediation so late in the process. She planned numerous strategies to accomplish what she thought was best for the community at the earliest stages—evacuating the Southbend neighborhood, closing Weber Elementary school, and stopping the BSTF from stirring up the chemicals to place them in the incinerator and thus releasing the chemicals into the air.[40]

Her accomplishments were eventually recognized. For instance ATSDR gave her the Auxiliary Mission Support Award which had only been given to agency employees before that; as Flickinger said of the marble plaque, "This is my proudest thing I've ever gotten." When she asked Barry Johnson, ATSDR chief why, he explained that she received the award for what she had "taught them about families living near toxic waste sites." In addition he noted that while they knew what each chemical could do to people, "they had never taken the synergistic and additive effects into account, especially with kids." And in Region 6 the next time the EPA came across a site near homes, they bought everyone out before trying to do remediation—a lesson they learned from Brio. She feared when the fight was over that she might have to move, that the community might never approve of her again. While she believes "the community never understood" the entire fight over Brio, almost everyone quickly accepted her. "People understood they built a $50 million incinerator but now they were tearing it down and they never used it. So then I was ok." Most concluded that she must have been right. Shortly thereafter she received approximately 90% of the votes cast in the South Belt area, becoming the first woman ever elected to the Board of Trustees of the San Jacinto College District. Her community had vindicated her.[41]

Endnotes

1   Interview of Marie Flickinger by author, March 17, 2010, Houston, Texas, in possession of author.

2   Interview of Catherine O'Brien by author, March 19, 2010, Pearland, Texas, in possession of author; Flickinger interview.

3   Handbook of Texas Online, s.v. "Oil and Gas Industry," http://www.tshaonline.org/handbook/ online/articles/OO/doogz.html (accessed March 15, 2010); Handbook of Texas Online, s.v. "Spindletop Oilfield," http://www.tshaonline.org/handbook/online/articles/SS/dos3.html (accessed March 16, 2010); Handbook of Texas Online, s.v. "East Texas Oilfield," http://www.tshaonline.org/handbook/online/articles/EE/doe1.html (accessed March 16, 2010); Handbook of Texas Online, s.v. "Texas City, Texas," http://www.tshaonline.org/handbook/online/articles/TT/hdt3.html (accessed March16, 2010); Handbook of Texas Online, s.v. "Petrochemical Industry," http://www.tshaonline.org/handbook/online/articles PP/dop11.html (accessed March 16, 2010); Handbook of Texas Online, s.v. "Environmental Health," http://www.tshaonline.org/handbook/online/articles/EE/sme2.html (accessed March 16, 2010). For a good overview of the oil industry in Texas, see Roger M. and Diana Davids Olien, *Oil Booms* Lincoln: University of Nebraska Press, 1982.

4   "Final Report: Feasibility Study Brio Refining Inc. and Dixie Oil Processors Site Friendswood, Texas," January, 1988, Book 21, pp. 2.5-2.7, Brio Repository, Parker Williams Library, San Jacinto College South, Houston, Texas (hereafter BR); Flickinger Interview; O'Brien interview.

5   Throughout the 1970s and into the 1980s the company refined many products from caustic materials to creosote to diesel. They received many types of waste from the PRPs. For a fuller listing of these chemicals and the times they were used, see Brio Site Task Force, "Final Report: Endangerment Assessment," January 1988, book 22, pp. 2.4-2.5, BR.

6   "Final Report: Feasibility Study Brio Refining Inc. and Dixie Oil Processors Site Friendswood, Texas," January, 1988, Book 21, pp. 2.2-2.5, BR; Flickinger interview; affidavit of Terry Pat White, March 23, 1993 in Brio Summit Book, BR; Special report by John McPherson, Channel 2 News, January 10, 1990, recorded in "Tar Wars" a video prepared by Marie Flickinger and David Flickinger, in possession of the author.

7   "Final Report: Feasibility Study Brio Refining Inc. and Dixie Oil Processors Site Friendswood, Texas," January, 1988, Book 21, pp. 2.5-2.7, BR; Flickinger Interview; O'Brien interview;

8   "Brio Refining Record of Decision" March 31, 1988, Book 1 section 13, BR; Harold Scarlett, "14 companies to fund study prior to Brio cleanup," *Houston Post*, May 17, 1985; Flickinger interview; O'Brien interview;

9   Harold Scarlett, "Residents told waste pits no threat," *Houston Post*, December 11, 1984; "Homeowners sue builders over abandoned dump site," *Houston Chronicle*, January 4, 1985.

10   "Homeowners sue builders over abandoned dump site," *Houston Chronicle*, January 4, 1985; "So. Bend homeowners win," *South Belt Leader* (hereafter SBL), May 2, 1985; "Ignorance is not bliss: Homeowners in Southbend cite health problems, blame 'abandoned refinery,'" *Houston Chronicle*, April 26, 1985; Originally the newspaper was named the *South Belt-Ellington Leader*. For this chapter the newspaper will be referred to as the *South Belt Leader* to avoid confusion.

11   Flickinger interview; O'Brien interview.

12   "Brio clean-up study underway," *SBL*, May 23, 1985; "So Bend air, water, soil found safe: officials," *SBL*, May 30, 1985; Flickinger interview; Margaret Ganter, "Official view not enough," letter to the editor, *SBL*, June 13, 1985; "An Open Letter to Southbend Residents," *SBL*, June 20, 1985; Fred Perry, "Little understanding of problems," letter to the editor, SBL, June 27, 1985; "Incineration not considered at Brio waste site," *SBL*, May 6, 1986; "Brio Site Task Force report made public, *SBL*, July 17, 1986; "Pits don't extend into Southbend," *SBL*, July 25, 1987.

13   Mary Ann Kreps, "Faith in EPA erodes over Brio cleanup," *Houston Chronicle*, February 4, 1990, Flickinger interview; "Hazards cited at Brio dump," *SBL*, October, 6, 1988; "Who's EPA protecting?" *SBL*, December 8, 1988.

14   Flickinger interview; "Hazards cited at Brio dump," *SBL*, October, 6, 1988; "Who's EPA protecting?" *SBL*, December 8, 1988.

15   Flickinger interview; "DOP assumed hazardous," *SBL*, February 16, 1989.

16   Trigg Gardner, "DOP tour enlightens residents," *SBL*, April 6, 1989; Gardner, "Revealed records contradict EPA," *SBL*, April 6, 1989; Flickinger interview. Ralph Lowe did not own DOP in 1975 when the

ball fields were built; he bought the site later.

17   Flickinger interview; "DOP assumed hazardous," *SBL*, February 16,
      1989; Marie Flickinger, "Editorial," *SBL*, February 16, 1989; "Tar
      Wars" a video prepared by Marie Flickinger and David Flickinger, in
      possession of the author. Thirteen minutes of the conversation that
      was recorded is included in the video "Tar Wars." The conversation
      was played while the video from the DOP site was showing, visually
      contradicting what the EPA officials were saying.

18   Trigg Gardner, "Revealed records contradict EPA," *SBL*, April 6, 1989;

19   Trigg Gardner and Marie Flickinger, "Former employees detail off-site
      dumping," *SBL*, April 27, 1989; Trigg Gardner, "Reaction to dumping
      draws concern," *SBL*, May 4, 1989; Rick Reynolds, "Seeking truths
      concerning Brio," letter to the editor, *SBL*, May 4, 1989; "City to check
      alleged dumpings," *Friendswood Journal*, May 10, 1989; Trigg Gardner,
      "Truck driver changes waste dumping locations," *SBL*, May 11, 1989;
      "Brio dump sites still a question with city officials," *Friendswood
      Journal*, May 17, 1989; Bill Dawson and Julie Mason, "Southbend
      contamination targeted," *Houston Chronicle*, June 2, 1989; Flickinger
      interview; O'Brien interview.

20   Trigg Gardner, "New toxic chemicals found at DOP site," *SBL*, April
      20, 1989; Trigg Gardner, "Unknown chemicals cause for concern,"
      SBL, April 20, 1989; Trigg Gardner, "'Priority Pollutants' perplex top
      officials," *SBL*, April 27, 1989; Trigg Gardner, "EPA's Superfund sites
      controversy continues," *SBL*, May 11, 1989;

21   "Barinka requests Leader records—Leader refuses," *SBL*, April 20, 1989;
      Flickinger interview.

22   Flickinger interview; "Tar Wars" a video prepared by Marie Flickinger
      and David Flickinger, in possession of the author; Marie Flickinger,
      "Editorial," *SBL,* February 16, 1989; Trigg Gardner, "EPA's Superfund
      sites controversy continues," *SBL*, May 11, 1989; Trigg Gardner, "Tar
      wars target DOP," *SBL*, May 18, 1989; "Softball moving; Pony Colt,
      Little League deciding," *SBL*, June 8, 1989; Alan Truex, "Local Little
      Leaguers strike out against toxic waste," *Houston Chronicle*, June 25,
      1989; Al Carter, "Where will the children play?" *Houston Chronicle*, July
      26, 1989; Trigg Gardner, "Petition seeking support," *SBL*, July 20, 1989;
      Trigg Gardner, "Committee says abandon ballpark," *SBL*, October 5,
      1989.

23   Morris Edelson, "Parents fear for health of children attending school
      near Brio waste site," *The Clear Lake Times*, (Houston), December 1,

1988; "H.E.L.P. goals outlined," letters to the editor, *SBL*, January 19, 1989; "Blame Brio not H.E.L.P.," letters to the editor, *SBL*, January 19, 1989; "Brio waste site to be dismantled under contract," *Houston Post*, July 20, 1989; Mary Ann Kreps, "Task force sets starting date for Brio work," *Houston Chronicle*, July 20, 1989; "Task force names contractor," *SBL*, July 20, 1989; Trigg Gardner, "DOP tests find harmful chemicals," *SBL*, July 20, 1989; Trigg Gardner, "Tests show trace of contamination," *SBL*, August 10, 1989; Marie Flickinger, "Brio contractor holds fine stigma," *SBL*, August 17, 1989; "H.E.L.P. seminar relates new living with toxics data," *SBL*, March 15, 1990.

24 Flickinger interview; O'Brien interview; "Goldman's unedited release," *SBL*, March 8, 1990; Harold Scarlett, "Industry group rips newspaper for account on state of aquifer," *Houston Post*, March 4, 1990; Beverly Miller, "Aquifer report is disputed," *Galveston Daily News*, March 6, 1990; "Brio Task Force calls foul in contaminated water claim," *Friendswood Journal*, March 7, 1990; "Goldman meeting angers parents," *SBL*, May 17, 1990; Trigg Gardner, "Brio needs reinvestigation," *SBL*, May 24, 1990; Marie Flickinger, "Brooks comes through," editorial, *SBL* May 24, 1990; Trigg Gardner, "USGS says 250-foot clay layer non-existent," *SBL*, June 28, 1990. In 1994 Goldman told the *Wall Street Journal* "I wish I'd never used the term [250 feet thick layer of non permeable clay]." She told them "what she actually meant was that there is a 'pretty good'layer of clay down below—which actually is permeable," Timothy Aeppel, "Superfund Site Spawns A Spate of Litigation, Though Not a Cleanup," *Wall Street Journal*, February 9, 1994.

25 Flickinger interview; O'Brien interview.

26 Julie Mason, "Huge suit by residents against Monsanto set," *Houston Chronicle*, October 17, 1989; Trigg Gardner and Marie Flickinger, "Records reveal Brio cover-up," *SBL*, October 19, 1989; Julie Mason, "Testimony starts in waste-site suit filed by 222 subdivision residents, " *Houston Chronicle*, October 19, 1989; Bruce Nichols, "Monsanto suit goes to trial," *Dallas Morning News*, October 19, 1989; Trigg Gardner, "Town meeting digs into Brio," *SBL*, October 26, 1989; Trigg Gardner, "Kaufmann files affidavit," *SBL,* November 2, 1989; Marie Flickinger, "Southbend is terminal," editorial, *SBL*, November 30, 1989; Trigg Gardner, "Documents reveal new story," *SBL*, December 14, 1989; Trigg Gardner, "New documents oversight called mistake," *SBL*, December 21, 1989; Bill Hensel, Jr., "Monsanto Co. ordered to pay $190,000 in toxic waste dump ruling," *Houston Post*, January 1, 1990; "Monsanto

withheld documents: judge" *Friendswood Journal*, January 3, 1990; Marie Flickinger, "Court fines Monsanto $190,000," *SBL*, January 4, 1990; Trigg Gardner, "As Slaughter vs. Monsanto trial rests More Brio cover-up surfaces," *SBL*, February 1, 1990; Julie Mason, "Monsanto cleared in homeowners' suit," *Houston Chronicle*, February 13, 1990; Bill Hensel, Jr., "State court clears Monsanto Co.," *Houston Post*, February 13, 1990; Trigg Gardner, "Jury vindicates Monsanto's role," *SBL*, February 15, 1990.

27   "Coalition seeking technical grant," *SBL*, May 18, 1989; Trigg Gardner, "TAG probes underway," *SBL*, August 17, 1989; Trigg Gardner, "OTA official names BRIO as problem case," *SBL*, November 9, 1989; Bill Odell, "You cannot depend on EPA for Answers: Hirschhorn," *Friendswood Journal*, January 12, 1990; Trigg Gardner, "Brio meeting riles citizens," *SBL*, January 18, 1990; Jim Morris, "Grant given for monitoring 2 cleanup efforts," *Houston Chronicle*, February 6, 1991; "H.E.L.P. receives EPA TAG grant," *SBL*, February 7, 1990; Flickinger interview; O'Brien interview; Marie Flickinger, "EPA-funded report blasts Brio testing," *SBL*, March 19, 1992; Joel Hirschhorn, "Final Report to H.E.L.P. on Definition of Site Problems and Clean-up Objectives for the Brio Refining Superfund Site, March 10, 1993, BR; Joel Hirschhorn, "Comments on 90% Remedial Design reports for the Brio Site Remediation, February 1, 1993, BR.

28   Trigg Gardner, "Informal health survey cites cancer correlation," *SBL*, June 15, 1989; C. H. O'Brien, "Help complete health survey," letter to the editor, *SBL*, April 4, 1991; "Health study group leaves," *SBL*, April 4, 1991; Trigg Gardner, "Health problems devastate South Canyon," *SBL* April 11, 1991; Marie Flickinger, "Health problems wreck South Canyon," *SBL*, April 18, 1991; Flickinger interview; O'Brien interview.

29   Flickinger interview; O'Brien interview; "ATSDR supports detailed Southbend health study," *SBL*, May 9, 1991; "Federal study shows health risk," *SBL*, October 17, 1991; Marie Flickinger, "Health Study to target Southbend," *SBL* November 21, 1991; Cheryl Bolen, "Health study to focus on former Southbend residents, children," *SBL*, May 7, 1992; testimony of David Satcher, Administrator, Agency for Toxic Substances and Disease Registry, Public Health Service, U. S. Department of Health and Human Services, before the Subcommittee on VA, HUD, and Independent Agencies, Committee on Appropriations, U. S. Senate, May 12, 1995, http://www.atsdr.cdc.gov/testimony/testimony-1995-05-12.html; testimony of Barry L. Johnson, Assistant Surgeon General, Assistant Administrator Agency

for Toxic Substances and Disease Registry, Public Health Service, U. S.
Department of Health and Human Services, before the Subcommittee
on Human Resources and Intergovernmental Relations, Committee on
Government Operations, U. S. House of Representatives, July 8, 1994.

30 Flickinger interview; O'Brien interview; Trigg Gardner, "Parents
    demand school closure," *SBL*, November 24, 1988; "Parent asks closure
    of school near waste site," *Houston Chronicle*, November 24, 1988; Trigg
    Gardner, "CCISD seeks further tests," *SBL*, December 1, 1988; Morris
    Edelson, "Parents fear for health of children attending school near Brio
    waste site," *The Clear Lake Times*, (Houston), December 1, 1988; Trigg
    Gardner, "Health Risks no option in transfers," *SBL*, September 28,
    1989; Trigg Gardner, "CCISD testing Weber," *SBL*, November 9, 1989;
    "Parents request school transfers," *SBL*, November 30, 1989; Beverly
    Miller, "Despite test results, some insist Brio site near CC school safe,"
    Galveston Daily News, December 22, 1989; Bonnie Pritchett, "Brio
    parents again seek kids' transfer," *Clear Lake Citizen*, January 23, 1990;
    Trigg Gardner, "CCISD refuses transfers," *SBL*, January 25, 1990; Trigg
    Gardner, "Teachers use Brio fears for Transfers," *SBL*, February 22,
    1990; Derek Rill, "School trash yields clues on toxic cite," *Houston Post*,
    May 30, 1990; Trigg Gardner, "Trash team ending CCISD raids," *SBL*,
    May 31, 1990; Special report by John McPherson, Channel 2 News,
    January 9-11, 1990, recorded in "Tar Wars" a video prepared by Marie
    Flickinger and David Flickinger, in possession of the author. The
    dumpster diving embarrassed CCISD because the women found many
    checks from vendors in envelopes that had never been opened, much
    less the checks cashed. They used this to help defeat a bond proposal
    at the same time. In addition they found love notes from a married
    employee to an employee of another school district about upcoming
    trysts at education conferences. When read without names at a board
    meeting, the district looked bad. At the same meeting they rolled in a
    "wheelbarrow" of checks according to Flickinger.

31 Stacy Gauldin, "Board member pulls children from Weber," *Clear
    Lake Times*, August 23, 1990; Trigg Gardner, "CCISD board member
    stands up for parents," *SBL*, August 30, 1990; Ruth Rendon, "Weber
    school transfers are approved," *Houston Chronicle*, September 26,
    1990; Stacy Gauldin, "CCISD to begin granting transfers," *Clear Lake
    Times*, September 27, 1990; "CCISD to allow Weber transfers," *SBL*,
    September 27, 1990; Derrick Rill, "Weber parents get OK to transfer
    children," *Houston Post*, September 27, 1990; Ruth Rendon, "Clear
    Creek grammar school to close," *Houston Chronicle*, January 28, 1992;
    William Pack, "Clear Creek will move students, staff," *Houston Post*,

January 29, 1992; "Weber to close August or sooner," *SBL*, January 30, 1992; Bill Odell, "Creek ISD lays plans to close Weber school," *Friendswood Journal*, January 31, 1992; Marie Flickinger, "Weber Elementary closes—Friday," *SBL*, March 26, 1992; William Pack, "Environmental concerns prompt Clear Creek board to close school," *Houston Post*, March 26, 1992; Marie Flickinger, "Special meeting— tough decision," signed editorial, *SBL*, March 26, 1992; Flickinger interview.

32 "*Leader* sets priorities," *SBL*, November 15, 1990; Marie Flickinger, "Toxic Waste—not the Leader—is the problem," editorial, *SBL*, October 15, 1992; Flickinger interview; O'Brien interview.

33 Doc Welby, "*Leader* distorts real Brio facts," letter to the editor, *SBL*, October 25, 1990; Doc Welby, "Apathy keeps Brio going," letter to the editor, *SBL*, November 1, 1990; J.J. Welby, "Welby Slams Flickinger," letter to the editor, *SBL*, May 7, 1992; James J. Welby, "Welby at it— again," letter to the editor, *SBL*, May 28, 1992; Flickinger interview; O'Brien interview;

34 Flickinger interview; O'Brien interview; "Getting the message across," *SBL*, October 25, 1990; Catherine O'Brien, "Varied segment signs petition," letter to the editor, *SBL*, November 1, 1990; Julie Mason, "Commissioners vote to file brief detailing Brio site cleanup concerns," *Houston Chronicle*, December 12, 1990; Bill Hensel, "County votes to oppose Brio Site cleanup pact," *Houston Post*, December 12, 1990; "County nixes Brio Consent Decree," *SBL*, December 13, 1990; "Brio Summit" notebook, BR; "Top officials to attend Brio Summit March 16," *SBL*, February 11, 1993; Marie Flickinger, "Community asked to be partners in Brio Summit," editorial, *SBL*, February 11, 1993; Marie Flickinger, "The question is—why?" editorial, *SBL*, February 18, 1993; "Brio Summit Monday, Tuesday," *SBL*, March 11, 1993;.

35 Cheryl Bolen, "Monsanto agrees to pay $39 million settlement locally," *SBL*, June 18, 1992; Ruth Rendon, "Monsanto settles Brio site lawsuits," *Houston Chronicle*, June 16, 1992; David Ellison, "$39 million settles Brio injury claims," *Houston Post*, June 16, 1992; Caleb Solomon and Christy Harlan, "Brio Toxic-Waste Complaint Is Settled; Agreements Now Total $207.5 Million," *Wall Street Journal*, June 19, 1992; Debbie Housel, "Settlement on Brio hits $207 million," *Houston Post*, June 19, 1992; Cheryl Bolen, "Brio Settlement a landmark deal," *SBL*, June 25, 1992; "Mortgage assumptions in settlement," *SBL*, June 25, 1992; "Total Southbend buyout considered," *SBL*, July 2, 1992; Cheryl Bolen, "Demolition set for Southbend," *SBL*, March 25, 1993.

36   Marie Flickinger, "Southbend air monitor finds high benzene," *SBL*,
     June 17, 1993; Marie Flickinger, "Brio chemicals found in Clear Creek,"
     SBL, July 1, 1993; Marie Flickinger and Cheryl Bolen, "Air, water toxins
     coming from Brio," *SBL*, July 8, 1993; Marie Flickinger, "Officials: Brio
     toxins offsite," *SBL*, July 22, 1993; Marie Flickinger, "Brio toxins in Clear
     Creek," *SBL*, November 25, 1993; Ruth Rendon, "State warning: Don't
     eat Clear Creek fish," *Houston Chronicle,* November 19, 1993; Douglas
     Freelander, "Officials warn against eating fish, crabs from Clear Creek,"
     Houston, Post, November 19, 1993; "Brio Task Force complies with
     cease-work order," *Friendswood Journal,* October 13, 1993; Cheryl
     Bolen, "Fine, evacuation, shutdown possible after Brio emission," *SBL*,
     October 14, 1993; Marie Flickinger, "Brio safety officer quits after
     emission," *SBL*, October 14, 1993; Cheryl Bolen, "Brio emission brings
     all parties together," *SBL*, October 21, 1993; Marie Flickinger, "Brio
     safeguards will now include siren, monitoring," *SBL*, October 28, 1993;
     "EPA stops Brio Work," *SBL*, March 17, 1994; William Furlow, "Work
     stops at Brio following release," *Friendswood Journal*, March 16, 1994;
     "2 vinyl chloride releases reported at Brio this week," *SBL*, April 7, 1994.

37   "New administration could decide against toxic incineration," *SBL*,
     December 17, 1992; "Washington responses from local Gore faxes,"
     SBL, Christmas Issue, 1992; Flickinger interview;

38   Cheryl Bolen, "Brio report could halt incineration," *SBL*, April 7, 1994;
     Flickinger interview;

39   Scott Harper, "EPA urges new tests at Brio site," *Houston Post*, April
     2, 1994; Marie Flickinger, "Complying with EPA recommendations,
     frequent toxic emissions may make incinerator unfeasible," *SBL*, April
     21, 1994; John Toth, "EPA considers containment of pollutants at Brio
     site," *Houston Chronicle*, May 17, 1994; Cheryl Bolen, "Brio incineration
     plan scrapped," *SBL*, May 19, 1994; Scott Harper, "Brio—it's a dirty
     job, and nobody's able to do it," *Houston Post*, May 19, 1994; Marie
     Flickinger, "Containment sought for Brio site," *SBL*, June 9, 1994;
     Marie Flickinger, "Residents say no to incineration," SBL, July 21, 1994;
     Marjorie Evans, "Incinerator being dismantled at Brio," Friendswood
     Journal, July 27, 1994; Flickinger interview.

40   Flickinger interview; Cheryl Bolen, "EPA report on Brio supports long-
     held community concerns," *SBL*, November 18, 1993; Marie Flickinger,
     Chemical companies speechless," editorial, *SBL*, April 7, 1994; Satcher
     testimony; Johnson testimony.

41   Flickinger interview; O'Brien interview.

CONTRIBUTORS

DR. WATSON ARNOLD, M.D., a specialist in nephrology and pediatrics, has practiced medicine in Fort Worth, Texas, for the past 42 years. He also holds the Ph D. in history from Texas Christian University. He currently serves as the President of the Board of Directors of the Texas State Historical Association.

MARK BEASLEY serves as an Associate Professor of History at Hardin Simmons University in Abilene, Texas. A native of Southern California, he specializes in modern American and Texas political history. He is currently completing work on a biography of former Speaker of the United States House of Representatives Jim Wright.

MICHAEL COLLINS is Professor Emeritus of History and Regents Professor at Midwestern State University in Wichita Falls, Texas. A Fellow of the Texas State Historical Association, past President of the Southwestern Social Science Association, and recipient of the Piper Professor Award, his publications include *Texas Devils: Rangers and Regulars on the Lower Rio Grande* (Norman: University of Oklahoma Press, 2008) and *That Damned Cowboy: Theodore Roosevelt and the American West* (New York: Peter Lang, 1989).

ARCHIE MCDONALD was Professor and Community Liaison at Stephen F. Austin State University in Nacogdoches, Texas. He served as Director of the East Texas Historical Association, 1971—2008. A past President and Fellow of the Texas State Historical Association, he has published more than 20 books, notably among them *William Barret Travis: A Biography* (Austin: Jenkins, 1976), and *Make Me a Map of the Valley: The Journal of Stonewall Jackson's Topographer, Jedediah Hotchkiss*, ed. (Dallas: Southern Methodist University, 1973). Along with Ben H. Procter, he also co-edited *The Texas Heritage*, Fourth edition (Arlington Heights, Ill.: Harlan Davidson, 2003).

DAVID MURPH is the former Director of Church Relations at Texas Christian University. Aside from holding the Master of Divinity degree from Lexington Theological Seminary. University, he also received his Ph. D. in history from Texas Christian University. His publications include *Before Texas Changed: A Fort Worth Boyhood* (Fort Worth: Texas Christian University Press, 2006). He is retired and lives with his wife, Jean, in Grapevine, Texas.

MARY KELLEY SCHEER, Associate Professor of History, serves as Chair of the Department of History at Lamar University in Beaumont, Texas. A member of the Board of Directors of the Texas State Historical Association, her publications include *The Foundations of Texas Philanthropy* (College Station: Texas A&M University, 2004), and coeditor and contributor for *Twentieth Century Texas: A Social and Cultural History* (Denton: University of North Texas Press, 2008). She was also a recipient of a Fulbright Scholar award in 2004 (Potsdam, Germany).

ROGER TULLER is an Associate Professor of History at Texas A&M University, Kingsville. A native of Illinois who specializes in the American West and in United States constitutional history, his publications include *Let No Guilty Man Escape: A Judicial Biography of Isaac C. Parker* (Norman: University of Oklahoma Press, 2000).

EDDIE WELLER is a Professor of History at San Jacinto College, South Campus. A past President of the Southwestern Social Science Association and current member of the Board of Directors of the Texas State Historical Association, his publications include *Joe T. Robinson: Always a Loyal Democrat* (Fayetteville: University of Arkansas Press, 1998.

CPSIA information can be obtained at www.ICGtesting.com
Printed in the USA
LVOW080827120513

333218LV00005B/5/P